John W. Baldwin

Baltimore

1976

ENGLISH SYNODALIA
OF THE
THIRTEENTH CENTURY

139

WORCESTER CATHEDRAL MS. Q 67, part of fo. 139 r *b*

(size of original). Cf. p. 59

ENGLISH SYNODALIA
OF THE
THIRTEENTH CENTURY

BY

C. R. CHENEY

WITH A NEW
INTRODUCTION
BY THE AUTHOR

OXFORD UNIVERSITY PRESS

Oxford University Press, Ely House, London W. 1

GLASGOW NEW YORK TORONTO MELBOURNE WELLINGTON
CAPE TOWN SALISBURY IBADAN NAIROBI LUSAKA ADDIS ABABA
BOMBAY CALCUTTA MADRAS KARACHI LAHORE DACCA
KUALA LUMPUR HONG KONG TOKYO

FIRST PUBLISHED 1941
REPRINTED LITHOGRAPHICALLY IN GREAT BRITAIN
AT THE UNIVERSITY PRESS, OXFORD
BY VIVIAN RIDLER
PRINTER TO THE UNIVERSITY
1968

INTRODUCTION TO THE NEW IMPRESSION

THIS work was originally designed to lighten the apparatus of a collection of the English Church councils, under preparation in the 1930s. But the editing was held up by the Second World War, and afterwards the editors' other activities caused further delay. As a result, the volume for which this work provides prolegomena did not appear until the year 1964: *Councils and Synods, with other Documents relating to the English Church*, vol. ii, A.D. 1205–1313, edited by F. M. Powicke and C. R. Cheney, in two parts (Oxford, at the Clarendon Press). Meanwhile, for twenty-three years, this book had to serve as the only guide to the most recent criticism of the corpus of English diocesan statutes. The old editions (where they exist) are full of gross inaccuracies and abound in false ascriptions, which have led to the misdating of statutes by decades, even by more than a century. In 1941 only a small number of copies of the book could be printed, and it has long been unobtainable. Its circulation was inevitably small. On the Continent the first reviews appeared in 1948, by Walther Holtzmann in the *Zeitschrift der Savigny-Stiftung für Rechtsgeschichte*, and by André Artonne in the *Journal des Savants*. These circumstances help to explain why some works published since 1941 in the field of church history are defective when they come to use diocesan statutes. They have too often continued to take old editions at face-value and have cited the statutes in ignorance of their origin, their interrelationship, and the textual problems.

The delay in the production of *Councils and Synods*, vol. ii, was not an unmixed evil. It at least enabled the author to look again at the evidence contained in this book and to make some further discoveries in manuscript collections. Today a thoroughly revised edition of the book would have to incorporate fresh material; it would also involve re-writing substantial parts of chapters IV and V; and throughout chapters III–V the references to *capitula* of the statutes would require re-numbering (for the old numeration has been superseded by a new one in *Councils and Synods*). Such revision is out of the question. The text itself therefore remains that of 1941, reprinted with only minor inaccuracies emended. The introductory chapter on the Diocesan Synod, which the late Hamilton Thompson commended in his review (*English Historical Review*, lviii, 1943), could be greatly enlarged, with more about procedure and more evidence of judicial and miscellaneous business; but it is doubtful whether this would seriously disturb the main lines of the picture. Chapter II, devoted to Diocesan Statutes in general, stands as a whole, though the statement on p. 31 that in the twelfth century 'the bishop does not use the synod to make known his superior's decrees or to legislate by his own authority' needs to be modified.[1] Chapters III to V still provide the necessary critical background to *Councils and Synods*, vol. ii, and will still be of service to the student of synods and statutes, so long as he takes account of the corrections already embodied in the latter work and of a few salient points brought out in the rest of this preface.

Statutes printed by Mansi under the title 'Concilium incerti loci' (xxii. 723) had not hitherto been connected with England and therefore were not mentioned in this book. They have since been found to belong to a series of statutes for the diocese of Canterbury issued by Archbishop Stephen Langton between July 1213 and July 1214 and have been printed in *Councils and Synods*, ii. 23–36. These show that English statute-making before the Fourth Lateran Council was more extensive than had been imagined, and disclose one of the most important sources of the statutes of Richard Poore, bishop of Salisbury.

The so-called 'Statuta legenda in concilio Oxoniensi', which had been briefly dismissed as an unofficial collection,[2] have been re-examined. This pointed to the original promulgation of a series, in the form of MS. Bodley 843, fols. 122r–125v, in some unidentified English diocese between the years 1222 and 1225.[3]

Further comparison of the statutes of Walter Cantilupe

---

[1] Cf. C. R. Cheney, *From Becket to Langton: English Church Government, 1170-1213* (Manchester, 1956), pp. 142–4.

[2] *Eng. Hist. Rev.*, l (1935), 395–8 and below, p. 44.

[3] *Ibid.*, lxxv (1960), 18–23 and *Councils and Synods*, ii. 139–54.

for Worcester (26 July 1240) with the undated statutes of Robert Grosseteste of Lincoln led to the conclusion that Cantilupe borrowed from Grosseteste. This reverses the order of these two highly important series of statutes as represented below. It is suggested that the Lincoln statutes were probably issued in 1239, in special general chapters held in the diocese of Lincoln, deanery by deanery, when the clergy met the bishop on visitation.[1]

Chapter IV below is also defective in the section relating to the statutes of Wells and York (below, pp. 97–103), because a manuscript of nearly identical statutes for the diocese of Carlisle was overlooked. Those statutes peculiar to the Carlisle manuscript are printed in *Councils and Synods*, ii. 628–30. The Wells, York, and Carlisle series all basically belong to the years 1258 and 1259; but the peculiar Carlisle statutes may be assigned to a later date or dates, perhaps to the early fourteenth century.

In chapter VI below various series of English statutes are mentioned (p. 142) without full discussion. These have all now been edited in *Councils and Synods*, ii, and the introductions to the texts in that volume may be consulted; the brief statutes of Llandaff (p. 142, n. 3) remain unprinted. A study of the Salisbury statutes attributed by Wilkins (*Concilia*, i. 713–20) to Bishop Giles of Bridport confirmed the view provisionally expressed on p. 49 below, that they 'have a more complicated history'.[2] Again, the process of editing the second series of Chichester statutes and those of York ascribed by Spelman and Wilkins to Archbishop William Greenfield reversed the relationship of these two series, established a much earlier date (1241–1255) for the core of the York series (the earlier of the two), and associated it with statutes of Durham and Dublin.[3]

All these changes mean that the chronological list of statutes on p. 36 below can be amplified and corrected, and in some cases limiting dates can be narrowed. It may be of service to readers to have before them a revised list:

[1] *Councils and Synods*, ii. 266.
[2] *Ibid.*, ii. 510–15, 549–67.
[3] See Cheney, 'A group of related synodal statutes'.

1213 × 1214   Canterbury I
1219   Worcester I
1217 × 1219   Salisbury I
?1224   Winchester I
?1222 × 1225   Synodal statutes
    for an English
    diocese
    (*Legenda*)
1222 × 1228   Canterbury II
1229   Worcester II
?1225 × 1230   *Constitutiones*
    cuiusdam
    episcopi
1228 × 1236   Durham I
1224 × 1237   Coventry
1225 × 1237   Exeter I
?1239   Lincoln
1240   Worcester III
c. 1229 × 1241   London arch-
    deaconry
1240 × 1243   Norwich

1238 × 1244   Salisbury II
?1247   Winchester II
1241 × 1249   Durham II
?1241 × 1249   Durham
    peculiars
1245 × 1252   Chichester I
1241 × 1255   York I
?1228 × 1256   Salisbury III
1239 × 1256   Ely
1257   Salisbury IV
?1258   Wells
1245 × 1259   London I
1245 × 1259   London II
1258 × 1259   Carlisle
1259   York II
1262 × 1265   Winchester III
1276   Durham III
1287   Exeter II
1289   Chichester II
1292   Chichester III

Since the book was first published the author has dealt with critical questions relating to English diocesan legislation in the following studies:

'The medieval statutes of the diocese of Carlisle', *Eng. Hist. Rev.* lxii (1947), 52–7.

'The earliest English diocesan statutes', *ibid.*, lxxv (1960), 1–29 [chiefly those of Canterbury, 1213 × 1214, Synodal statutes, 1222 × 1225, and Constitutiones cuiusdam episcopi, ? 1225 × 1230].

'A group of related synodal statutes of the thirteenth century', in *Medieval Studies presented to Aubrey Gwynn, S.J.*, ed. J. A. Watt, J. B. Morrall, and F. X. Martin (Dublin, 1961), pp. 114–32. [Durham II, York I, Chichester II, and Dublin.]

'Rules for the observance of feast days in medieval England', *Bulletin of the Inst. of Hist. Research*, xxxiv (1961), 117–47.

'The so-called statutes of John Pecham and Robert Winchelsey for the province of Canterbury', *Journal of Eccl. Hist.*, xii (1961), 14–34 [discusses diocesan statutes which came to be treated as provincial legislation].

'William Lyndwood's Provinciale', *The Jurist*, xxi (1961), 405–34 [deals with diocesan statutes which were given provincial currency by Lyndwood].

Statute-making in the English Church in the thirteenth century', in *Proceedings of the Second International Congress of Medieval Canon Law, Boston College, 12–16 August 1963* (Città del Vaticano, 1965) pp. 117–47, 485–7.

'Aspects de la législation diocésaine en Angleterre au xiiie siècle', in *Études d'histoire du droit canonique dédiées à Gabriel Le Bras* (Paris, 1965), i. 41–54 [deals with statutes which concern the instruction of the clergy and parochial finance].

Since 1941 various scholars have thrown light on texts and topics discussed in this book. The following may be mentioned: Professor D. W. Robertson jr. made use of the synodal statutes extensively in three essays, on 'The *Manuel des Péchés* and an English episcopal decree', *Modern Language Notes*, lx (1945), 439–47, on 'The cultural tradition of *Handlyng Synne*', *Speculum*, xxii (1947), 162–85, and on 'Frequency of preaching in thirteenth-century England', *ibid.*, xxiv (1949), 376–88. Father Leonard E. Boyle, O.P., in 'The *Oculus sacerdotis* and some other works of William of Pagula', *Trans. of the Royal Hist. Soc.*, 5th series, v (1955), 81–100, drew attention (p. 90 n. 1) to the origin of the 'instructions to parish priests' which I failed to identify below (pp. 112, 115, 147); they are extracts from the *Oculus sacerdotis*, dextera pars. Mrs. Dorothy Owen discusses the practice of 'Synods in the diocese of Ely in the later Middle Ages and the sixteenth century', in *Studies in Church History*, vol. iii, ed. G. J. Cuming (Leiden, 1966), 217–22.

The bibliography on pp. 153–8 below could be largely augmented by reference to the work on continental synods which has appeared since the Second World War. Fortunately this has now been brought together (with the earlier literature of the subject) in the admirably comprehensive *Bibliographia synodorum particularium* of Jakub T. Sawicki (Monumenta Iuris Canonici, Series C: Subsidia, vol. ii, Città del Vaticano, 1967). It may nevertheless be worth while to call attention to a few of the recent works which have advanced the study of diocesan statutes in Europe. Professor Sawicki has himself produced an unequalled series of texts and studies on Polish synods in the ten volumes of his *Concilia Poloniae* (1948–63) and in numerous essays. A great bibliographical undertaking initiated by the late André

Artonne in post-war France has borne fruit in a *Répertoire des statuts synodaux des diocèses de l'ancienne France du xiiie à la fin du xviiie siècle*, by André Artonne, Louis Guizard, and Odette Pontal (Paris, Institut de Recherche et d'Histoire des Textes, 1963). On a smaller scale, from opposite ends of Europe come articles by P. Isaias Da Rosa Pereira on 'Sinodos da diocese de Lisboa. Notas históricas', *Lumen*, xxv (1961), 385–98 and 'Sínodos medievas Portugueses (Séculos xiii–xv)', in *Proc. of the Second Intern. Congress of Med. Canon Law* (Città del Vaticano, 1965), pp. 457–66, 486 and a valuable monograph by Professor Sigurd Kroon, *Det svenska prästmötet under medeltiden* (Acta historico-ecclesiastica Suecana, no. 18, Stockholm, 1948).

PREFACE

THE following essays are the outcome of ten years' study of English diocesan legislation of the thirteenth century; they form, as it were, prolegomena to the edition of the English Church Councils which is now in preparation. They do not attempt to describe fully each set of episcopal statutes or to comment upon the historical interest of particulars contained in them. Such matters as these must await full publication of the texts. At present, the object is simply to observe and illustrate the way in which the statutes were fashioned and the influence of certain series upon others. The introductory chapter on diocesan synods is designed purely to place the synodal statutes in their right setting.

While it is not likely that the discussion will interest more than a limited number of specialist students, and while it is certain that it leaves untouched much that is most interesting in the statutes, there yet seems reason for recording these dry facts and dubious conjectures. For the statutes cannot be used properly until their provenance and their inter-connexion have been understood. Through lack of this understanding, generations of historians and ecclesiologists have misused them in the past. Faith in the ascriptions and dating of the old editors of the *Concilia* is hard to break down. Even the most modern and useful works inevitably suffer from an inadequate realization of the problems which the documents present. The material with which the writers could have formed juster views has not been to hand, and it is high time that the results already reached should be published.

At the beginning of the eighteenth century William Wake recognized the importance of the statutes made in English diocesan synods, and observed: 'of these we have several collections already published in the volumes of our councils, and many more there are still remaining in the registers of our churches.' The second volume of Spelman's *Concilia* had in fact contained eleven sets of thirteenth-century synodal statutes, including the highly important ones of

Richard Poore and of Peter Quivil. Wilkins, working with Wake's materials, added five more sets to the number; but his texts were often bad, and much remained unpublished. It is a scandalous reflection upon English scholarship that since the time of Wilkins's *Concilia* practically nothing has been done to improve the texts or the ascriptions of the published statutes, while only two sets unknown to Wilkins have been edited, and badly edited at that. We are now in a position to add at least eight new sets to those already published. As each of these is known only from one manuscript, it is highly probable that others still lurk unidentified in libraries, while some sets which once existed are irretrievably lost.

It cannot be claimed that the present essays do more than marshal some of the evidence and expose the baselessness of some past assumptions. For two reasons, in particular, the conclusions tentatively set forth here are liable to error. First, the connexion between certain English and continental statutes makes ideally necessary an equally exhaustive survey of French and German *synodalia*. But this work has yet to be undertaken systematically by continental scholars. Heinrich Finke dealt critically with some of the problems in his *Konzilienstudien* in 1891, but in Germany he has only been followed by a few studies dealing with particular dioceses separately. In France the way was prepared in 1911 by Mlle Dobiache-Rojdestvensky's work on *La vie paroissiale*, but there has been no adequate continuation. No finality can be reached until the manuscript tradition of all this continental material has been sifted and compared, and in the present state of world affairs this is impossible. A second marked deficiency of the present study is its failure to use such arguments for dating as might be derived from the theological and canonistic content of the statutes. At the best of times this is likely to be difficult, and for one who is not an expert highly dangerous. It has therefore seemed preferable to proceed as far as possible by other ways in the hope that the work of experts will add precision to these conclusions rather than overturn them.

A word must be said about the system of quoting statutes in this book. For the convenience of readers, references are generally given to printed editions, where these exist. Quotations, however, generally follow the manuscripts in text and orthography, as they are likely to appear in a new edition. Where the printed text now available presents a distinct version, the manuscript authority for the reading quoted is expressly stated; in other cases it has not seemed necessary to encumber the notes with variant readings or references to the manuscript authorities which are fully described in the course of the work. The punctuation and use of capitals in the manuscripts have not been observed.

Finally, I wish to express my gratitude to those who have helped me with their criticism and advice, in particular, Mr. R. W. Hunt, Mr. W. A. Pantin, Professor F. M. Powicke, Mr. R. W. Southern, and my wife. The cathedral chapters of Hereford, Salisbury, and Worcester kindly sent manuscripts for my use to other libraries; so also the Right Reverend the Bishop of Lewes, the Earl of Leicester, the trustees of the late Hon. Lionel Tollemache, and the university librarians of Aberdeen and of Durham. The Dean and chapter of Worcester kindly permit me to reproduce in facsimile a part of their MS. Q 67. I am particularly grateful to the Delegates of the Press for undertaking to publish this book.

C.R.C.

CONTENTS

I

INTRODUCTION : THE DIOCESAN SYNOD

THE diocesan synod, in the period with which these studies are concerned, was already an institution of venerable age, and one whose functions and composition depended rather upon tradition than upon positive enactments. From some scraps of laws and exhortations together with the historical evidence of synods held in different times and places, we can gain an idea of the traditional character of the synods of the later Middle Ages. Custom, it is true, produced many variations in different times and places, in respect of frequency, composition, and business transacted. But the same principles, the same possibilities, were usually recognized. The evidence suggests that the legal character of the diocesan synod did not change vastly from century to century. The contrary opinion was indeed held by Rudolph Sohm, but his views on the nature and authority of ecclesiastical assemblies have not found general acceptance.[1] For the purpose of understanding the circumstances and authority of synodal legislation,[2] it seems permissible first of all to generalize upon the conduct of synods without too strict a regard for time or place. The particular historical evidence of the twelfth and thirteenth centuries can follow after.

The canonists have already prepared the way. The commentaries which had grown up in the later Middle Ages around the statements of the canon law were harvested by a Savoyard priest of the early sixteenth century, Enrico de Botteo (d. 1544). His treatise *De synodo episcopi* was first published at Lyon in 1529. It indulges in excessive detail and leaves nothing to chance. The author tells us he fears prolixity—'inimicam naturae meae'—and well he might.

---

[1] For recent discussion of them in relation to the medieval evidence see Boye's study in *Ztschr. der Savigny-Stiftung*, pp. 135 *seqq.*, and the work of Barion, pp. 122 *seq.*, 166 *seqq.*

[2] This term is convenient, but can only be used with caution. Strictly speaking, the synod was not a legislative assembly and its members did not give legal force to the statutes published by the bishop. Cf. Hauck, *Kirchengesch.*, v. 180; Benedict XIV, *De synodo diœcesana*, bk. xiii ch. 1 and ch. 2 § 1; and below, pp. 8–10.

Every conceivable part of the subject finds a place, at least once, in Botteo's book. Still, for all its tediousness, it provides a comprehensive statement of legal opinions. Others dealt systematically with the same subject after Botteo, some of them at even greater length.

For the purpose of this study we have confined ourselves to three works only, which cover the ground in different ways. While Botteo is indispensable for his full references to canonistic authorities (together with some notes on the abuses of his day), Bartolomeo Gavanti, *consultor* of the Congregation of Rites early in the seventeenth century, had for the main object of his *Praxis exactissima diœcesanæ synodi* (Rome, 1628) that it should serve bishops who wished to know how to conduct a synod. The work is particularly useful for the details about the preliminaries of a synod and for the collection of formulas contained in its fourth part. Finally, the great work of Pope Benedict XIV, *De synodo diœcesana*, deserves attention.[1] It is immensely long and extremely diffuse: the publishers of the second edition claimed truly that it dealt with the whole episcopal office and concerned all orders of Christian society. Despite its many irrelevancies, it is valuable for its careful historical survey of the law and practice of synods. Here it comes into line rather with the historical method of Thomassin, who had devoted a few useful pages to diocesan synods,[2] than with the canonists of earlier days. In using Benedict XIV's work for a study of the Middle Ages we must, of course, remember the more thoroughly centralized administration of the post-Tridentine Church, which explains some differences between Botteo and the eighteenth-century pope.[3]

The modern literature of synods is very extensive, but comparatively little of it is concerned with the diocesan

---

[1] First published at Rome, 1748. The second edition of 1755 is much enlarged and has a dedication by the publishers to the Empress Maria Theresa. The selections published in English translation in 1926 include very little of the parts relating to synodal statutes; the appendix on 'The diocesan synod in Anglo-Saxon times', by C. E. Douglas, is amazingly mistaken.

[2] *Anc. et nouv. discipline*, pt. II, bk. iii chs. 73–5 (vol. v pp. 355–65).

[3] Cf. Addleshaw, 'Diocesan synods', p. 266. This essay gives a very good and clear account of the law as found in Botteo and Benedict XIV.

synod of the Middle Ages.[1] All else is put in the shade by the great work of Hinschius. Both as a legal and as an historical study of the various forms of synodal assembly in the Church, the third part of the second section of the first book of his *System des katholischen Kirchenrechts*, published in 1882, remains the classic exposition of the subject. Any summary account of the diocesan synod, such as is here attempted, must necessarily be under a heavy debt to Hinschius.

The medieval diocesan synod appears in the records under many titles[2]; on the one hand, the terms *generale presbiterorum concilium* and *synodus diocesana* indicate more or less exactly the scope of the assembly, whereas such titles as *synodus episcopi* emphasize the authority that governed its action. The two questions of scope and authority are complementary. Stutz observes that in the early Church the relations of bishops of different sees were controlled by laws, but that for the ecclesiastical hierarchy within each bishopric there was no law but the bishop's will.[3] It follows from this that while in ecumenical and provincial councils the bishops who participated contributed to the authority of the assembly's acts, the clergy who attended a diocesan synod under the presidency of the bishop were under the jurisdiction of the bishop and formed a merely consultative

[1] Hauck's article 'Synoden' in Herzog-Hauck, *Realencyklopädie* spares little space for the diocesan synod; but his historical contributions to the subject in *Kirchengesch. Deutschlands* are of first importance. For the early Middle Ages they are supplemented by the lists of Werminghoff and Boye, by Boye's article in *Ztschr. der Savigny-Stiftung*, and by the works of Barion and De Clercq. Werminghoff, *Verfassungsgesch.*, pp. 219–20, gives a useful brief statement of the nature of diocesan synods in medieval Germany, following Hinschius very closely and adding a bibliography of works on particular German dioceses. For other recent works on particular dioceses and periods see the bibliography below, pp. 153–8.

[2] Hinschius, iii. 586, 591. Cf. Wake, *State of the Church*, p. 25. Wake suggests (*ibid.*, p. 24) that the term *synodus* was also used for assemblies smaller than the general synod of the diocese; he gives no evidence, but we may compare references cited here, below, p. 5, p, 20 n. 11, p. 28 n. 4.

[3] 'Kurz, die ganze bischöfliche Kirche, die Kirche im engeren Sinn, wurde vom Bischof nicht nach Rechtsgrundsätzen, sondern nach freistem Ermessen regirt.' U. Stutz, *Die Eigenkirche als Element des mittelalterlich-germanischen Kirchenrechtes* (Berlin, 1895), p. 13. Cf. C. H. Turner in *Cambr. Med. Hist.*, i. 147–8 and E. W. Watson, *ibid.*, vi. 528–9.

body. This accords with the generally accepted view of the origin of the diocesan synod. It did not 'represent' the bishop's subjects or the Christian community of the diocese: it grew out of the *presbiterium*, or body of priestly helpers, ordained to aid the bishop and called together occasionally by him for consultation.[1] If custom established that the core of the diocesan synod should be this assembly of priests of the diocese, the bishop as ordinary could in theory and often did in fact summon others to his synod for such purposes as seemed good to him. His was the authority in the synod, he could prescribe the matters for transaction, and decide with whom he would consult. Those he summoned were there to give him, in the words of Innocent III's decretal, 'due obedience and reverence'.[2]

As to the objects of the synod, Benedict XIV quotes approvingly the statement of an earlier canonist: ' Episcopalis synodus instituta est quatuor ex causis . . . . Primo, ut depravata corrigantur: secundo, ut ignorantes instruantur: tertio, ut regulæ morum, statutaque formentur: quarto, ut quæ in provinciali synodo decreta sunt, in episcopali publicentur.'[3]

The thirteenth-century canonist, Hostiensis, was responsible for a further distinction on the nature of the assembly. He declares that it is mixed in nature: for in so far as it is a synod (or, as Panormitanus glosses his words, *respectu convocationis*) it is *de lege dyocesana*, but in so far as judgements are given therein and things ordained it is *de lege iurisdictionis*. He illustrates his point with the case of a monastery exempt from the ordinary of the diocese as regards the payment of synodal taxes and so on ; its abbot may yet be obliged to attend the synod in respect of non-exempt over whom he has cure of souls.[4]

---

[1] 'Sie haben nicht . . . die Bedeutung einer Repräsentation von kirchlichen Körpern, sind vielmehr, wie dies auch ihr Ursprung ergiebt, aus dem Presbyterium des Bischofs herausgewachsen, und nehmen neben ihm nur die Stellung einer berathenden Versammlung ein.' Hinschius, iii. 328 ; cf. *ibid.*, 583 n. 3.

[2] *Decretales*, i. 33, 9 'Quod super his' (Innocent III to the archbishop of Rossano, 31 Dec. 1199 : Migne, *Patr. lat.*, ccxiv. 823, Potthast, *Regesta pont.*, no. 919).

[3] *De synodo diœcesana*, vi. 1 § 4, quoting Erasmus Chokier, *De iurisdictione in exemptos*. Cf. David Wilkins, in *Concilia*, i p. vii.

[4] Commenting on *Decretales*, i. 33, 9 : Hostiensis, fo. clixr*b* ; Panormitanus, ii. 112v*b*. Cf. Benedict XIV, i. 4 §§ 3–4.

This distinction drawn by Hostiensis emphasizes an important point. One may classify the business of the synod as administrative or judicial or legislative, but in most, if not in all, of these activities the pastoral element is evident. As in his visitation of the diocese, all aspects of the bishop's pastoral office are illustrated in the synod. As in his visitation, he has to instruct, to correct, and to adjudicate. The two processes of visitation and synodal action are indeed closely bound together. 'The gathering of the clergy to one centre', says Frere, 'and the journey of the bishop round the different centres were each the counterpart of the other.'[1] With slight, but pardonable, exaggeration Bishop White Kennett emphasized this in his primary visitation charge at Peterborough in 1720:

' It is well known', he says, ' that an episcopal visitation was from the beginning, and is still in effect, a diocesan synod, prorogued by the bishop from place and time to other place and time, wherein the bishop is to preside and his clergy to appear and assist; and so jointly to enquire, to inform, to examine, reprove, correct and amend all persons, manners and things within the proper cognizance of the bishop.'[2]

The confusion of the two processes occasionally causes some ambiguity of nomenclature. For a bishop, calling together the clergy and people of an archdeaconry or deanery as he went on circuit, might call the assembly a synod, although it did not represent the whole diocese. This may be the type of assembly which, according to Alexander, bishop of Lincoln, was wont to be held in parish churches of his bishopric;[3] and this may be what is meant by *synodus provincialis* in the Lincoln Cathedral statutes of 1214.[4] So

---

[1] *Visitation articles*, i. 29. Cf. Benedict XIV, i. 2 § 2.

[2] Quoted by Norman Sykes, *Church and State in the eighteenth century* (Cambridge, 1934) p. 137. Maskell's objections to Kennett and Stillingfleet have no weight (*Monumenta rit.*, i. cclxxx seqq.). Botteo (fo. 381ra § 1) uses the parallel of the law of visitation to show that the holding of synods is part of the bishop's right as ordinary and that he can therefore delegate the presidency of it. See also Cheney in *Eng. Hist. Rev.*, l. 206–7.

[3] See below, p. 20.

[4] In which the chaplains of prebends need not plead in a case unless it be brought to the bishop by way of appeal. The *synodus provincialis* is probably held within the archdeaconry (the archdeacon being described as *archidiaconus provincialis*), but contrasts with the *provinciale capitulum*, the archdeacon's chapter (*Lincoln Cathedral statutes*, ii. 140). We must, however, admit that *synodus* was

also the term *testes synodales* is often used to mean witnesses at the bishop's visitation: they act thus in the parochial visitations of Exeter, for example, at Culmstock in 1301.[1] If these *testes* were appointed in the synod to bear witness at the visitation, the two processes had indeed merged into one.

We see the pastoral aspect of the synod again in the ceremonial which formed the framework of its sessions. The medieval liturgical books of the Latin Church which are known as Pontificals provide, among other episcopal services, the forms proper to the assembly, including processions, special prayers, and exhortations.[2] It is true that some early pontificals which have come down to us entitle this section ' Qualiter concilium agatur provinciale', whereas the title of provincial council is rarely recorded for a diocesan synod,[3] and that they draw on the rules for the conduct of provincial assemblies laid down in the Fourth Council of Toledo. But the text of the liturgy suggests,

sometimes applied to archidiaconal assemblies as well as to the smaller synods of the bishop (cf. *Hist. et cart. S. Petri Glouc.*, ii. 167–9).

[1] *Register of Walter de Stapeldon, bishop of Exeter*, ed. F. C. Hingeston-Randolph (London, 1892) p. 130.

[2] It may suffice to cite a few examples without attempting to establish pedigrees and relationships. The *Liber pontificalis ordinis* (1292–5) of Durandus ' Speculator', bishop of Mende, was the basis of the *Pontificale romanum* as revised late in the fifteenth century. In part iii of Durandus occurs 'Ordo ad consilium seu synodum celebrandum': cf. P. de Puniet, *The Roman pontifical, a history and commentary*, trs. M. V. Harcourt (London, 1932) pp. 37–43 and H. Leclercq, ' Pontifical', in Cabrol and Leclercq, *Dictionnaire d'archéologie chrét. et de liturgie*. An edition of Durand is planned for the Vatican series of *Studi e testi*. Another short 'Ordo ad celebrandum synodum' occurs in the Metz pontifical of 1302–16: *The Metz pontifical*, ed. E. S. Dewick (Roxburghe Club, 1902) cols. 59–62. The order ' Qualiter concilium agatur provinciale prima secunda et tercia die' in the twelfth-century *Pontifical of Magdalen College*, ed. H. A. Wilson (H. Bradshaw Soc. 39, 1910) pp. 54–6, cf. 262–3, occurs without much variation in other early texts including that printed by Spelman (*Concilia*, ii. 1–3) and Wilkins (*Concilia*, iv. 784–6) and in the later *Liber pontificalis of Edmund Lacy bishop of Exeter*, ed. Ralph Barnes (Exeter, 1847) pp. 53–6. In the form of these texts it is clearly designed for a diocesan synod. English MSS. of the eleventh and fifteenth centuries preserve another 'Ordo qualiter ab episcopo synodus agatur' printed by Maskell, *Mon. rit.*, i. 218–24; cf. Henderson, *Liber pont. Chr. Bainbridge* (Surtees Soc., 61, 1875) p. xxix.

A fine representation of the bishop in the opening procession of a synod heads the 'Ordo' in the Metz pontifical (fo. 98, plate 83). Woodcuts from the *Pontificale romanum* of 1520 and 1572 are reproduced in *Pontifical services*, iv, ed. Athelstan Riley (Alcuin Club coll., xii, 1908) figs. 101–5.

[3] Cf. *Eng. Hist. Rev.*, l. 196, 197 n. 1.

by its constant use of the word 'synod' in preference to 'council' and by its reference to the bishop as president, that the form had been worked over at an early date to serve for a diocesan synod. The insistence upon correct dress and order of sitting,[1] the preference for the bishop's cathedral church as the place of session,[2] bring into relief the hierarchical position of the bishop and his spiritual functions in the synod. The pontificals direct that to close the proceedings the bishop shall admonish the clergy and instruct the people and close his sermon with the remission of sins.[3] At this point it should, however, be noted that the diocesan celebrates his synod as ordinary, not as one consecrated to the episcopal office. According to Botteo, 'potestas congregandi synodum non confertur in consecratione episcopi, et non est de his quæ sunt ordinis, sed est de his, quæ sunt iurisdictionis'. Whence it comes about that not only may a bishop-elect celebrate a diocesan synod, but a bishop may delegate the presidency to a vicar-general or other official, or the synod may be celebrated *sede vacante* by the appropriate authority.[4]

The duty of pastoral instruction appears prominently in the use of the synod to publish the canons of general and provincial councils. Already demanded in the Sixteenth Council of Toledo (A.D. 693),[5] this was again ordered in the Fourth Lateran Council,[6] and is stressed by later canonists. Such publication as this did not add in any way to the validity of the laws, nor did the bishop thereby exercise legislative power. But by insisting that their clergy should listen to the recital and exposition of the canons[7] and even take away written copies from the synods,[8] diocesans were

---

[1] Botteo, fos. 384vb–385rb §§ 8–33 ; Gavanti, part i ch. 13 ; Thomassin, II. iii. 75 § 6 (vol. v p. 362b, cf. p. 363b). A constitution of Pope Clement IV (1266) described the sort of mitre which a mitred abbot was permitted to wear in episcopal synods. *Reg. Pontissara*, ii. 754 (Potthast, *Reg. pontificum*, 19801).

[2] Cf. Benedict XIV, i. 5 § 6.

[3] 'Postea vero episcopus moneat clerum et doceat populum, atque in fine predicationis remissionem peccatorum faciat.' *Pontifical of Magdalen Coll.*, p. 56.

[4] With due modification of rites. Botteo, fo. 379rb §§ 31, 32.

[5] *Decretum*, i. 18, 17.

[6] *Decretales*, v. 1, 25. Cf. *Eng. Hist. Rev.*, l. 209.

[7] Botteo, fo. 385rb § 36.

[8] Cf. *Eng. Hist. Rev.*, l. 212–13.

combating that ignorance of the faith and the law which constituted so grave a problem in the medieval Church.

On the judicial side, the synod was a recognized occasion for the bishop to correct the faith and morals of his subjects. This might be done by following up the *comperta* of a visitation, or as the result of reports made by *testes syno-dales*[1] on the basis of previous inquiry, or after a *scrutinium*[2] conducted in the synod itself. Accusations were made, compurgators received, and penalties inflicted. The procedure was not peculiar to the synod, but could be carried through there with fitting solemnity and accorded well with the aims of the synod. Prayers in the pontificals implore the aid of the Holy Spirit in the doing of justice: 'esto solus et suggestor et effector iudiciorum nostrorum'.

The jurisdiction of the bishop in civil causes was at all times considerable, and in certain periods is prominent in synodal records. All manner of litigation concerning ecclesiastical property, as well as all other classes of action claimed for the courts christian, came before him or his deputies. He heard the disputes of rectors and their vicars, the claims of 'appropriating' monasteries, tithe suits, and many other matters. Besides this, he provided an important court of record, which witnessed transactions between individuals, and lent his authority to the transference of lands and churches to ecclesiastical corporations.

Finally, the bishop used his synod to make and publish statutes for his diocese. Both Botteo and Benedict XIV give more extended treatment to this than to any other part of their subject. Botteo attaches importance to the word *statuta* as the correct title for a bishop's legislation; he does not sanction *constitutiones* or *canones*, although he has to admit that some jurists have used the words. Practice in the Middle Ages had varied: all these words, and *decreta* and *precepta* besides, were used apparently indifferently;

---

[1] Cf. Council of Basel (1433) session 15. On their duties see Botteo, fos. 385vb–386ra §§ 58–74; on their appointment and summons, Gavanti, i. 33 note 10 and iv. 3 § 2. Benedict XIV, who deals fully with the matter (iv. 3 § 8), says how hard it is to find good men to undertake the task. See also Van Espen, part i, tit. 18 ch. 3 (vol. i pp. 158–9) and *Eng. Hist. Rev.*, l. 204–6.

[2] See especially Gavanti, i. 23 § 11 and (for articles of inquiry) iv. 4 § 6. Benedict XIV says that the synodal scrutiny was often omitted: v. 3 §§ 5–7.

and Benedict XIV later on preferred the word *constitutiones*.[1] There seems no legal or historical justification for the distinction which M. Jusselin wishes to make between 'statuts' and 'constitutions';[2] we shall do well to adhere to 'statutes' as a convenient term to which none can take exception.

The canonists are agreed that the bishop's is the authority which makes the synodal statutes binding.[3] It is not for the assembly to frame the statutes, for the bishop could with equal right compose them without reference to a synod or dispense against statutes made with his synod:[4] the main object of issuing the statutes in a synod is to ensure publicity. Not only does the bishop ensure by this means that copies of the statutes are diffused: they become immediately binding upon those who heard them published, whereas the law would otherwise allow the lapse of some months before they took effect.[5] But the bishop is expected to take advice in the framing of his statutes and in some cases the law demands that he do so. Normally, he will make use of the same machinery which directs his judicial action in the synod: the *testes synodales* and the *scrutinarii*[6] will be called upon to advise and regard will be paid to the findings of visitations. In the post-Tridentine Church, preliminary meetings of the bishop with regular prelates and committees of theologians and canonists were also recommended.[7] But it seems that the bishop might call these

---

[1] Cf. Botteo, fo. 387ra §§ 108–9 and Benedict XIV, bk. i ch. 3. The gloss on *Decretales*, i. 33, 2 uses the words *decreta, constitutiones, canones episcopales* for a bishop's statutes.

[2] 'Les véritables statuts complets commencent toujours par un traité sur les sacrements, fond permanent que conserve toute nouvelle édition ; les constitutions synodales, au contraire, apparaissent généralement comme des additions à ce fond, elles ne sont pas toujours reproduites dans la suite des temps, ou ne le sont qu'en partie.' Jusselin, 'Statuts synodaux . . .' p. 72.

[3] Cf. Botteo, fo. 387ra §§ 103–4.

[4] *Ibid.*, fo. 387rb § 111 and fo. 405vb § 9.

[5] *Ibid.*, fo. 404vab §§ 1–5.

[6] 'Antequam dimittatur synodus, valde utile erit ut hi præfecti [scrutinarii] conveniant coram episcopo et summarie referant communiorem statum totius cleri, quod si quid in communi monendum erit, decreto opportuno imminenti malo provideatur, antequam discedat clerus.' Gavanti, part i, ch. 23 § 11.

[7] *Ibid.*, part i, chs. 4–6. 'Ex his [congregationibus] et ex visitatione proxima civitatis et diœcesis, opera prædictorum consultorum haurienda est materia decretorum synodi, quæ debet esse de iis, in quibus ut plurimum peccatur' (*ibid.*, i. 4 § 7). 'Distribui possunt diversi tituli materiarum synodalium prædictos inter

committees together for information rather than for advice. It was otherwise when he consulted his cathedral chapter. Here the law laid upon him the explicit obligation to discuss his proposed statutes on matters of major importance.[1] Even so, Botteo thought it very doubtful whether the bishop was obliged to follow the advice which he received from his chapter. Gavanti is careful to say that the chapter should be summoned to a synod 'ut de canonicorum consilio stabiliantur [decreta] *non autem de consensu*'.[2] Benedict XIV maintains, with great display of authorities, that the chapter has a right to be consulted but no *votum decisivum*.[3]

The statutes lawfully promulgated in a synod were perpetually binding on the subjects of the diocesan and his successors.[4] His subjects, for this purpose, are deemed to be all those who are under his diocesan jurisdiction in so far as they are not exempt by privilege. Thus, exempt persons who offend against the statutes in non-exempt places within the diocese are bound by the statutes.[5] Laity as well as clergy are bound, since they too are subjects of the bishop *ratione delicti*.[6]

As regards scope, the diocesan statute is invalid if it is contrary to the common laws of the church or to the laws of the particular province of the Church, or if it is prejudicial to the bishop's superiors, pope or archbishop or primate.[7]

consultores; ut quisque suggerat, quod in domino expedire iudicaverit' (*ibid.*, i. 6 § 1). Cf. Benedict XIV, vi. 1 § 1.

[1] Cf. *Decretales*, iii. 10, 4 and gloss; Botteo, fo. 382ra § 26 and fos. 387vb–388ra §§ 137–42.

[2] Gavanti, i. 6 § 8, with notes on various opinions.

[3] 'Nisi in casibus a iure expressis': bk. xiii ch. 1 *passim*, esp. §§ 6, 9. The question is part of the much broader one of the entire relations of bishop and chapter, which need not be touched on here; cf. Panormitanus i. 76c (on *Decretales*, i. 4, 9 Cum consuetudinis) and Hinschius, iii. 595. Dr. Claude Jenkins seems to rate the counsel-taking rather too highly when he likens it to the action of provincial councils: 'It was possible also for him [the bishop] to promulge in his diocesan synod ordinances of a more general application for the well-governing of clergy and people in the same way that archiepiscopal constitutions were promulged in the provincial synod. There was probably less of autocracy about such a proceeding in either case than might at first appear.' *Episcopacy ancient and modern*, ed. C. Jenkins and K. D. Mackenzie (London, 1930) p. 81. Cf. *Eng. Hist. Rev.*, l. 200.

[4] Botteo, fo. 404vb § 6. Botteo deals at length (fo. 402 §§ 50–66) with the conditions in which a synodal statute may lapse through desuetude and when the rules of lawful prescription can be applied. Cf. below, pp. 98 and 139.

[5] *Ibid.*, fo. 400vb § 5.   [6] *Ibid.*, fo. 400ra §§ 3–4.   [7] *Ibid.*, fo. 390ra § 13.

Benedict XIV adds a caution to bishops against making in their synods theological decisions on matters not defined by the Apostolic See.[1] Within these limits, the pastoral office of the bishop permits him to deal with all sorts of questions concerning the cure of souls. To borrow the same writer's words : 'asserimus debere episcopum in sua synodo constituere, quæ ad vitia coercenda, virtutem promovendam, depravatos populi mores reformandos, et ecclesiasticam disciplinam aut restituendam, aut fovendam, necessaria et utilia esse judicaverit.'[2] It may often happen that the bishop finds it unnecessary for this purpose to issue new legislation : he will be content to reiterate certain sections of the common law or provincial canons or statutes of his own predecessors. He may issue these selections under his own name, with such explanations of doubtful points as he thinks desirable.[3] He may also add penalties where the law states none, or may add anathemas and pecuniary penalties beyond those imposed by the canon.[4]

Undoubtedly one of the main uses of the synodal statutes was the opportunity they offered for simple exposition of matters dealt with too briefly or too obscurely in the canons.[5] This copying, which is sanctioned by law and very often found in practice, has sometimes misled modern scholars to depreciate unduly the diocesan statutes. The fact that the two most explicit statements in the *Corpus Iuris* on episcopal synods[6] are exclusively concerned with the publishing of provincial canons has contributed to the error. But the older canonists clearly attached great importance to the independent power of the diocesan bishop in this respect, and historical considerations suggest that they were

---

[1] *De Synodo diœc.*, vii. 1 § 1.   [2] *Ibid.*, vi. 1 § 1.

[3] Botteo, fo. 392va § 95 ; cf. Gavanti, i. 6 § 4 and Benedict XIV, vi. 1 § 2. The bishop's 'declaratio seu interpretatio' will only bind his subjects (Botteo, fo. 392vb § 100), and if the pope revoke the original law the bishop's statute is thereby revoked (*ibid.*, fo. 393ra § 103).

[4] Botteo, fo. 393 §§ 106–28. The author protests against the abuse of these. powers in his day (§§ 113, 128).

[5] Gavanti insists that statutes should be written in Latin, but may be glossed in the vernacular by the bishop when they are recited in synod (i. 6 §§ 6–7, cf. i. 22 .§ 2).

[6] *Decretum*, i. 18, 17 'Decernimus ut dum' (16th Council of Toledo, 693) ; *Decretales*, v. 1, 25 'Sicut olim' (4th Lateran Council, 1215).

right. As Schulte points out, in respect of practical details, in the Middle Ages and even more since the Council of Trent, the legal structure conformed to the diocese rather than the province.[1] Great latitude was allowed to local custom in regard to rites, payments to the Church, remuneration of the clergy. The diocesan synod could reconcile custom and law on these points better than could the provincial council. Therefore Botteo held that, while a bishop's statutes ought to be interpreted if possible to conform with the common law, if the words do not follow precisely the terms of the common law, they ought to be interpreted so that they add to rather than are identified with it.[2] A bishop may even, subject to certain restrictions, make statutes conformable to custom, and derive authority for them from custom, although the custom be contrary to law.[3] He may also modify the operation of a law in circumstances which the law does not specify, so long as he can allege a reasonable cause.[4] The other conditions of diocesan legislation discussed by Botteo seem to be of less significance; it may be remarked that the question was gravely discussed by canonists, whether a bishop's sumptuary laws were valid against a husband's desire to see his wife well dressed. Zanetus says: 'uxor debet potius obedire marito quam episcopo, quando ornatus non est de se peccatum, alias secus.'[5]

After this short survey of the synod's business—inquiry, instruction, correction, and law-making—we can amplify a little our first statement about the composition of the assembly. The authority of the bishop was such that it is doubtful whether he could be forced to summon any particular person or class of persons, unless it was his cathedral chapter, which had the right to attend if its interests were

[1] 'Die Rechtsbildung hinsichtlich der praktischen Einzelnheiten ist schon im Mittelalter und noch mehr seit dem Tridentinum nicht nach Provinzen, sondern nach Diözesen erfolgt.' *Gesch.*, III. i. 90.

[2] Botteo, fo. 407r §§ 7–10, citing Panormitanus on *Decretales*, i. 3, 18, who does not explicitly refer to bishops' statutes (i. 45, cf. i. 75vb on *Decretales*, i. 4, 8).

[3] Botteo, fo. 393ra § 104. On the other hand, 'statutum contrarium consuetudini quod reducit nos ad ius commune debet valere' (*ibid.*, § 105).

[4] *Ibid.*, fo. 391vb §§ 62 *seqq.*   [5] *Ibid.*, fo. 394rb § 138.

concerned;[1] but this question can seldom have had more than an academic interest. Of more practical importance was the bishop's power to compel attendance.

Throughout the Middle Ages uncertainty persisted on this point. The pastoral purposes of the synod suggest that its most ancient and important element were priests with cure of souls. But if the purposes were broadly interpreted, the bishop might wish to summon all sorts and conditions of men. The decree of the Sixteenth Council of Toledo (A.D. 693) incorporated in the *Decretum* of Gratian (i. 18, 17) does indeed demand that the bishop shall bring together 'omnes abbates, presbyteros, diaconos atque clericos, seu etiam omnem conventum civitatis ipsius ubi praeesse dignoscitur, necnon et cunctam dioecesis suae plebem'. The pontificals, repositories of early traditions, allow for the presence of deacons and subdeacons, and of layfolk 'bone conversationis vel qui electione concilii interesse meruerint'.[2] But these regulations can have borne scant resemblance to the practice of the medieval Church. It was absurd to think of mobilizing annually in the cathedral church almost the whole population of a diocese. Other customs prevailed, and the canonists of the later Middle Ages palpably rely to a great extent on custom.[3] They got little help from the common law: the *Decretales* only yielded an ambiguous text about the attendance of abbots for them to gloss, and when Innocent IV and Panormitanus refer to *Decretum*, i. 18, 17, they both ignore its reference to the laity.[4] All that we can do is to state the canonists' opinions and relate them to the practice recorded in the twelfth and thirteenth centuries.

The canonists would permit the bishop to compel all with the cure of souls to attend his synod, unless they have special

---

[1] *Ibid.*, fo. 382ra §§ 24, 26.

[2] *Pontifical of Magdalen Coll.*, p. 54. By an early misreading of the Council of Toledo, the medieval pontifical texts read 'electione coniugali'. The pontificals demand that the laity withdraw while the clergy's *querelae* are being heard.

[3] Cf. Botteo, fo. 382rb § 37.

[4] Gloss on *Decretales*, iii. 5, 29 'Grave nimis': Innocent IV says 'Ad episcopale autem concilium vocandi sunt abbates sacerdotes et omnem clerum civitatis et diocesis convocare debet episcopus'; cf. Panormitanus, vol. vi fo. 36rb.

Decretum, i. 18, 16, which demands the attendance of clerks, abbots, and monks, is spurious (see Friedberg's edition).

privilege. Even those ruling parishes within exempt jurisdictions were liable to be called;[1] also, monks and canons
holding parochial cures.[2] Botteo shows that the decretal
'Quod super his' of Innocent III, so frequently glossed
by canonists, which demanded the attendance of abbots,
stated no simple rule. Abbots need not attend the synod
without a special summons, unless they have cure of souls
over the bishop's subjects.[3] Even abbots thus obliged need
not attend in person unless they exercise their cure personally.[4] But Benedict XIV, looking back to the pre-Tridentine
period, found many indications that non-exempt abbots
were commonly expected to attend episcopal synods.[5] For
them, as for other classes of persons whose attendance might
be required, custom counted for much and might create
a duty.[6]

Others besides those with cures were commonly summoned, and if summoned, bound to attend. Firstly, all
secular prelates subordinate to the bishop; 'for', says
Botteo, 'the bishop who presides in the synod and has
ordinary jurisdiction ought to conduct everything with their
advice'.[7] Secondly, the bishop might (according to Innocent
IV's commentary) summon all priests without cure and all
clerks holding 'simple benefices'.[8] Panormitanus agrees
with this in general but would limit it to occasions when
the bishop wishes to publish statutes concerning the whole
clergy or proceed to the reformation of manners.[9] The
cathedral chapter might be exempt from regular attendance
because its members had not the cure of souls; but the

---

[1] Botteo, fo. 381vb § 16; Benedict XIV, bk. iii ch. 5.
[2] Botteo, fo. 381va § 9. Gregory IX complained that certain prelates forced
Mendicant friars to attend their synods. *Decretales*, v. 31, 17 and gloss 'ad
synodos'.
[3] *Ibid.*, fo. 381va § 6 and *Decretales*, i. 33, 9 gloss. Cf. *Decretum*, i. 18, 11
and gloss: the ascription of the decree to the Council of Tours is wrong; it occurs
in the penitential of Theodore. *Die Canones Theodori Cantuariensis*, ed. P. W.
Finsterwalder (Weimar, 1929) pp. 254, 272, 313.
[4] Botteo, fo. 381va § 7. Cf. Benedict XIV, iii. 1 § 11.
[5] Benedict XIV, iii. 1 § 1.
[6] Botteo, fo. 382rb § 37; Benedict XIV, iii. 6 § 5.   [7] Botteo, fo. 381va § 14.
[8] 'Qui instituuntur perpetuo in oratoriis et capellis.'
[9] Innocent IV on *Decretales*, iii. 5, 29 'Grave nimis'; Panormitanus on the
same (vol. vi fo. 36rb) and on *Decretales*, i. 33, 9 'Quod super his' (vol. ii
fo. 112vb); Botteo, fo. 381vb §§ 17–18; Benedict XIV, bk. iii ch. 6.

bishop was expected to seek the chapter's advice for so many purposes, and especially for the making of statutes, that the canons were generally summoned and, being summoned, ought to attend.[1] The last class which remains to be considered is the laity. The bishop might seem to have as much reason to summon them as to summon any class of his subjects; but the canonists generally held that he should only do so when he had provincial statutes to publish or when other special business required their presence.[2] In any case they were present as auditors only, and should be excluded from those sessions which concerned the correction of the clergy.[3] Finally, it is obvious that the judicial purpose of the synod at all times might bring to it individuals, ecclesiastical and lay, to appear in litigation.[4]

As the composition of the synod depended on local custom or the special needs of the moment rather than on any general enactment, so with its time and period of session. Until the thirteenth century the ancient custom of the Church, as represented by the pontificals, was based upon the early regulations for provincial councils; these decreed that two councils be held annually, in summer and in autumn.[5] But whether this custom was ever generally observed we cannot say. The decree 'Sicut olim' of the Fourth Lateran Council (*Decretales*, v. 1, 25) contented itself with demanding annual synods: this remained the common law requirement, while commentators recognized that the decree did not prevent a second annual synod where this was usual.[6] The Council of Basel, in its fifteenth session, decreed that the diocesan synod should be held 'at least once a year, where twice a year is not customary'. Most of the pontifical services allow for a synod of three

[1] Botteo, fo. 381v*b* §§ 22–6 ; Benedict XIV, bk. iii ch. 4.

[2] Benedict XIV (iii. 9 § 8) fears that summoning of laymen may establish a customary claim to attend.

[3] Botteo, fo. 382r §§ 33–5, citing Panormitanus, Andreas, and others.

[4] Botteo, fo. 382r*b* § 39.

[5] 'Sancta sinodus bis in anno decrevit habere concilia, unum estate, aliud tempore autumni.' *Pontifical of Magdalen Coll.*, p. 54; cf. the texts in distinctio 18 of the *Decretum*.

[6] Cf. Benedict XIV, i. 6 §§ 1–3. The legate Courçon's council at Paris, which in more than one detail anticipates the Fourth Lateran Council, demanded episcopal synods 'saltem semel in anno'. Mansi, *Concilia*, xxii, col. 843.

days, but this created no general rule; nor, so far as we know, did any general rule exist.[1]

Does the diocesan synod as represented in liturgy and law bear much resemblance to the actual assemblies of the Middle Ages? To generalize even over a comparatively short period is dangerous, so various was custom at different times and places; but even so, some correspondence can be established between the system described above and the conduct of synods in the twelfth and thirteenth centuries in England, France, and Germany. Despite scantiness of records, we can safely say that the institution was active. In this period, at least, there seems no justification for a recent statement that 'in the Middle Ages the bishop used [the synod] as part of his visitation, but there is no evidence that it was more than a somewhat formal meeting only occasionally summoned'.[2] The terms in which the records refer to synods suggest that they were common occasions for all kinds of business envisaged by the canons.

While our information about continental synods is far more copious than that about English ones, we cannot be sure that they were most thriving abroad. It seems rather to be the result of the habit of some continental legislators: whereas the English bishops seldom mention the synod in their synodal statutes, French and German prelates describe the procedure fairly fully, with instructions to priests about their dress, about their journey, and about the provision for the parishes in their absence. Interesting as these details are, they will only be mentioned here when they are thought to throw light upon English usage. The evidence for English diocesan synods is mainly found in charters, judgements, and compositions. As these documents seldom bear full dating clauses we are unable to say what was the usual time of meeting or how many synods were held annually. We have records of synods held in

---

[1] The Salisbury pontifical in Brit. Mus. Cotton MS., Tib. C. 1 gives a form for synods to last four days: Henderson, *Liber pont. Chr. Bainbridge* (Surtees Society, 61, 1875) p. xxix. The Council of Basel leaves the matter open: 'Quæ synodus saltem biduo vel triduo duret, vel prout necessarium episcopis visum fuerit.'

[2] Dr. C. F. Garbett, in *Episcopacy ancient and modern*, ed. C. Jenkins and K. D. Mackenzie, p. 101.

April at Bath in 1220, at London in 1250, and at Exeter in 1287;[1] on 6 May at York in 1158;[2] on 8 May and 17 May at Worcester in 1229 and 1233 respectively;[3] about 25 May at Rochester in 1225;[4] on 14 June at Exeter in 1133;[5] and on 26 July at Worcester in 1240.[6] Autumn synods are often recorded about Michaelmastide, as in the dioceses of Exeter 1169,[7] Lincoln 1192,[8] Norwich 1201,[9] Worcester 1219, 1220, and 1252;[10] synods of Chichester meet on 6 October 1289 and 14 October 1292;[11] at Winchester the synodal statutes order an annual synod on the Thursday before St. Denis (9 October);[12] synods of Canterbury 1187[13] and Rochester 1244[14] meet about All Saints. At Norwich in 1255 there were customarily two synods a year, the Easter one and the Michaelmas one, and this custom obtained a century later.[15] From these miscellaneous indications one may infer that an autumn synod was usual but that except in Exeter, Norwich, Rochester, and Worcester there is nothing to suggest the holding of a second synod in the year. The earlier synod, the 'summer synod' of which the pontificals speak, might be held at any time from April to July, usually following Easter or Whitsun. Fourteenth-century evidence adds Durham, Ely, and York to the number of dioceses which held two synods annually.[16]

[1] *Hist. MSS. Commission Report, Wells,* i (1907) 52 ; Brit. Mus., Harl. MS. 3697 fos. 46, 49 ; Wilkins, ii. 161b.

[2] *Hist. et cart. S. Petri Glouc.* (Rolls series) ii. 107.

[3] *Annales monastici,* i. 73, 90, iv. 425.

[4] Wharton, *Anglia sacra,* i. 393.

[5] Stenton, 'Acta episcoporum' *Cambr. Hist. Journal,* iii. 10.

[6] Wilkins, i. 665 (morrow of St. James), *Annales mon.,* iv. 432 (St. Anne's day).

[7] A. Morey, *Bartholomew of Exeter* (Cambridge, 1937) p. 147.

[8] *Cart. of Osney,* ed. H. E. Salter (Oxf. Hist. Soc.) iv. 431–3.

[9] Oxford, Bodl. Norfolk rolls, 82c.

[10] *Annales mon.,* i. 65, iv. 411, i. 150.   [11] Wilkins, ii. 169, 183.

[12] (1262–7) : *Reg. Joh. Pontissara,* i. 239.

[13] *Epistolæ cantuarienses* (Rolls series) p. 155.

[14] Matth. Paris, *Chron. majora* (Rolls series) iv. 393.

[15] Wilkins, i. 708–9. A late twelfth-century deed refers to two synods a year, without recording dates : Norwich Cathedral muniments, 'Norwich misc.' box, N. 676. References to the Michaelmas synod and to the Easter synod occur in 1201 (Bodl., Norfolk rolls 82c) and 1277 (Bodl., Norfolk ch. 625) respectively. References to the Easter and Michaelmas synods occur in the early fourteenth-century episcopal registers : *ibid.,* Register i fo. 9r, Register ii fos. 82r, 83v.

[16] Wilkins, ii. 416b ; *Vetus liber arch. eli.,* pp. 16, 26 (? late thirteenth cent.)

In most French dioceses, but not in all,[1] there were supposed to be two synods a year; a spring or summer synod which commonly followed Easter or Whitsun, and an autumn or winter synod,[2] usually after St. Luke's or All Saints. In Germany there is little to suggest that two synods a year were a common custom in this period.[3] The autumn synod was apparently the more common and was held in September or October; another synod, if at all, about Eastertide.[4]

The synod appears to have been a regularly recognized obligation, and its summoning in this period apparently was not so remarkable as to occasion comment; but we cannot be sure that the regulations were perfectly maintained in any province of the Western Church.[5] In England we can point to a handful of documents executed in synods of the twelfth and thirteenth centuries;[6] to statements of obligation or exemption and excuses for absence, which

and *Sacrist Rolls of Ely*, ed. F. R. Chapman (Cambridge, 1907) ii. 16 (1302–3); Wilkins, iii. 69*b*.

[1] At Cahors a Whitsun synod only was held, and at Meaux only a synod in the third week of September. Dobiache-Rojdestvensky, pp. 47, 49–50.

[2] 'Yemalis' at Mende. Durandus, *Instructions*, p. 95. 'In synodo hyemali celebrata die martis post festum omnium sanctorum': Carcassonne, 1295. Dobiache-Rojdestvensky, p. 34.

[3] Hinschius thought it was becoming commoner in the thirteenth century (*System*, iii. 588, 591). Hauck is sceptical (*Kirchengesch.*, v. 169). Schreiber produces no evidence for his statement that ' in general, in the twelfth and thirteenth centuries, two diocesan synods were held each year ' (*Kurie und Kloster*, i. 216 n. 3).

[4] Cf. Hauck, *Kirchengesch.*, iv. 8 and v. 167–70 notes. Dom Berlière's hypothesis that pentecostal processions to cathedral churches originally coincided with synods held at Whitsun supposes a more general custom of Whitsun synods than he can find evidence of. Berlière, ' Les processions des croix banales ', pp. 426–8.

[5] Cf. Dobiache-Rojdestvensky, pp. 47–8 ; Hauck, *Kirchengesch.*, iv. 7–8 and v. 166–8. In Poland diocesan synods rarely met : Vetulani, p. 398.

[6] Canterbury (1189 × 1190) J. Thorpe, *Reg. roffense* (London, 1769) p. 49. Coventry and Lichfield (1129 × 1138) *Reg. antiquiss. Lincoln*, ed. C. W. Foster (Linc. Rec. Soc.) ii. 8 no. 317 ; (1149 × 1161) Brit. Mus. Cotton ch. xiii. 6 (19) ; (1161 × 1179) Brit. Mus. Harl. MS. 3650 fo. 37v. Exeter (1133 and 1169), above, p. 17 n. 5 and n. 7 ; (1171) G. Oliver, *Monasticon diœcesis exon.* add. supp. p. 5. Hereford (1137) Wilkins, i. 413 ; (1148 × 1163) *Cart. S. Petri Glouc.*, i. 253, iii. 6. Lincoln (*c.* 1155) *Transcripts of Gilbertine charters*, ed. F. M. Stenton (Linc. Rec. Soc.) p. 5 ; (1192) above, p. 17 n. 8. Llandaff (1146) *Cart. S. Petri Glouc.*, ii. 55 ; (1149 × 1161) *ibid.*, ii. 52, 54. Norwich (1201) above, p. 17 n. 15. St. Andrews (*c.* 1148) *Early Scottish charters*, ed. A. C. Lawrie, p. 166. Winchester (1167 × 1179) Brit. Mus. Lansdowne MS. 416 fo. 46v. Worcester (1092) Wilkins, i. 369–70. York (1144 × 1147) W. Farrer, *Lancashire pipe rolls*, &c., pp. 280–1.

argue the existence of synods;[1] and to a few incidental references.[2] The series of synodal statutes begins in the second decade of the thirteenth century. These bear witness to more frequent synods than their number at first suggests, since statutes often show signs of re-handling in successive synods. But as evidence of frequency, all this, it must be admitted, is inconclusive.

The pontificals in use in England at this time prescribed a form of liturgy for three days' sessions,[3] but no record proves the practice or gives any clue. Continental records suggest a shorter procedure. We possess several accounts of the way in which synods should be conducted: in the statutes of Odo de Sully, bishop of Paris at the beginning of the thirteenth century,[4] in those of a bishop of Cambrai about the end of the century,[5] and in the pontifical of Metz.[6] None of these proves that a synod was meant to last longer than one day. The *constitutiones* of Durandus allow for sessions of two days for the diocesan synods of Mende, and two days was the normal duration elsewhere in France.[7] For the diocese of Rouen explicit record fortunately survives for a series of synods held in the time of Archbishop Rigaud (1248–75). Here the archbishop's register records, year after year, in summer and in autumn,[8] a synod held

---

[1] Below, pp. 22–3.
[2] Bath and Wells (1192 × 1206) *Hist. MSS. Comm. Report, Wells*, i (1907) 30. Canterbury (1187) above, p. 17 n. 13. Chichester (1148 × 1154) *Chronicon mon. de Bello* (Anglia christiana Soc., 1846) pp. 68–71. Coventry and Lichfield (? 1189) *Rotuli curiæ regis*, ed. F. Palgrave, i. 66; (1193 × 1205) *Hist. MSS. Comm. Various coll.*, i. 238; Norwich (late twelfth century) above, p. 17 n. 15. St. David's (1100 × 1135) *Cart. S. Petri Glouc.*, i. 265. [3] Cf. above, p. 15.
[4] Mansi, xxii. col. 675. Found in an enlarged form preceding the statutes of the diocese of Meaux (Martène and Durand, iv, col. 891).
[5] Gousset, ii. 441.
[6] *The Metz pontifical*, ed. E. S. Dewick, cols. 59–62. So also the later pontifical of Poiters (now lost): see H. Leclercq, 'Pontifical' in *Dict. d'archéol. chrét. et de liturgie*, xiv (1939) col. 1444.
[7] 'Statuimus et ordinamus ut omni anno synodus paschalis celebretur in ecclesia Mimatensi, vel ubi episcopus ordinaverit, feria quarta et quinta hebdomade illius qua cantatur *Ego sum pastor bonus*. Yemalis vero synodus celebretur eisdem diebus semper in ea hebdomada in qua festum beati Luche evangeliste occurrerit' (Durandus, *Instructions*, p. 95). In 1289 the statutes of Rodez order synods to be held in this diocese twice a year, on Tuesdays and Wednesdays (Martène and Durand, iv, col. 673).
[8] 'Synodus estivalis' and 'synodus penthecostes' (Rigaud, *Regestrum*, pp 368, 403); 'synodus hiemalis' (Pommeraye, *Concilia rotomag.*, p. 252).

on one day followed by the *synodus decanorum* on the next.[1] The first day's proceedings were clearly the most solemn, described as *maior* or *sacra synodus*,[2] celebrated in the cathedral church, with mass[3] and a sermon by the archbishop,[4] and to it came the abbots.[5] The synod of the deans, on the the other hand, was held in the archbishop's hall or some other room,[6] and was concerned with disciplinary cases and the promulgation of statutes. This Norman practice is noted here for its own interest, not because it can be regarded as throwing any light at all on English custom.

There is nothing in the records of this period to present a violent contrast between practice and the canonists' statements regarding the composition of the synod and the formalities observed there. If the cathedral church was the favourite place of session,[7] other meeting-places might be chosen: Derby, by the bishop of Chester,[8] Cardiff by the bishop of Llandaff;[9] and Alexander, bishop of Lincoln, reserved the right to hold his pleas, synod, and chapters in the parish church of Peterborough 'sicut alie parrochiales ecclesie episcopatus Linc' in quibus hec fieri solita sunt'.[10] In the fourteenth century the diocesan synod of Ely commonly met in the Augustinian priory of Barnwell.[11] The earliest recorded case in England of the delegated

[1] A synod of the 'maior archidiaconatus' of Rouen was usually held on the day before, which was a Monday (cf. *Regestrum*, p. 38).

[2] *Ibid.*, pp. 38, 75 &c., 228 &c. Sometimes the whole three days' proceedings are described as 'sacra synodus'. *Ibid.*, p. 263.

[3] *Ibid.*, p. 75.   [4] *Ibid.*, p. 190.   [5] *Ibid.*, pp. 276, 322.

[6] 'Aula nostra Rothomagensi' (*ibid.*, p. 252); 'camera nostra iuxta capitulum ecclesie' (*ibid.*, p. 322); 'camera sociorum nostrorum' (*ibid.*, p. 378); 'camera inferiori' (*ibid.*, p. 446), &c.

[7] e.g. Bath (1220) above, p. 17 n. 1; Chichester (1289 and 1292) above, p. 17 n. 11; Coventry (? 1189) above, p. 19 n. 2; Exeter (1133) above, p. 17 n. 5; (1287) Wilkins, ii. 130*b*; Lincoln (*c.* 1155) above, p. 18 n. 6; London (1250) above, p. 17 n. 1.

[8] (1129 × 1138) above, p. 18 n. 6.

[9] (1149 × 1161) above, p. 18 n. 6.

[10] *Reg. antiquiss. Linc.*, i. 36 no. 52.

[11] *Sacrist rolls of Ely*, ed. F. R. Chapman, ii. 71; *Ely diocesan remembrancer*, July–Aug. 1892, p. 760; *ibid.*, Jan.–Feb. 1894, p. 181, &c. Cf. Durandus, above, p. 19 n. 7 and above, p. 7 and Hauck, *Kirchengesch.*, v. 170. Monasteries obtained exemption from the holding of synods in their churches: e.g. Westminster, Holtzmann, *Papsturkunden*, i. 552 no. 262; Bury, *Pinchbeck register*, ed. F. Hervey, i. 7.

presidency over a synod seems to be the synod of Canterbury over which the bishop of Rochester presided at All Saints 1187.[1] In vacant sees, the later practice, which is witnessed by numerous commissions and one full record of proceedings, was for the official *sede vacante* to summon and celebrate the synod.[2]

The law which bade the bishop summon all his subjects to the synod was interpreted with latitude. Durandus ordered to be summoned 'all those, both secular and religious, who by law or custom are bound to come to the synod of Mende',[3] and other injunctions are equally vague. The statutes of Odo, bishop of Paris, speak of the abbots and priests who are bound to attend the synod, and of the priests, especially those with cure of souls.[4] Odo also envisages the presence of layfolk, scholars, and other clerks in the preliminary stages of the synod. The only persons specifically mentioned in the Metz *Ordo* are abbots, archdeacons, and deans; while a bishop of Münster can speak of the prelates, religious and secular, and the entire clergy of the city and diocese as giving their consent to statutes made in a general synod.[5] Bishop Richard Kellaw of Durham in 1312 demanded the regular attendance at synods twice a year of 'omnes abbates, priores, archidiaconi, præpositi, rectores, vicarii, et capellani parochiales civitatis et diœcesis Dunelm' et alii, qui tenentur synodo huiusmodi

---

[1] *Epistolæ cantuar.*, p. 155. In Archbishop Rigaud's absence the treasurer of Rouen presided at the summer synod of 1258 (*Regestrum*, p. 308 cf. p. 520). The dean of Münster presided ' vice et auctoritate [episcopi] ' in a synod of 1296 (*Westfälisches Urkunden-Buch*, iii, ed. R. Wilmans (Münster, 1859–71), part i, p. 804 no. 1540). In the fourteenth century the bishops of Ely delegated the presidency on various occasions to the prior of Barnwell and sacrist of Ely, the sacrist and the bishop's officials, the subprior of Ely and the bishop's officials (*Ely diocesan remembrancer*, July–Aug. 1892, p. 760; *ibid.*, May–June 1895, p. 91; *ibid.*, June–July 1895, p. 109).

[2] Churchill, *Canterbury administration*, i. 184, 198, 216, 337, ii. 100. The only thirteenth-century record is the composition of Archbishop Boniface with Worcester 1268, whereby the prior became official *sede vacante* (*ibid.*, ii. 60). The record of the Ely synod held by the archbishop's official in Barnwell priory in 1401 is printed from Arundel's register *ibid.*, ii. 144–5.

[3] Durandus, *Instructions*, p. 96.

[4] Mansi, xxii, cols. 675–6. Archbishop Rigaud in 1257 orders the rural deans to summon ' omnes abbates, priores, presbyteros et omnes alios qui debent synodum '. *Regestrum*, p. 276.

[5] (1282). *Westfälisches Urkunden-Buch*, iii part i p. 620 no. 1182.

interesse de consuetudine vel de iure."[1] Archdeacons were an indispensable class of 'inferior prelate', and appear commonly as witnesses to synodal *acta*.[2]

Prelates found themselves obliged in certain circumstances to attend synods in other dioceses than their own. This obligation was incurred by cathedral chapters and monasteries when they had jurisdiction over distant churches. For such persons to neglect a summons might lead to the sequestration of their churches, as the dean of St. Paul's found to his cost in 1239, when he was prevented by illness from attending the bishop of Salisbury's synod and failed to send his excuse. The bishop sequestrated his church, and the intercession of the legate Otto, at Temple Dinsley, was invoked to appease him.[3] It is not surprising that some great religious houses, as we shall see, obtained special exemption from this duty.

'Cum abbates de iure ad synodum venire teneantur...', says the bishop of Angers in 1298.[4] The fact that papal privileges of monastic exemption often specify exemption from attendance at synods shows that it was regarded then as a common-law obligation.[5] Schreiber, who has dealt fully with this question, cites the significant limitation of privi-

---

[1] Wilkins, ii. 416*b*.

[2] e.g. Coventry and Lichfield (1161 × 1179) above, p. 18 n. 6; Exeter (1169) above, p. 18 n. 6; Lincoln (*c*. 1155) above, p. 18 n. 6; Norwich (1201) above, p. 17 n. 15.

[3] The church through which the dean—here called ' dean of London '—incurred the obligation is not named in the legate's letter. Otto writes to the bishop : ' Cum discretus vir decanus London' ad synodum vestram venire nequiverit, nec eciam se excusaverit, diversis negociis impeditus, et vos eius inpotenciam nescientes propter hoc ecclesiam suam duxeritis sequestrandam, paternitatem vestram affetuose rogamus quatinus dictum sequestrum nostrarum precum intuitu relaxetis . . .'. Dated at Diniflee, 10 kal. September 1239. Salisbury, Dean and Chapter Muniments, Liber evid. C p. 170 (formerly fo. 67v) no. 228. The original at Salisbury is said (*Hist. MSS. Comm. Report, Var. Coll.*, i. 350) to be dated at Dinoflet ' apparently near Dumfries', 22 Sept. 1239, but the place is in Herts.

[4] Bouchel, p. 891.

[5] See above, p. 14. e.g. exemption of Westminster. Holtzmann, *Papsturkunden*, i. 552 no. 262, and cf. D. Knowles in *Downside Rev.*, l (1932) 206. Regular prelates appear as witnesses to synodal *acta* at Exeter (1169) above, p. 17 n. 7 ; Hereford (1137) Wilkins, i. 413.

While the attendance of abbesses at synods seems to have passed unnoticed by the canonists, it was at least sometimes demanded in medieval Germany. Schreiber, *Kurie und Kloster*, i. 218 n. 3. Abbesses were also expected to appear in the synod of Reims (*c*. 1330). Gousset, ii. 535.

lege in a bull of Celestine II to the non-exempt house of Stablo: 'abbas ad nullius nisi diœcesani episcopi synodum ire cogatur.'[1] St. Peter's abbey, Gloucester, enjoyed a similar limited privilege. Between 1139 and 1148 Gilbert Foliot, as its abbot, was on his way to the bishop of Hereford's synod when he found himself obliged to send a letter of excuse in his stead; but when Gilbert became bishop of Hereford, he and his chapter granted to his successor at Gloucester permanent exemption from the duty to attend.[2] The abbey of Gloucester, itself in the diocese of Worcester, was only concerned with the bishop of Hereford's synod on account of its parish churches in the diocese of Hereford. It still was obliged to attend the Worcester synod. The same duty was even enforced upon exempt houses on ac-count of the churches they controlled within their own diocese. In the mid-twelfth century the abbot of Battle contumaciously ignored several summonses to the episcopal synod of Chichester, and apparently royal help sustained him despite his excommunication by the bishop. But times changed and the canon law came into its own. When in 1235 the matter became one for canonical decision, it was ordained that the *decanus leugæ* of Battle should, as officer of the exempt jurisdiction of the abbey, be bound to come to the bishop's synod 'auditurus eius precepta et nullum iudicium subiturus.'[3] Again, Evesham established, albeit on shaky foundations, its own exemption from episcopal control; but Innocent III so interpreted its forged privi-leges as to involve the abbot in attendance at the bishop of Worcester's synods in respect of churches in the Vale of Evesham.[4] Even Coggeshall, a house of the Cistercian Order, which was usually considered exempt,[5] might undertake

[1] Schreiber, i. 216. For the whole question see *ibid.*, i. 216-24.
[2] Migne, *Patrol. latina*, cxc, col. 788 letter 64; *Cart. S. Petri Glouc.*, i. 253, iii. 6.
[3] *Chron. mon. de Bello*, pp. 68-71, 192; Cheney, *Episcopal visitation*, 41-2.
[4] *Chron. abbatiæ de Evesham* (Rolls series) pp. 182-3; *Decretales*, v. 33, 17; Alexander III gave Reginald, bishop of Bath, power to censure abbots, priors, and other persons bound to attend his synod, who absented themselves without canonical excuse (1178). C. M. Church, *Early hist. of ch. of Wells* (London, 1894) p. 368. At a Benedictine General Chapter of the province of Canterbury *c.* 1252 'Abbas de Alincestre [Alcester] se excusat per laicum propter synodum episcopi Wygorniensis.' Pantin, *Chapters*, i. 47.
[5] Cf. Hauck, *Kirchengesch.*, v. 172 n. 4 and Schreiber, i. 222-4. There was

to attend synods and chapters in the diocese of London 'ratione delicti in Lond' diocesi perpetrati', on account of its portion in the parish church of Coggeshall.[1] After 1228 a special agreement governed the synodal duty of the priors of Binham and Wymondham. They must come or send proctors or excusatory letters and sit among the other priors in the synod of Norwich; but without doffing their travelling attire, hooded and spurred.[2] The alternative of sending a proctor was probably common for the heads of religious houses. Bishop Oliver Sutton of Lincoln tried to force the abbot of St. Albans to send a proctor to his synod celebrated at Aylesbury.[3]

As for the attendance of priests, we have in addition to the evidence stated above the statutes of Worcester (1229) and Chichester (1244 × 1253)[4] to the effect that all priests with cures must attend. These usually included regulars with cure of souls and the priests subject to exempt houses.[5] Other priests leave few traces in synodal records. The statutes of Clermont (1268) order all priests to come to the customary summer synod, and to the winter synod only those with cure of souls.[6] In the fourteenth century the numbers

an injunction by the General Chapter of the Order as late as 1273: ' Item abbatibus Lemovicensis diœcesis, ne accedant ad episcopales synodos, nisi causa fidei prædicationis, vel etiam si episcopali debeant fungi officio, per capitulum generale inhibetur.' *Statuta cap. gen. ordinis cisterc.*, ed. J. M. Canivez, iii (Louvain, 1935) 120, ch. 25. Once they began to control parish churches, Cistercian abbeys were likely to be treated by bishops in the same way as exempt Benedictine houses, such as Evesham.

[1] 1223 × 1225. *Early charters of St. Paul's*, ed. M. Gibbs (Camden 3rd series 58) p. 252 no. 314. Cf. exemption from attendance at synods, &c. (except assemblies *pro fide*) confirmed for Cistercian abbots of England in 1244, and for Netley in particular in 1245. *Cal. pap. letters*, i. 205, 212.

[2] *Gesta abbatum S. Albani* (Rolls series) i. 278.

[3] *Ibid.*, i. 457. Cf. a proxy by the prior of Bradenstoke in 1320. *Cal. of the reg. of John de Drokensford* (Somerset Rec. Soc., vol. i, 1887) p. 178. The *Sacrist rolls of Ely*, ed. F. R. Chapman, ii. 8, 16, 31, 71 show that from 1291-2 several obedientiaries of Ely sometimes attended the diocesan synod together; and in 1418 it was stated that the subprior and two monks were wont to attend. *Cal. patent rolls 1416-22*, p. 183. I am obliged to the Reverend Seiriol Evans for calling my attention to this evidence. [4] Wilkins, i. 626b, 693b.

[5] Cf. above, p. 14, and see Schreiber, i. 221, ii. 62, and J. F. Lemarignier, *Étude sur les privilèges d'exemption . . . des abbayes normandes* (Paris, 1937) p. 225. But Lucius II in 1144 freed priests and parishioners of Cluny from attendance at any synod save that of the pope or the abbot. G. Letonnelier, *L'abbaye exempte de Cluny* (Ligugé, 1923) p. 30.

[6] Mansi, xxiii col. 1185.

were sometimes reduced by an order to rural deans to summon only a proportion of the parish priests,[1] but evidence for this practice in England is not forthcoming. Statutes enforce the regulations of the pontificals about the dress of prelates and priests in synods. But again, the fullest evidence is continental. Odo of Paris demands that priests shall wear albs and stoles at the Easter synod, surplices and stoles only at the September one. Later French statutes, including those of Meaux, give more elaborate instructions.[2] In twelfth-century England occurs the solitary case of Henry de Manscell, suspended by the bishop of Coventry because he did not appear 'in habitu sinodali coram eo in sinodo'.[3] In the middle of the next century the bishop of Norwich ordered: 'quod decani rectores vicarii et capellani in superpelliciis ad minus vel alias in albis vel capis sericis intersint nostris sinodis sub pena canonica eis super hoc infligenda'.[4] That some sort of order of precedence was observed in the seating arrangements is shown by the abbot of Evesham's right to have first place after the bishop in the synod of Worcester, and the prior of Bath's right in the synod of Bath.[5]

It is doubtful whether simple clerks or laity were expected to attend synods regularly. They appear sometimes as witnesses to synodal *acta* of the twelfth century,[6] but are not mentioned in the synodal statutes of the thirteenth. Probably customs changed during this period as the synod came to be more specialized in its activities. This change in the normal business of the synod must be considered next.

[1] Hauck, *Kirchengesch.*, v. 173 notes 4 and 5; Gousset, ii. 441.
[2] Cf. Martène and Durand, iv. 891; Hauck, *Kirchengesch.*, v. 171 n. 3; Gousset, ii. 535; and above, p. 7.
[3] *Hist. MSS. Comm. Report, Various coll.*, i. 238.
[4] Durham, Bishop Cosin's library, MS. V. v. 7 fo. 141v, cf. Wilkins, i. 735a.
[5] *Chron. abb. de Evesham*, p. 183 (*Decretales*, v. 33, 17) cf. *Ann. monastici*, iv. 411; *Hist. MSS. Comm. Report, Wells*, i (1907) 52, A.D. 1220. Cf. the claims of the provosts of Bonn and Xanten to sit on either side of the archbishop of Köln 'in generali synodo et ceteris conventibus publicis' (A.D. 1138) Hauck, *Kirchengesch.*, iv. 8 n. 1; and the arrangement at Reims (c. 1330) Gousset, ii. 535. See also above, p. 14.
[6] 'Et multis aliis clericis et testibus laicis . . . [eight of them named]' (Exeter, 1133) Stenton, *Cambr. Hist. Journal*, iii. 10; 'Et multis aliis clericis et laicis' (Canterbury, 1189 × 1190) Thorpe, *Reg. roffense*, p. 49; layfolks named (Lincoln, c. 1155), Stenton, *Gilbertine charters*, p. 5.

In the twelfth century the diocesan synod was an assembly in which the bishop confirmed the more solemn legal acts of his subjects, heard their disputes, and administered ecclesiastical discipline. Arrangements about property between the bishop and his chapter, the transference of a monastery from one religious Order to another, might suitably have their solemn enactment in a synod. If a monastery were founded by a layman or endowed with a parish church, the gift might be confirmed by the diocesan in the presence of his subjects.[1] Examples of this practice in the late eleventh century are recorded in the *Liber vitæ* of Durham.[2] When Earl Waltheof had given the church of Tynemouth to Durham, 'donationem Walcherus episcopus in plena synodo petente et presente ipso comite Waltheswo [*sic*] cum omni clero sui episcopatus confirmavit'; some years later 'Gwillelmus episcopus ecclesiam predictam sua auctoritate monachis sancti Cuthberti in perpetuum confirmavit et omnes qui eam sancto Cuthberto vel monachis ei servituris in posterum auferrent, in synodo perpetuo anathemate condempnavit'. Thus, a century later, the church of Rochester obtained confirmation of all its lands, churches, and privileges from Archbishop Baldwin, fortified with an elaborate *sanctio* clause and given at Canterbury in the synod in the first year of King Richard.[3] The synod might be chosen for a transaction, even when bishop's confirmation was not sought. It was 'in communi sinodo' at Lincoln, about 1155, that Supir de Bayeux made a grant in alms to the nuns of Sixle, 'presentibus multis et audientibus', including the subdean and chancellor of the cathedral church.[4] The desire for publicity apparent in all these documents suggests the motive which, in the secular sphere, produced the witnessing of private charters in the shire or hundred court,[5] with the added force of the ecclesiastical anathemas which might accompany the synodal confirmation. For these

[1] Hinschius, iii. 587 n. 1.
[2] *Liber vitæ ecclesiæ dunelmensis* (Surtees Soc. 136, 1923) i fo. 46v. This and the related documents are now held to be later fabrications: *Durham Episcopal Charters 1071–1152*, ed. H. S. Offler (Surtees Soc. 179, 1968), p. 45.
[3] Thorpe, *Reg. roffense*, pp. 48–9.
[4] Stenton, *Gilbertine charters*, p. 5.
[5] Cf. Bracton, *De legibus . . . Anglie* (Rolls series) vi. 138 (bk. iv ch. 15).

reasons, too, the synod was the obvious place to publish privileges and penalties. So in 1187 the monks of Canterbury cause a papal indult to be read solemnly in their diocesan synod,[1] and about 1203 Bishop Savaric excommunicates in his synod those who invade the property of the church of Wells.[2]

The deed by which John de Gray, bishop of Norwich, in his Michaelmas synod of 1201, established a vicarage in the church of Ludham comes in a different category of administrative acts. In form a grant of the church to St. Benet of Holme, it was in fact erecting a vicarage with a fixed portion of one hundred shillings.[3] It may be compared with the notification by Robert, bishop of Hereford, that the abbot of Conches has appeared in his synod at Hereford in 1137 and admitted liability for an annual pension to the church of Leominster in lieu of tithe.[4]

These last two agreements may actually conceal cases of synodal litigation and judgement. The hearing of pleas in the synod seems to have been common in this period. The earliest English example is also one of the best recorded: the dispute ('quæstio') between the priests of St. Helen's and St. Alban's churches heard in Wulfstan's synod at Worcester, in the crypt, in the year 1092.[5] It broadened into a general inquiry into the parochial rights of the cathedral priory in the city of Worcester, and resulted in a solemn judgement by the bishop:

Hoc igitur testimonium ego Wlfstanus verum comprobans, litem presbyterorum sedavi, et veram comprobationem testimonio hujus sanctæ synodi literis nostris et sigillo corroboravi ; cavens, ne amodo de his rebus in hac sancta et matre ecclesia inter monachos et alias quaslibet personas dissensio, sive scandalum oriatur. Servantibus haec vita æterna donetur in cælestibus. Qui autem fregerit, vel in pejus mutaverit, cum diabolo et angelis ejus perpetuis damnetur cruciatibus.

---

[1] *Epist. cantuar.* (Rolls series) p. 155.

[2] *Hist. MSS. Comm. Report, Wells,* i (1907) 30. Cf. *Annales monastici,* i. 73.

[3] Bodleian, Norfolk roll 82c, printed without dating clause in Dugdale, *Monasticon* (1817–30) iii. 91 n. 29. Cf. the earlier documents relating to Ludham church in *Reg. of St. Benet of Holme,* ed. J. R. West (Norfolk Record Soc. 1932).

[4] Wilkins, i. 413.

[5] *Ibid.,* i. 369–70 ; cf. R. R. Darlington, *The vita Wulfstani of Wm. of Malmesbury* (Camden 3rd series, 40, 1928) pp. xxv n. 1, xxxvii.

A dispute over rights in the chapel of Combe Martin, interesting for the form of *finis* and *concordia* which its settlement takes, was decided by the bishop of Exeter in his synod in 1133,[1] and at about the same time (1129 × 1138) the bishop of Chester gave notification of a *finis concordie* reached in his synod, also concerning the obedience of a chapel.[2] The cases recorded in the Gloucester Abbey cartulary, from the dioceses of Llandaff and St. David's, have the added interest that they show procedure in the synod consequent upon a mandate of the archbishop and a royal writ respectively.[3] If such cases as these were all collected and studied as they deserve, there can be no doubt that they would throw light on the interaction of ecclesiastical and lay courts and on the evolution of procedure in the latter. Here they are only cited to illustrate the judicial function of the synod.

' Iudicio synodi ', ' totius synodi iudicio ' are the phrases sometimes employed in these documents.[4] Taken by themselves, they would suggest that the synod was a court in which the suitors were the judges.[4] But if in these cases of ' recognition ' the bishop may be regarded as announcing the judgement of the court, he does at the same time do more. He is *iudex ordinarius*, and the recognition is confirmed by his authority. Wulfstan's control over his synod appears in various words of his charter of 1092. ' Hanc conventionem confirmavi ego Rogerus Cestrensis episcopus in sinodo meo [*sic*] ', says the bishop of Chester. If others are mentioned in synodal decisions, they appear as advisers or witnesses. Thus at Exeter in 1133: ' confirmavi mea auctoritate et tocius ecclesie nostre consilio . . . coram prefatis personis sub testimonio nostre synodi '.

What of the correction of manners, which is numbered among the purposes of the synod? The law demanded it,

---

[1] Stenton, *Cambr. Hist. Journal*, iii. 10.

[2] *Reg. antiquiss. Lincoln.*, ii. 8–9 no. 317.

[3] *Cart. S. Petri Glouc.*, ii. 52, 54 ; *ibid.*, i. 265.

[4] Cf. Pollock and Maitland, i. 548 *seqq.*, ii. 622 *seqq.* on suitors and recognitors in lay courts. Note the phrases : ' per ipsam synodum recognitum fuit' (*Cart. S. Petri Glouc.*, i. 265) ; ' recognitum est coram nobis in plena synodo ' (Morey, *Bartholomew of Exeter*, p. 147) ; ' hanc recognitionem et concessionem fecit ipse Fulcho coram nobis et coram omni sinodo apud Bomin ' [not certainly a diocesan synod] (Oliver *Monasticon exon.* add. supp. p. 5).

the pontifical *Ordo* found a place for it, but our records provide very little evidence in the period under review. At a much earlier date, *testes synodales* had been appointed to delate offenders to the bishop, and it is interesting to speculate on the possibility that the accusing jury which King Henry II wished the church courts to adopt derived from this source and operated in the diocesan synods of the twelfth century.[1] But positive proof there is none. An interesting twelfth-century tradition recalled the support given by Earl Waltheof to the bishop of Durham in his disciplinary work, but unfortunately recorded no details:

Fuerunt autem amicissimi sibique mutuo acclines Walcherus episcopus et Waltheovus comes. Unde una cum episcopo et in synodo presbyterorum residens, humiliter et obedienter prosequebatur quicquid pro corrigenda in suo comitatu Christianitate statutum ab episcopo fuisset.[2]

Infringements of the law of marriage would naturally be included in this sort of ecclesiastical business. That in the twelfth century a prelate might judge matrimonial cases in his synod appears from a letter of Pope Alexander III. This describes the trial by Richard, archbishop of Canterbury, and the consequent appeal to Rome, of a husband and wife accused of marrying within the prohibited degrees:

Archiepiscopus presentibus memorato viro et muliere in plena sinodo cepit rem ipsam discutere, et de ea cognatione seniores et prudentiores producti sunt testes, in quorum audientia contrahendi matrimonii fuerat denuntiatio celebrata. . . . Cum autem super hoc in sinodo multipliciter decertatum fuisset, sepe nominatus A. futurum divortium veritus pro se et uxore sua in vocem appellationis prorupit.[3]

Unfortunately we are not told how these proceedings were initiated; they seem to presuppose the machinery for collecting *fama publica.*

When we descend to the thirteenth century, Hauck cites one shred of evidence in the shape of a complaint made at

---

[1] Const. Clarendon ch. 6 (Stubbs, *Sel. charters*, 9th ed., p. 165); cf. Pollock and Maitland, i. 151–2 and Haskins, *Norman institutions*, pp. 226–8.

[2] *Symeonis Dunelmensis opera* (Surtees Soc., 51, 1868) i. 93 (Rolls series, ii. 200).

[3] Alex. III to the bishop of Worcester (1174 × 1181), in 'Collectio Wigorniensis' part i no. 48 (*Zeitschr. der Savigny-Stiftung für Rechtsgeschichte*, liii, Kanon. Abt. xxii (1933) 88–9).

Regensburg in 1209 that parish priests and deans conceal each other's offences and will not denounce them in the synod.[1] The Council of Narbonne 1227 orders the appointment of *testes synodales* in each parish to report to the bishops ' de hæresi et de aliis criminibus manifestis ';[2] the diocesan statutes of Salisbury provide for the appointment of two or three inquisitors in each deanery who shall report excesses to the bishop.[3] But here is no hint of using the synod as a place of trial or correction. The material in the register of Achbishop Rigaud of Rouen is much more to the point. For this shows actual cases of individuals summoned to answer for their offences in the synod,[4] and receiving sentence there.[5] It is worth noticing that in this solitary record of actual practice, there is no case of the accusation of a layman, and nothing to prove the existence of procedure by *testes synodales*. In regard to the first point, we may perhaps infer that the relations with the lay power made it advisable to bring charges against laymen in a more strictly constituted court, and that the archdeacon's jurisdiction counted for a good deal; ' For er the bisshop caughte hem with his hook, They weren in the erchedekenes book.' Regarding *testes*, Rigaud had experimented in their use for the provincial council and the experiment had failed, as later canonists say it often failed.[6] His disciplinary procedure in the synod seems rather to be the outcome of his visitations.[7] As visitation became more general, so might this form of synodal action, and so the thirteenth century may mark an advance upon the twelfth. But having regard to the scantiness of our evidence for this activity and to the competition of the regular courts of bishop and archdeacon, we can hardly suppose that the discipline of individuals

---

[1] Hauck, *Kirchengesch.*, iv. 9 n. 1.

[2] Mansi, xxiii. 24. The order is reminiscent of the third decree of the Fourth Lateran Council and of the decree of the Council of Verona 1184. Cf. L. Tanon, *Hist. des tribunaux de l'Inquisition en France* (Paris, 1893) pp. 276–81.

[3] Ch. 44. *Salisbury charters*, p. 144. Cf. *Eng. Hist. Rev.*, l. 204.

[4] *Regestrum*, pp. 138, 346, 581, 590, 614. Cases in which a day for purgation was appointed in synod, *ibid.*, pp. 322, 415, 434, 546, 614. Cf. *Visite pastorale du diocèse de Lyon 1378–1379* (*Bulletin de la Diana*, xxvi, 1937) ed. Abbé Merle, pp. 320, 330, 333.　　　　[5] *Regestrum*, pp. 291, 347, 434, 502, 614.

[6] Cf. *Eng. Hist. Rev.*, l. 205 and above, p. 8 n. 1.

[7] *Regestrum*, pp. 138, 346–7.

occupied much time in the diocesan synod. The chief advantage of using this assembly for the purpose must have been the presence in it of a large body of clergy who were potential witnesses or compurgators.

The character of synodal business in the twelfth century explains sufficiently why all classes of persons might be found in attendance. Regular prelates and layfolk often had as much interest in attending as had the parish priests. But while the business touched all classes, it generally concerned individual persons and corporations. There was very little of it that had a general bearing, very little in which the bishop treated his flock as a whole. While his synodal acts emphasize his ordinary jurisdiction throughout the diocese, the bishop does not use the synod to make known his superiors' decrees or to legislate by his own authority. That only happens in the following century, when these activities come to surpass in importance the older functions of the diocesan synod.

It has been seen[1] that one of the original purposes of the diocesan synod was to communicate to the clergy and laity at large the decisions of the councils of the Church. Examples of the practice are found in the early Middle Ages,[2] but by the twelfth century, to judge by the silence of the records, the practice may have ceased. Innocent III's decree was intended to revive it. Our evidence for its use comes entirely from the period after the Fourth Lateran Council. Not only were canons of general, legatine, and provincial councils published in the next diocesan synods. Had this been so, there would have been many diocesan synods with nothing of the sort upon their agenda. Perhaps by a wide interpretation of the decree *Sicut olim*, perhaps following the example of the religious Orders, prelates ordered the recitation of canons at every synod. There

---

[1] Above, p. 7.

[2] e.g. the account in the letters of Ratherius of his diocesan synod at Verona. Ratherius called it in order to publish canons against incontinent clergy issued in the council of Ravenna at which he had been present. Migne, *Patr. lat.*, cxxxvi, cols. 679–80, cited by Boye.

Ch. 3 of the canons published under King Edgar suggests that the Anglo-Saxon Church at this time had diocesan synods annually, in which legislation was promulgated : cf. Darlington, in *Eng. Hist. Rev.*, li. 412.

was no general rule, and the need for a wide knowledge of certain sections of the law produced rules for the repetition of select chapters. While the canons of Oxford 1222 were to be recited in bishops' synods 'as it should seem expedient', the excommunication clause was to be recited therein every year. The legate Ottobono ordered the archbishops and bishops to have his statutes read diligently word by word in their synods every year, and Pecham renewed this order.[1] A fifteenth-century manuscript collection of English canons[2] has an illuminating note on the continuance of this practice:

> Nota constituciones recitandas in sinodo, scilicet Othonis c. *de archidiaconis.* Et Oxon' c. *ut archidiaconi,* et c. *presbiterorum.* Io. Stratford' c. *statuimus* et c. *avida* et c. *humana.* Et Othon' ad baptismum et constitucio *licet ad profugandum.* Et in constitucionibus Redyng' c. iiii. Et Peccham c. iii. Et Ottoboni c. *ingredientibus.*

A council of Bordeaux, held at Cognac in 1262, shows comparable procedure in the south of France:[3]

> Statuimus ut constitutiones provinciales annis singulis in synodis publicentur et maxime illæ per quas pœnæ transgressoribus infliguntur.

The Metz pontifical shows that in the early fourteenth century it was customary in at least one diocese to recite in synod particularly important extracts from the Decretals:[4]

> Legatur fides catholica, hec est decretalis que sic incipit: *Firmiter credimus.* Postea alique alie de etate et qualitate preficiendorum, de vita et honestate clericorum, et alie prout episcopus viderit expedire.

France also supplies evidence of an extension of this practice; in the 'Measures taken by the Prelates of France against the Friars', edited by Dr. A. G. Little,[5] we see how the parish priests were to be warned and protected against

---

[1] Wilkins, i. 593*b*, ii. 15*b*, 51*b*; cf. *Eng. Hist. Rev.*, l. 395–8.

[2] Peterhouse MS. 84 fo. 175*ra* and Cambridge, Univ. libr. MS. Gg. 6, 21 fo. 61v. The latter is the Moore MS. known to Wilkins as 'Eliensis 235'. The references can be easily traced in Lyndwood's and Athon's collections.

[3] Mansi, xxiii, col. 1109; Bouchel, p. 890, reading 'transgressionibus'. Cf. the council for Tours 1336, Bouchel, p. 896.

[4] *The Metz pontifical*, col. 61. The occasional use of diocesan synods as preparation for rather than as consequence of other councils should not be overlooked. Cf. *Eng. Hist. Rev.*, l. 206.

[5] Published in *Miscellanea Francesco Ehrle* (Rome, 1924) iii. 49 *seqq.*; dated *c.* 1289–90.

the friars' encroachments by means of synodal pronounce-ments. The papal decrees on confession and absolution were to be read and explained with an interpretation favourable to the seculars; friars to whom episcopal licence was granted were to be named in the synod; there, too, other confessors for reserved cases were to be appointed.

Not content with publishing and glossing the decrees of their superiors, bishops of the thirteenth century add to them by making statutes within the limits set by the common law. This development deserves separate treatment. In concluding this chapter it is simply desirable to observe that, as its legislative importance increased, so the judicial activity of the synod diminished. Synodal decisions of the kinds noted above are extremely rare in the thirteenth century. The change reflects more than one aspect of ecclesiastical movements of the age. The emergence of the bishop's official and the establishment of distinct episcopal courts, the growth of a cancellarial office in the registry, made it unnecessary to occupy the time of the synod with lawsuits and concords. With a better system of written record, less importance was perhaps attached to the public transference of rights and property. Disputes on the old subjects had increased rather than diminished but, partly for that very reason, they could now be dealt with by new administrative machinery which worked all the year round. A direct in-dication of the tendency is in the statutes of the diocese of Rodez, 1289:[1] 'Nullus causas inducat ad synodum quæ alio tempore coram nobis vel officiali nostro possent facilius et commodius expediri.' The laity thus had less occasion to attend the synod, and this at a time when, for many other reasons, the distinction was hardening between clergy and laity, between the laws of the Church and those of the State. As the synod came to exercise its pastoral function more efficiently and more thoroughly in a smaller sphere, it appeared as a purely clerical institution.

[1] Martène and Durand, iv, col. 674 ; cf. Hauck, *Kirchengesch.*, v. 175 n. 4.

II

DIOCESAN STATUTES

NOTHING more clearly illustrates the influence of the papacy on the local Churches in the thirteenth century than does the new statute-making activity of the bishops; nothing more clearly shows how that influence enhanced the authority of bishops in their dioceses.[1] It may, indeed, be argued that since the bishop legislated only for his subjects on matters within his competence, limited by the restraints of papal and metropolitan authority and exempt jurisdictions, the impression left by episcopal statutes distorts the truth. But there is more serious distortion in a picture drawn solely from the records of appeals and special privileges. These loom large in cartularies and registers and the *Corpus iuris*, but they must be seen in their proper setting. They are, however numerous, the exceptions to a common law and custom, clearly though less copiously recorded in the diocesan statutes of the thirteenth century. These statutes were generally issued in the diocesan synod. While, in the past, the diocesan synod had been a recognized and usual part of the machinery of Church government, it had not normally been a statute-making body. Bishops had seldom ventured to legislate for their whole dioceses. In this respect the Fourth Lateran Council marks a development, and was probably anticipated by only a very few French and German prelates of the preceding generation. In Germany this type of legislation is seldom found before the Council;[2] in Poland diocesan synods, rare throughout the thirteenth century, are not found at all until 1227.[3] Mlle Dobiache-Rojdestvensky is not quite correct in stating that we have no French synodal statutes from the first twenty years of the thirteenth century; for those of Odo de Sully (1196 × 1208) precede the Fourth Lateran Council.[4] But her general contention is

---

[1] Cf. Cheney, *Episcopal visitation*, ch. 2.
[2] Cf. Hinschius, iii. 587; Hauck, *Kirchengesch.*, iv. 9; and Bierbaum, p. 385.
[3] Abraham, 'Ius canonicum particulare in Polonia', p. 409.
[4] *La vie paroisssiale*, p. 48.

approximately true and emphasizes the barrenness of the period 'ante concilium'. In England, likewise, no sign has been seen of diocesan statutes before 1215.

The next generation bore fruit of this sort in most parts of the Western Church. In Germany the second half of the thirteenth century saw diocesan synods publishing particularly comprehensive collections of statutes, and the same is noted in France.[1] In both these countries statute-making activity continued through the fourteenth century; but the work was usually confined to collecting, conflating, and systematizing earlier statutes. In Gabriel Cossart's view they were of small importance: 'Nimia eorum esset moles, fructus exiguus.'[2]

In England activity was most intense in the mid-thirteenth century. Already before the archbishop of Canterbury convened a provincial council in accordance with the Fourth Lateran decree, two of his suffragans had issued statutes for their dioceses. Those of William de Blois, bishop of Worcester, which were published in 1219, were confined to very short injunctions, mostly on administrative matters. Those of Richard Poore, bishop of Salisbury, were formed on a more comprehensive plan. Both these dioceses produced other statutes later in the century. Bishop William de Blois greatly enlarged his first series ten years later, and his successor Walter de Cantilupe issued an important series in 1240. Poore's statutes for Salisbury were supplemented by Bishop Robert of Bingham (1238 × 1244) and Bishop Giles of Bridport (1257 × 1262). The archdiocese of Canterbury may have had its own series before the death of Stephen Langton. By this time Peter des Roches had composed his statutes for the diocese of Winchester (probably in 1224), and these were followed by an extensive second series between 1247 and 1249, and by a third between 1262 and 1265. By this time, before the legatine council of Ottobono, most of the other English dioceses had made at least one contribution to the local

---

[1] Hauck, *Kirchengesch.*, v. 146. Note 1 gives a list of diocesan statutes 1250–1400 not found in Hartzheim's *Concilia*. Dobiache-Rojdestvensky, p. 48.

[2] Labbe and Cossart, *Concilia*, xi, col. 1467, cited by Dobiache-Rojdestvensky, p. 7.

literature of canon law. A chronological list of statutes will show roughly the extent of the development:[1]

1219 Worcester I		1238 × 1244	Salisbury II
1217 × 1221	Salisbury I	1247 × 1249	Winchester II
1222 × 1228	Winchester I	1244 × 1253	Chichester I
1222 × 1228	Canterbury	1255 Norwich II	
1229 Worcester II		1252 × 1258	Bath and Wells
1224 × 1237	Coventry and Lichfield	1245 × 1259	London I
		1245 × 1259	London II
? 1222 × 1237	Exeter I	? 1259 York	
? 1228 × 1237	Durham I	1258 × 1260	Durham II
1240 Worcester III		1257 × 1262	Salisbury III
1240 × 1243	Lincoln	1262 × 1265	Winchester III
1240 × 1243	Norwich I	? 1241 × 1268	Ely

After this time there is a distinct slackening of production; the only notable statutes from the rest of the thirteenth century being those of Ely (possibly soon after 1268), Exeter 1287, Chichester 1289 and 1292, and Durham 1274 × 1283. This slackening need not be interpreted as the sign of declining zeal. The bishops of the earlier generations had legislated against the ignorance and indiscipline of their clergy, and their statutes could be revived and reiterated. Many of them were equally relevant to a new age; some of them were of singular literary merit, not likely to be surpassed. The manuscript tradition shows that if production of new statutes had slackened almost to stopping point by the middle of the fourteenth century, the copying and quoting of the old went on.

These considerations of date obviously affect the questions: What was the usual subject-matter of the statutes? Had the bishop-legislators a common purpose? If not some papal decree, surely some concerted policy, or urgent and widespread needs prompted the activity? The dates suggest dependence upon Innocent III's great general council, and historians and canonists have talked as though the sixth decree were the whole cause of the synodal activity of the bishops. It is desirable to be a little more

---

[1] The list gives only the supposed first recensions of the statutes. The dates attributed to them depend in most cases for their justification on arguments in later chapters. For a corrected list, see above, p. viii.

precise. What precisely did the sixth decree demand of bishops? It demanded that they should meet annually in provincial councils to legislate for whole provinces and should make use of their diocesan synods annually for the publishing of general and provincial canons. Clearly, Innocent III had no idea of laying down new rules for the celebration of diocesan synods. The decree does not so much as mention legislation by the bishop for his diocese. The conclusion is unavoidable that Innocent III only mentioned the synod in decree 6 because it was a piece of existing machinery which had once been used, and could be used again, for publishing general and provincial canons. If, then, we are to connect the development of synodal statutes with the Fourth Lateran Council, in accordance with the chronological evidence, it must rather be because the Fourth Lateran Council was itself the most universal expression of needs acutely felt by many churchmen of the day, and because diocesan legislation was itself a response to those needs.

The parochial ministry, instruction of and by the clergy, the disputes between lay and ecclesiastical courts: these were matters which had engaged the attention of the papacy constantly between the Lateran Councils of 1179 and 1215. But they were matters upon which the parish clergy needed guidance from the diocesan bishops. In the period between the two great Lateran Councils, the episcopate was awakening to this work, and episcopal statutes are the result.

At first one is surprised by the absence of diocesan legislation on these topics in the twelfth century, for the clergy probably stood as much in need of instruction then as later, and there were equally zealous prelates. The sudden development of the early thirteenth century is explicable by a change in the conception of the diocesan structure. The patronage of parish churches and chapels, and rectorial rights in them, had, in the past hundred years, been transferred in enormous numbers from lay control to the control of religious corporations. Possessed of many powers and responsibilities in the ministry of parishes, appropriating monasteries naturally left the imprint of their custom and rite upon the countryside which they controlled. The influence may not often have gone very deep; but in so far as the parochial clergy of the twelfth century escaped the old isolation of hereditary livings, they perhaps depended on the custom of cathedral or monastery rather than on distinctly diocesan traditions.[1] Then came, to supplement the old reform movement against heredity in benefices, a great new drive to secure ordained vicarages and a permanent ministry in appropriated churches.

Late in the twelfth century the papacy was active in maintaining and defining the control of diocesan bishops over the presentation to Church benefices. From all points of view it seemed desirable that the diocesan should exercise some pastoral control over the clerks installed by lay patrons and by the monasteries who came increasingly to replace the laymen. So it was considered necessary to insist upon the rule of presentation to the bishop.[2] It was exceedingly important that the presentee should have been regularly ordained. Besides the validity of his orders, his competence for the ministry ought also to be established. Finally, the bishop ought to ensure by formal inquiry and ordinance that churches would not lie vacant for long at a time, and that the priests who were eventually installed would receive adequate income. All these matters called for the local application of the universal law of the Church and for authoritative statements of local custom. The whole subject is one which constantly recurs in the diocesan statutes.

An inspection of thirteenth-century records must convince any reader that the examinations of ordinands and presentees to benefices did not secure a well-educated priesthood. The diocesans had to cope with beneficed clergy who were ignorant, even illiterate. Consequently, some episcopal statutes (of which Richard Poore's are the best example) try to give a simple exposition of the chief articles of faith, or at least a summary account of the seven

---

[1] Cf. below, p. 101.
[2] Cf. *Decretales*, III. 7, 3 (Alexander III to archbp. of Canterbury and suffragans).

sacraments. At the same time, priests are exhorted to instruct their parishioners in these matters, simply and in the vernacular. If the parish priest often resembled his flock by ignorance of elementary theological teaching, he was also often assimilated to the laity in his dress, his recreations, and his relations with women. Diocesan statutes repeat the canons on these matters, adding special prohibitions and penalties of their own.

Another class of statutes invariably appears in diocesan legislation of the thirteenth century. It is that which regulates the duties of the laity towards the clergy. Within its scope come the complicated question of tithe and that of mortuary payments, the customary oblations of parishioners at stated seasons, the free gifts expected at marriages, burials, and so forth. It also includes the highly important statutes which declare the occasions for ecclesiastical censures.

These topics are not the only ones which may be found in the diocesan statutes, nor do they indicate the whole scope of a bishop's rights and duties as conceived in the thirteenth century. They do, however, include all that needed most urgently to be brought home to the parish clergy, whether by promulgation in synods or by other means. Some few bishops make general statutes concerning the monastic life, others give ordinances to the officials of their courts and to archdeacons and deans in their synodal statutes. But there was other machinery for this. Thus Walter de Cantilupe ends his synodal statutes by saying: ' Que autem circa viros religiosos statuenda decrevimus in eorum proponimus capitulis publicare.'[1] The synod, then, retained its original concern with priests who have the cure of souls, and the statutes generally reflect this preoccupation.

The character of diocesan statutes changed during the hundred years or so which followed the Fourth Lateran

---

[1] Wilkins, i. 676a. In his synodal statutes for Exeter 1287, Peter Quivil abstains from legislating for the religious of his diocese, since they have enough guidance from their Rules, the decrees of the fathers, legatine and provincial canons, ' et correctiones quas facimus circa personas eorum in visitationibus nostris quasi singulis annis'. *Ibid.*, ii. 160b (ch. 54).

Council. The growing resistance to lay encroachments on ecclesiastical privilege, which is visible in the development of provincial canons in this period, is reflected in the increase of diocesan statutes about tithe and other debatable topics. At the same time, the solid core of didactic material which we find in Poore and Cantilupe and others seldom finds its counterpart in statutes of the latter years of the thirteenth century; and this for several reasons. In some dioceses earlier statutes were available which remained binding upon later generations. Robert of Bingham, bishop of Salisbury, refers explicitly to those of Poore, requiring them to be read.[1] Walter de Cantilupe confirms the statute on festivals made by his predecessor in the see of Worcester.[2] Rather than revise throughout a well-made series of statutes, some bishops were content to add new chapters from time to time, as occasion demanded. Elsewhere it is probable that recourse was had to miscellaneous collections, circulating under the name of *statuta sinodalia* or *statuta legenda in sinodo*. These confined themselves generally to material on the sacraments and on the conduct of parish priests. One such collection, composed from sources which cannot all be identified, seems to have become attached to a selection of the canons of Oxford 1222. We have no reason for associating them with this council, or with official publication in any diocese. But the large number of manuscripts of the 'Oxford' *legenda* suggests that they were pretty well known.[3] Late in the thirteenth century Archbishop Pecham's canons of Lambeth 1281 covered some of the same ground and added a useful catechism which parish priests might use for the regular teaching of their flock.[4] The wide diffusion of these canons throughout England dispensed with the need for similar didactic material in diocesan statutes.

But meanwhile several bishops were supplementing their statutes in a new way. Possibly stimulated by the friars'

---

[1] Below, p. 74.

[2] Wilkins, i. 675*b*. Cf. below, p. 95.

[3] Cf. *Eng. Hist. Rev.*, l. 395–8.

[4] Wilkins, ii. 54*b*–56*b*: the passage beginning 'Ignorantia sacerdotum'. The whole section was taken over by John Thoresby, archbishop of York in 1367. Cf. *The Lay Folks' Catechism* (Early Eng. Text Soc., o. s. 118).

manuals on confession and penance,[1] bishops produce official handbooks for their clergy, which they are obliged to possess and digest, and bring, like synodal statutes, to all synods. A reference to this sort of 'compendiosus tractatus' in the canons of Basel (session xv, 1433) suggests that by then the practice had extended widely. In the thirteenth century the finest example is to be seen in the double work of Durandus of Mende who, in the words of his epitaph, 'instruxit clerum scriptis monuitque statutis'.[2] Written originally between 1292 and 1296, the work was rescued from oblivion at the beginning of this century. The prologue describes its two parts as *Instructiones* and *Constitutiones*; in the former, Durandus recommends the priests of his diocese to follow his instructions that they may achieve 'vita et conversatio irreprehensibilis' and 'scientia commendabilis'; in the latter he makes orders in the usual manner of episcopal statutes.[3] While the *Constitutiones* are themselves singularly comprehensive, and include a great deal about the divine office and the administration of sacraments, the *Instructiones* give the theological background and much practical advice in a homiletic form. They are more discursive and much longer than the statutes: Durandus finds it convenient in his statute on penance to give a cross-reference to his instructions for further details.[4]

The work of Durandus for his diocese of Mende claims first place because of its bulk and excellence. We do not need, however, to go to the south of France for more humble specimens of the same type. English bishops were interested in this sort of literature from a much earlier time. Bartholomew, bishop of Exeter, had composed a penitential,[5] and Richard Poore, before he became a bishop, had persuaded Robert of Flamborough to write a *Summa de*

---

[1] See Dietterle, 'Die Summae Confessorum', and Mandonnet, 'La Summa de Pœnitentia magistri Pauli presbyteri S. Nicolai', *Aus der Geisteswelt des Mitte-alters* (Studien und Texte Martin Grabmann . . . gewidmet [*Beiträge zur Gesch. der Philos. und Theol. des Mittelalters*, Supplementband III] 1935) i. 532.

[2] *Histoire littéraire de la France*, xx. 431.

[3] Durandus, *Instructions*, pp. 9, 95.

[4] *Ibid.*, p. 130.

[5] Edited in A. Morey, *Bartholomew of Exeter*, pp. 163–313.

penitentia which itself owes something to Bartholomew's work.[1] A little later we find official manuals on penance in England. It is not always realized that the text printed by Wilkins as constitutions of Alexander of Stavensby, bishop of Coventry, in fact comprises three distinct short works, which are clearly distinguished by the bishop himself. After an address to his archdeacons, Stavensby gives a series of short statutes which, though they show unusual originality in expression, conform to the usual contemporary pattern. At the end, the bishop orders that they be observed and copied:

. . . simul cum sermone de septem criminalibus peccatis, que ad vos mittimus, et hoc cum quodam tractatu modico de confessione. Hec serventur et scribantur, sicut vultis quod ecclesie vestre non suspendantur, cum ad ecclesias vestras accesserimus vel per nos vel per nuntium nostrum.[2]

Manuscripts, which contain the statutes also contain these other works,[3] and they are found together without the statutes in a thirteenth-century manuscript from Bury St. Edmunds.[4] It should be observed that Stavensby does not explicitly claim authorship of these little treatises; his close associations with the Dominicans suggest that writings so much in keeping with the work of the Order may have been produced by friars in the bishop's service.[5] Stavensby's neighbour, Walter de Cantilupe, bishop of Worcester, was apparently himself the author of a treatise which was circulated in the same way. In his statutes of 1240 the bishop states that in order that priests shall know how to instruct their parishioners in the right method of confession and how to make inquiries and injunctions, he has made a treatise on confession:

---

[1] Cf. below, p. 54.

[2] Wilkins, i. 642*a* gives an imperfect text. The above is taken from Aberdeen Univ. MS. 137 fo. 6*rb*–6*va*, a xiii c. MS. which belonged in the xv c. to St. Paul's Cathedral, London.

[3] Aberdeen Univ. MS. 137 fo. 2r; Balliol Coll. MS. 228 fo. 216*vb*; Worcester Cathedral MS. F 71 fo. 294r; Brit. Mus. Cotton MS. Vesp. E. III fo. 142r. The first two MSS. set the treatise on penance first.

[4] Brit. Mus. Royal MS. 8 B. IV fo. 81r. Probably the two treatises occurred separately in a MS. at Peterborough Abbey: cf. Gibbs and Lang, p. 29 n. 7 and M. R. James, *List of MSS. formerly in Peterborough Abbey library*, pp. 75–6.

[5] Cf. Gibbs and Lang, pp. 29–31.

Quendam tractatum de confessione fecimus, quem sciri [A; B: scribi] ab omnibus capellanis precipimus et etiam observari in confessionibus audiendis, quia longum esset ipsum in presenti synodo publicare.

In a later chapter of his statutes he makes orders for this *tractatus penitentialis* to be copied and expounded.[1] A third, and lengthy manual was published in 1287 by Peter Quivil, as a supplement to his synodal statutes of Exeter. He describes it as a *summula*, drawn from various treatises, and orders all parish priests to obtain and copy and study it within the next six months.[2]

With the adding of such means as these for the general instruction of the parish clergy, as well as the gradual accumulation of collections of old statutes, the need for comprehensive new series disappeared. When a bishop of the fourteenth century wishes to issue supplementary statutes and censures for observance throughout his diocese, he generally does so by the medium of mandates addressed to his clergy. Thus Ralph of Baldock, bishop of London, sends out one circular in 1311 and another in 1312, addressed to the archdeacons, deans, and beneficed clergy of his diocese, ordering them not to receive unauthorized *questores*. In 1311 he orders the official of the archdeacon of London to prohibit unauthorized confessors and orders him to publish a condemnation of sorcerers and magicians. Another of his mandates to the same official is concerned with wrestling-matches in churches and cemeteries: it repeats and expands one of the statutes of his predecessor, Fulk Basset.[3] Similar letters were circulated to archdeacons and their officials by John de Sandale, bishop of Winchester in 1317 'ad monendum omnes rectores Wintoniensis diocesis quod non reponant fructus suos alibi quam in solo ecclesiastico', and by Henry Burghersh, bishop of Lincoln,

---

[1] Wilkins, i. 669*b*, 676*a-b*. It is probably this work which appears in the *Cat. of the libr. of Syon monastery*, ed. M. Bateson (Cambridge, 1898) p. 191, though the index (followed by Tanner, *Bibliotheca britannica*, p. 355) attributes it to William [de Blois], bishop of Worcester.

[2] Wilkins, ii. 162-8; cf. ii. 144*a*.

[3] *Reg. R. de Baldock episc. London.*, ed. R. C. Fowler (Canterbury and York Soc., 1911) pp. 134, 152, 140, 144, 145. Cf. *Eng. Hist. Rev.*, xxx. 297 (ch. 65).

in 1322 and 1323, to declare the excommunication of those
who withheld oblations due to the church of Lincoln.[1]

This change in the procedure of publishing, as well as
in the character of, episcopal statutes, may be due to the
decline of diocesan synods; but without more evidence it
would be dangerous to suppose that it was dictated by
anything other than the possibilities of better archidiaconal
machinery. In any case, it emphasizes the point which has
been observed in the last chapter: a bishop could as well
issue statutes on his own initiative as he could 'in plena
sinodo'. The method of publishing the statutes does not
suggest any active participation by the bishop's subjects.
We know, to be sure, far too little about the preliminaries
of synodal action at this time: the bishop might discuss
measures with his chapter beforehand,[2] or with the deans
in the synod.[3] But the orders eventually promulgated are
merely 'read and published' in the synod. The terms of
thirteenth-century statutes bear this out. The bishop of
Chichester says: 'in sancte synodi presentia quedam duximus proponenda';[4] some few legislators go further and
speak of the advice (*consilium*) or approval of the synod,[5]
while the statutes of Wells are issued 'presentis synodi
sacrosancte interventu consilio et assensu'.[6] Seldom are
enactments made by authority of the synod. The fullest
example is that of Walter of Suffield, whose statute for
the diocese of Norwich has the following introduction:

Nos Walterus de Suthfeld episcopus Norwicensis in synodo sancti

[1] *Reg. of John de Sandale* (&c.), ed. F. J. Baigent (Hants Record Soc., 1897),
p. 41, cf. p. 49; *Lincoln Cathedral statutes*, i. Liber Niger, ed. H. Bradshaw and
C. Wordsworth (Cambridge, 1892) pp. 332–4, 345–6. These are simply cited
as examples of a common fourteenth-century type. Cf. examples from Rouen
and Amiens 1305, printed by Dobiache-Rojdestvensky, pp. 183–6.

[2] As at Paderborn 1324: 'Postquam cum præsulibus ecclesiæ et canonicis
pertractasset ea, quæ in synodo proponenda . . .', quoted by Hauck, *Kirchengesch.*,
v. 181 n. 2. Cf. above, p. 10.

[3] As at Rouen 1262: 'Locuti fuimus cum decanis nostris in camera inferiori,
et ordinavimus, inter alia, quod . . .' Rigaud, *Regestrum*, p. 446. Cf. the procedure at Evreux in 1268 and Mlle Dobiache-Rojdestvensky's comment thereon:
La vie paroissiale, p. 54 n. 1, and *ibid.*, pp. 53–7.

[4] Wilkins, i. 688a.

[5] Worcester: *ibid.*, i. 625b; Salisbury: *ibid.*, i. 717 and Harl. MS. 52 fo. 119v;
Durham: Wilkins, ii. 28a.

[6] Vatican MS. Ottobon. lat. 742 fo. 109rb.

Michaelis presidentes, de consensu capituli nostri diocesani et presentis synodi autoritate, omnibus existentibus in sancta synodo in hoc consentientibus diffinimus. . . .

This certainly suggests the bishop's desire to increase the force of his statute by synodal authority; but it is exceptional and contrary to the opinion of later canonists, and Hinschius denies that even here the words necessarily signify a *votum decisivum*.[1] Other indications of the bishop's sole authority are to be seen in the power of interpretation and emendation which Peter Quivil of Exeter and Durandus of Mende expressly reserve, when they publish their statutes.[2] Finally, it is evident that even in the period of greatest synodal activity, bishops occasionally issued whole series of statutes or instructions without referring them to a synod. No less than three pronouncements of Robert Grosseteste, the statutes of Alexander of Stavensby, and a set of *articuli* sent out by John Pecham come into this category of circular letters.[3]

In order that his statutes may be well known, the bishop commonly enjoins that all parish churches shall possess them.[4] It is in compliance with this injunction that inventories of church property found in the churches of St. Paul's and the archdeaconry of Ely contain 'statuta sinodalia'.[5] Certain statutes—ones which were not likely to need revision—were ordered to be inscribed in a missal

[1] Cambridge Univ. Libr., MS. Ii. 3, 7 fo. 143v, cf. Wilkins, i. 708–9; Hinschius, iii. 595 n. 2. The document bore the seals of both bishop and cathedral chapter; the advice of the chapter is mentioned in Salisbury statutes, Wilkins, i. 715a. Cf. Exeter, *ibid.*, ii. 151a and London, *Eng. Hist. Rev.* xxx. 294 (ch. 44).

[2] Wilkins, ii. 160b; Durandus, *Instructions*, p. 146.

[3] Grosseteste, *Epistolæ*, pp. 72, 154, 317; Wilkins, i. 640; *Reg. epist. J. Peckham* (Rolls series) iii. 948–50.

[4] Salisbury: below, p. 60; Winchester: MS. Hatton 92 fo. 161v; Chichester: Wilkins, i. 693b; Worcester: *ibid.*, i. 626b, 676b; Norwich: *ibid.*, i. 735a; Durham: *ibid.*, i. 708b; London: Bishop of Lewes' MS. fo. 8v; York: MS. Lansdowne 397 fo. 252v; Exeter: Wilkins, ii. 161b. Cf. fourteenth-century visitation articles (? dioc. Salisbury) in MS. Harl. 52 fo. 26.

[5] *Visitations of churches belonging to St. Paul's* (Camden Soc., N.S. 55) pp. 2–62 *passim*; *Vetus liber eli.*, pp. 30–147 *passim*. Cf. the complaints made in the dioceses of Grenoble and Lyon: *Visites pastorales . . . des évêques de Grenoble* (*Docs. hist. sur le Dauphiné*, 4e livraison, 1874, ed. C. U. J. Chevalier, pp. 44, 45, 52, etc.; *Visite past. du diocèse de Lyon, 1378–1379* (*Bulletin de la Diana*, xxvi, 1937) pp. 240, 241, etc.

or other service-book of the church;[1] but in other statutes we hear of the *libellus* or *quaternus sinodalis*,[2] to be kept by the parish priest and brought to synods, there to be corrected and augmented from time to time.[3] It was the duty of the priests to read and expound the statutes periodically to their parishioners.[4]

As in the case of provincial canons, the suffragans were responsible for publication in their dioceses, so for the diocesan statutes bishops used the machinery of the archdeaconries: some mandates were directed to the archdeacons, and even those with a more extended address probably circulated through the same channels. The archdeacons and rural deans were told to recite synodal statutes in their chapters,[5] and to see that their subjects obtained copies. Thus Richard Poore orders:

quod archidiaconi constitutiones istas, pro communi utilitate editas et pro correctione excessuum et reformatione morum promulgatas, faciant inviolabiliter observari, transgressoribus debitam penam infligentes; provisuri nichilominus quod prescriptas constitutiones transcriptas et correctas habere faciant decanis, et decani sacerdotibus aliis infra festum proximum sancti Michaelis.[6]

Walter de Cantilupe went further to demand that the parish clergy should be examined at local chapters in their knowledge of the statutes.[7]

French records show the same procedure as in England, and add more precise details. The same importance is given to the deans in the diffusion of statutes. The rural deans and archpriests of the diocese of Angers are ordered in 1262 each to obtain a copy of the *præcepta synodalia* at

---

[1] Bishop of Lewes' MS. fo. 5v; *Reg. ep. J. Peckham*, iii. 948–50.
[2] Dobiache-Rojdestvensky, pp. 47, 48, 55.
[3] Wilkins, i. 693*b*.
[4] Every Sunday: Bishop of Lewes' MS. fo. 5v; MS. Harl. 3705 fo. 13; Durandus, *Instructions*, p. 146. The vernacular to be used: MS. Lansdowne 397 fo. 252v; Wilkins, ii. 161*b*.
[5] Winchester: MS. Hatton 92 fo. 161v; Salisbury: MS. Harl. 52 fo. 121v.
[6] Worcester Cathedral MS. Q 67 fo. 144v. Cf. London: Bishop of Lewes' MS. fo. 8v; Durham: Wilkins, i. 708*b*; Norwich: *ibid.*, i. 735*a*, and below, Ch.V, p. 129. A time-limit is also stated in York: MS. Lansdowne 397 fo. 252v; Worcester: Wilkins, i. 676*a*.
[7] Wilkins, i. 676*a–b*. Cf. Gousset, ii. 613, 617; Dobiache-Rojdestvensky, p. 55 n. 2; Hauck, *Kirchengesch.*, v. 179 n. 4, 181 n. 3.

each synod, from the bishop or the archdeacons.[1] The *synodus decanorum* which appears in Rouen in the time of Archbishop Rigaud is to be seen in the ' præcepta decanis facta post synodum hyemalem' of 1245. In that year the deans were told to correct the *præcepta sinodalia* recited in the synod according to the authentic copy, and were within a month to have all priests' copies corrected according to their own corrected copies.[2] These 'corrections' imply the re-editing of existing statutes, and may be compared to the explicit order of the synod of Tournai 1481 that when parish priests come to the synod they are to bring the synodal statutes and 'if it shall happen that additions or subtractions or alterations be made to them, they may emend their copies after the bishop's exemplar'.[3]

These details about the publication of statutes throw light upon the present state of the texts. The textual problems which arise almost entirely concern those statutes which were issued in synods. We can easily imagine that in such a process of compilation a single series of statutes would gradually be transformed, swelled by additions, and modified by corrections. As these changes were announced in successive synods, parish priests would modify their *libellus sinodalis*, deleting, interlining, adding marginalia. Extensive additions might be inserted at what seemed to the copyist to be appropriate points in the original text, or might form a solid appendix at the end. The process of re-touching was continually going on and—we may reasonably suppose—with varying amount of inaccuracy. We do not hear of any special measures taken in England (as they were occasionally taken in France)[4] to see that priests obtained properly authenticated copies. Only one episcopal register—that of Pontissara of Winchester—contains synodal statutes, and these were not first issued by Pontissara. One text of the Ely statutes has the recommendation of being in a register of the archdeaconry of Ely. But very few surviving copies of synodal statutes can lay claim to

---

[1] D'Achery, *Spicilegium*, i. 728a, cf. 729a.
[2] Pommeraye, *Rotomag. concilia*, p. 252.
[3] Gousset, ii. 769.
[4] Dobiache-Rojdestvensky, p. 56.

this official character. We may even doubt whether bishops always kept adequate record of their own and their predecessors' synodal pronouncements. The contrary is certainly suggested by the preamble of the bishop of Châlons to his statutes of 1281:

Mandata synodalia quæ per diversos caternos et cedulas erant confuse superflue et inordinate diffusa . . . duximus compilanda,[1]

and Archbishop Rigaud, who enregistered the canons of his provincial councils of Rouen, only summarized in his register the *mandata* and *præcepta* given in his *synodus decanorum*. Instead of official copies, then, we are confronted with texts which may be derived from official sources but may go back ultimately to the casual copying of a parish priest. Examples of the divergences which occur will appear clearly in the discussion of the statutes for the dioceses of London and Norwich, and it is not hard to see how these first arose. The copyists of the archetypes might fail to attend some synods and so might omit some of the additions. They might, for the same or some other reason, fail to notice excisions and alterations in the first edition, ordered in later synods; and even when they agreed in making the same additions, they might insert them at various points in the original series. This process of accumulation and corruption may often be observed, even though the details of the process are obscure, in those statutes of which more than one text survive. But a remarkably large number of our synodal statutes are known only by a single text, and it is important to recognize that these may well exhibit the same characteristics: in other words, they too perhaps present us with a series which was never published as a whole by one bishop and which is, instead, an incomplete conflation of several issues.

Since the occasion of issue and the nature of the assembly did not seriously affect the validity of the statutes, these facts were seldom recorded.[2] The long series of Norwich statutes furnishes a good example: one manuscript alone gives us the meagre and possibly inaccurate information

---

[1] Dobiache–Rojdestvensky, p. 36.
[2] This is not true of some French dioceses. Cf. *ibid.*, pp. 33, 37.

that these are synodal statutes 'alias in synodo promulgata per Walterum quondam Norwyc' episcopum et additiones postea per Symonem successorem suum'. That the statutes usually attributed to Giles of Bridport, bishop of Salisbury, have a more complicated history is suggested by the title in one manuscript: 'statuta dominorum episcoporum Sar'.'[1] Errors arising from the incorporation of late additions in earlier statutes are so common as scarcely to need illustrating. A copyist was content to add to a text of Richard Poore's statutes the excommunication clauses of Reading 1279, without troubling to note that this was not part of the original issue. A more serious error has been fostered by the attribution of Grosseteste's statutes to a synod of Ely more than a century after his death. It is one of the main purposes of the following chapters to date the origins of some of the synodal statutes.

The most obvious question about the genesis of the diocesan statutes has yet to be raised: Who wrote them? This question has been deliberately left to the last because we are incapable of answering it. We may be made tolerably certain by the reputation of certain prelates that they actually composed their statutes: Durandus is a case in point. But if we ask what evidence usually exists for supposing that bishops wrote the statutes attributed to them, the answer is: None. There is, of course, no doubt that bishops like Richard Poore, Alexander of Stavensby, Robert Grosseteste, had all the necessary qualifications. This is not enough. The more learned a bishop was, the more scholarly assistants he was likely to have in his service. When we find likeness between the bishop of Salisbury's statutes and the writings of the contemporary sub-dean of Salisbury,[2] we must admit that we move on unstable ground. Diocesan business constantly caused chancellors and officials to speak in the bishop's name: why should they not do so in diocesan statutes?[3] In a later·age it was the registrar of the diocese of Worcester who, at the request of Archbishop Thomas Arundel, in 1404, framed

---

[1] Cambridge, Emmanuel Coll. MS. 27 fo. 172v.   [2] Cf. below, p. 54.
[3] Cf. the judicious remarks of Canon Deedes about the authorship of the third Winchester series. *Reg. Pontissara*, i. xlii.

in elegant terms a provincial canon 'ad orandum pro episcopis defunctis'.[1] If, to avoid intolerable circumlocution, we refer to a bishop as author of the statutes which he promulgated, this must be taken as a mere form of words.

[1] 'Constitucio provincialis ad orandum pro episcopis defunctis per G[ilbertum] de Stone rudi modo concepta de mandato reverendissimi patris domini Thome Arondell' archiepiscopi.' *Inc.*: 'Oriens ex alto . . .'. Bodley MS. 859 (S.C. 2722) fo. 41v. We do not know whether this form was adopted; cf. Wilkins, iii. 278, 282, 305.

III

THE STATUTES OF RICHARD POORE, BISHOP OF SALISBURY, AND RELATED TEXTS

THE statutes attributed to Richard Poore, bishop successively of Chichester, Salisbury, and Durham, have already been recognized as the most widely influential among English diocesan statutes of the thirteenth century. Reacting against undue neglect of this important series, the most recent writer on the subject goes so far as to conclude: 'that the Bishop of Salisbury, and not the Archbishop of Canterbury, was the great influence behind the movement towards the issuing of episcopal codes of statutes in the reign of Henry III. . . . By about the year 1240 Richard seems to have been generally recognized as the great authority on diocesan constitutions; the rest of the constitutions issued by bishops in the reign of Henry III are all based on the Salisbury constitutions.'[1] This, it will be seen, is to rate their importance too high. And since the nature of their influence in some directions has been exaggerated and in other directions ignored, the whole question of sources, texts, and derivatives deserves fresh study.

The common ascription to Richard Poore has fairly good manuscript authority, and the internal evidence of the statutes supports it. Their earliest recension was obviously framed for the diocese of Salisbury, it uses the Fourth Lateran Council, and it does not refer to the Council of Oxford of 1222. To argue from silence is usually dangerous for establishing a *terminus ad quem*; but the canons of Oxford were so widely diffused and the occasions when they might have been cited so frequent in the statutes of Salisbury that the argument seems valid here. The date must therefore be 1216 × 1221. It is just possible that the statutes were first issued by Bishop Herbert Poore in a synod of 1216, but all later recensions agree in attributing them to Bishop Richard, Herbert's brother, and it is more

---

[1] Miss Lang, in M. Gibbs and J. Lang, *Bishops and reform, 1215–72*, pp. 117, 120–1.

in keeping with what we know of the character and training of the two men that Richard should have composed
and issued them. While his reputation as author of other
works rests on dubious evidence, Richard had at least had
an academic education, as *conscholaris* with Thomas of Marl-
borough and pupil of Stephen Langton,[1] and had plenty
of practical experience in the working of ecclesiastical law.
He had attended the Fourth Lateran Council, and had
probably known personally all the contemporaries whose
works are quoted in these statutes. All the conditions
seem satisfied. If Richard's authorship be accepted, the
statutes must be dated 1217 × 1221.

The work has a homogeneity and plan which suggest
that it is mainly an original composition; it is also on a
bigger, more comprehensive scale than most of the surviving sets of synodal decrees, English or foreign. It aims
at providing a modicum of doctrinal instruction and practical advice for priests as well as at publishing decrees
with canonical force. The work of the theologian and the
canonist is blended in a way not uncommon in the products
of the Paris schools of the late twelfth century; and to the
academic and juristic elements are added precepts of a sort
which one would expect from a prelate faced with practical
problems, careful about his pastoral duties and administration. These statutes may indeed be differentiated from
some others of their age by their insistence upon elementary truths and common difficulties: the author has saved
space by avoiding those contingencies which seldom arise
and which were so much beloved by contemporary writers
of treatises on the sacraments. Thus Poore refrains from
copying from the source of his statutes on the Eucharist
the usual minute regulation respecting flies and spiders in
the chalice: another English bishop put it all in.[2] Furthermore, he does not concern himself much with the diocesan
officials, the cathedral clergy, or the regulars. The conduct and training of the parish priests is his main business.
The statutes open with a section relating particularly to the

---

[1] Gibbs and Lang, pp. 25–7.
[2] Cf. Statutes of Odo, bishop of Paris, ix. 24 (Mansi, xxii. 682) and the statutes
for the diocese of London, ch. 43 (*Eng. Hist. Rev.*, xxx. 294).

secular clergy, their ordination, and their pastoral duties (chs. 1–14).[1] The rest of the statutes are mostly built up round the discussion of the other six sacraments: these occupy chs. 15–61 and 77–91, in which short homiletic passages introduce decrees. Other chapters concerning the church fabric, the holding of benefices, prebendal rights, preachers, &c., are fitted into two sections, chs. 70–6, 92–108, without any obvious reason for their sequence. But in general the arrangement is systematic and the whole ordered by the idea which Poore expresses in the last chapter: 'ut sacerdotes, ipsas [constitutiones] frequenter habentes pre oculis, in ministeriis et dispensationibus sacramentorum sint instructiores, et in fide catholica bene vivendo firmiores.'

THE SOURCES OF POORE'S STATUTES

On investigating the sources, one is at once confronted with a difficulty in the shape of the well-known 'statuta legenda in concilio Oxoniensi'. The text printed under this misleading title by Wilkins (*Concilia*, i. 593), as well as some earlier similar texts,[2] contains much material found in Poore's statutes. But so long as the date and formation of the 'Legenda' remain beyond the hope of conjecture, the parallels cannot be treated as sources for or derivatives from Poore's work. A second difficulty arises with regard to the numerous *Summæ* and treatises on sacraments which Poore may be expected to have known. The influence of such works is fairly clear in various sections of the statutes, and they may well have provided the immediate source of some citations of the fathers, Ambrose, Gregory, and others; but close verbal parallels could alone determine which of these works the bishop most employed, and such evidence has not been found. It is, however, worthy of remark that two writers of *Summæ* were certainly known personally to Poore. Robert of Flamborough, who is re-

---

[1] References in this book to the chapters of Poore's statutes follow the numeration in *Salisbury charters*. In the forthcoming edition the chapters will be differently numbered, with a concordance.

[2] Cf. *Eng. Hist. Rev.*, l. 395–8, and above, p. 40.

garded as among the earliest authors of a new type of penitential literature, wrote his *Summa*, according to Dietterle, between 1207 and 1215.[1] In his preface he addresses the person who had prompted the work : 'Hilaris ergo et letus et securus aggredi temptabo quod petistis, decane salubergensis.'[2] If the dean of *Salisbury* be intended, it is almost certainly Richard Poore, who held the dignity from 1198 to 1214. Such a connexion seems entirely suitable. The two men wrote with similar purposes ; and the mixture of theological and legal matter which has been observed in the statutes was typical of both.[3] A writer on penance whose work was probably more widely diffused than Robert of Flamesbury's had a yet closer connexion with Salisbury in this period. Thomas de Chabham, who wrote the well-known *Summa de casibus penitentie*, was a clerk of Bishop Herbert Poore, and apparently subdean of Salisbury from about 1214 to 1230.[4] Without doubt he and his diocesan, Richard Poore, must have discussed the questions of priestly conduct about which each was writing ; whether one stimulated the other to write it is impossible to say. But again, we see that the author of the *Summa* had the same practical interests as the framer of synodal statutes : 'subtilitates et inquisiciones theoricas pretermittemus' says Thomas de Chabham, 'et comparaciones et consideraciones practicas que ad audiendas confessiones et ad iniungendas penitencias sacerdotibus necessarie sunt diligencius prosequamur.'[5]

The only source of a distinctly homiletic nature so far identified is the original of Poore's introductory remarks about baptism in ch. 20 : these prove to be taken entirely from a decretal letter of Innocent III, which Poore may have known by its inclusion in *Compilatio III*.[6]

---

[1] J. Dietterle, 'Die Summae Confessorum ', p. 373 ; cf. Teetaert, *La confession,* p. 234.

[2] So Dietterle's text; Brit. Mus. Royal MS. 15 B. iv fo. 146r reads *saluberiensis*.

[3] 'Man darf die Summae confessorum nicht verwechseln mit den rein juristischen oder rein theologischen Summen. Ihre Verfasser bewegen sich zu gleicher Zeit auf dem juristischen und theologischen Gebiete.' *Ibid.*, pp. 354–5.

[4] Cf. J. C. Russell, *Dictionary*, pp. 158–9, and Teetaert, *La confession.* pp. 347–51.

[5] *Summa de casibus*, Brit. Mus. Royal MS. 11 A. vi fo. 3rb.

[6] *Compilatio III*, iii. 34, 1 ; *Decretales*, iii. 42, 3 ; Potthast, 1479.

Fortunately we have firm evidence of the origin of many of the statutes, and we find that this work which at first impresses by its arrangement and homogeneity is in fact a mosaic carefully contrived with the help of at least four main canonical sources. Rather more than half the whole number of chapters are verbatim copies or slightly modified versions of canonical matter which Poore found at hand. First and foremost, the Fourth Lateran Council. Poore had attended the General Council and presumably brought away with him its decrees. It is reasonable to see in Innocent III's legislation the main stimulus to Poore's composition of statutes.[1] Poore's own statutes exploit the Lateran decrees very fully, as well as drawing thrice upon the Third Lateran Council of 1179.[2]

The next source from which Poore drew extensively was the latest series of English provincial canons: those of Archbishop Hubert issued at London in 1200. Sixteen chapters are taken wholly or in part from this source. Thus, it may be remarked in passing, Hubert's canons came to be passed from one diocese to another without any mark of origin. Otherwise they were probably little known, and have only survived in the manuscripts of Roger of Hoveden's chronicles and in a poor early thirteenth-century text from St. Bartholomew's, Smithfield.[3]

Another eminently suitable source, to swell the sacramental teaching, was provided by the statutes attributed to Odo de Sully, bishop of Paris 1196–1208.[4] They appear to be the immediate source of seventeen chapters of Poore's statutes. These statutes of Bishop Odo had even wider ramifications than had Poore's. They fall into two parts: the first, entitled 'Prohibitiones et præcepta observanda ab omnibus sacerdotibus', begins with rules for holding a synod and proceeds with six long chapters upon the sacraments (the sacrament of Orders being omitted); the second part begins 'Hic incipiunt communia præcepta synodalia'

---

[1] Cf. Gibbs and Lang, pp. 108–21.

[2] Chs. 97, 102–3. In accordance with the practice of the time, this General Council was called the First Lateran Council: 'Quoniam in concilio lateranensi primo dinoscitur esse statutum' (ch. 103); cf. Cheney, 'La date de composition du "Liber Poenitentialis",' pp. 402–3.

[3] Cf. *Eng. Hist. Rev.*, l. 388–9.   [4] Mansi, xxii. 675.

and covers topics of great variety, including some additions to the preceding chapters on the sacraments. Until the manuscript tradition of these statutes has been elucidated, it would be dangerous to dogmatize about their date. It may be that the evidence of Odo's authorship is none too strong; and certainly the second part is probably a later issue than the first.[1] The facts remain that they bear no trace of the Fourth Lateran Council and may well be dated before November 1215, that they mention explicitly the church of Paris, and that one section of the second part is cited as of Paris in the 'Liber penitentialis' of Peter de Poitiers.[2] Either these Paris statutes share a common source with Poore's statutes or are themselves the parent ; for a comparison of the related texts shows that they cannot be derived from Poore. The cumulative evidence, though not conclusive, points to direct parentage. For the same material which composes the sacramental section of Odo's statutes occurs in fragments in many other places. The bishop of London's statutes, framed a generation after Poore's, not only use Poore's statutes but also independently take almost all of Odo which Poore had rejected. Sections of both parts 1 and 2 are used in statutes of Rouen, dated at some time later than 1215.[3] They are adopted, almost in their entirety, by the bishops of Chartres.[4] The statutes of Trier of 1227 have likewise been shown to have for their *Hauptquelle* the statutes attributed to Odo,[5] while a few years later they provided a nucleus for synodal statutes of Mainz (1233).[6]

---

[1] Cf. Heydenreich, ' Zu den Trierer Synodalstatuten ', p. 484.

[2] Probably composed soon after 1215. Cf. A. Teetaert, ' Le *Liber Poenitentialis* de Pierre de Poitiers ', *Aus der Geisteswelt des Mittelalters* (Studien und Texte Martin Grabmann . . . gewidmet [*Beiträge zur Gesch. der Philos. und Theol. des MA*, Supplementband iii] 1935), i, 323 and Cheney, *loc. cit.*, pp. 401–4.

[3] Mlle Dobiache-Rojdestvensky offers good reasons for supposing that these Precepta antiqua of Rouen are earlier than Archbishop Peter de Collemieu (1235–45), under whose name they appear, and dates them at ' commencement du treizième siècle '. She fails to notice that they reproduce verbatim several canons of the Fourth Lateran Council (*La vie paroissiale*, pp. 41–4).

[4] Jusselin, *loc. cit.* Several other series of statutes in the collection of Martène and Durand come from the same source ; e.g. the statutes of Autun, *Thesaurus*, iv cols. 467 *seqq.*

[5] Heydenreich, 478–85.

[6] *Ibid.*, 484. Cf. H. Finke, *Konzilienstudien*, pp. 35–6 ; if Finke's view be

Poore's own early connexion with the schools of Paris and the general fame of Bishop Odo's statutes sufficiently explain borrowings from this source. To the same reasons one may ascribe the traces of Robert de Courçon's legatine canons, issued in Paris and Rouen, in 1213 and 1214.[1] Poore may well have known the great cardinal-legate as a teacher in the schools, and this legislation of his circulated widely enough to reach Poore in his later days when, as bishop, he passed between England and Rome. If one is surprised that only four chapters of Poore's statutes show traces of Courçon's, it should be remembered that the legatine decrees dealt mainly with subjects outside the scope of the Salisbury statutes and that when they were used by Poore he could and did draw upon the decrees of the Fourth Lateran Council 'de vita et honestate clericorum'.

THE MANUSCRIPTS OF POORE'S STATUTES

If we eliminate for the moment manuscripts of statutes copied or derived from the Salisbury series, the following four manuscripts remain:

A. Worcester Cathedral Library, MS. Q 67 fo. 138r.
No title. *Inc.* 'Cum nec rugam . . .'. The statutes occur at the end of a small quarto volume containing various works : sermons, the 'Speculum ecclesie' of St. Edmund Rich, &c., written in several hands, xiii c. and xiv c. So far as a tight modern binding permits one to see, the statutes form a separate section, and are written in a hand different from the others of the volume. The statutes are written in two columns, in a small neat hand of the early part of Henry III's reign. Most of the original red chapter headings have been modified, deleted, or erased. Notes appear to be in two hands (A², A³). The bottom and outside edges of most of the leaves have suffered from damp and so some marginal notes may be lost. Some notes on the inside edges cannot be read because of the tight binding. There is no indication of provenance of the statutes; on fo. 145v, perhaps part of the same section, is copied a letter of John XXII to the bishop

---

accepted, this section of the 1233 statutes came from an earlier council of Mainz, 1200 × 1230. Hauck's arguments for a much earlier origin (*Theologische Studien Th. Zahn dargebracht*, p. 83) never seemed strong and break down when confronted with the evidence of Bishop Odo's statutes.
[1] Mansi, *Concilia*, xxii. 818 ; Hefele-Leclercq, *Hist. des conciles*, v. ii. 1308 ; Finke, *Konzilienstudien*, pp. 45–6.

of London on behalf of William de Cotton (or Totton), priest of Norwich diocese. Another section of the book, consisting of sermons, belonged in xiv c. to ' domino Willelmo Brimpene, capellano de Helnestowe [? Helstone, in Lanteglos by Camelford, Cornwall] ' (fo. 49r). There is no record of the date at which the volume reached Worcester.

B. Salisbury Dean and Chapter Muniments, Liber evidenciarum C p. 367 (formerly fo. 172r), no. 493.

Title: 'Constituciones R' episcopi Sar' '. *Inc.* 'Cum nec rugam . . .'. The statutes form the first gathering of a collection of provincial and diocesan canons, and are in a hand different from the others in the collection. While the rest is in hands of the second half xiii c. (probably before the Council of Reading 1279), the hand of the Salisbury statutes appears to belong to the first half xiii c. It is an aquiline bookhand, with titles in red, and red and blue initials. A late xiii c. annotator on p. 367 attributes these statutes tentatively to Bishop Robert of Bingham,[1] and a xv c. annotator writes above the title : ' Constituciones Ricardi Sar' episcopi '. Whatever the origin of the whole collection, which includes one series of Winchester statutes and an extract from another, it was apparently an integral part of this important capitular muniment book before the end of the xiii c. It seems highly probable that the collection was made for the cathedral chapter or for a member of the chapter. This text was printed fairly accurately[2] by W. D. Macray in *Charters and documents of Salisbury*, pp. 128–63 and is the best edition at present available.

C. Oxford, Corpus Christi College MS. 360 fo. 62r.

Title : ' Constituciones bone memorie domini Ricardi Sar' episcopi' to which a xvii c. hand (possibly Dugdale's) has added ' Poore' after ' Ricardi ' and ' circa annum domini 1217 '. *Inc.* ' Cum nec rugam . . .'. The statutes begin a new section of the manuscript, and there is no indication that in the Middle Ages it was bound with the first section: Bartholomew of Exeter 'de fatalitate'. Poore's statutes occupy one gathering and part of a second in which they are followed by statutes of Bishop Giles of Bridport and of the diocese of Winchester, in other nearly contemporary hands. The rest of the volume is occupied by the ' Summa Ricardi de sacramentis ' (fo. 79) and the ' Summa Willelmi de Montibus ' *Qui bene presunt* (fo. 100), each of which begins a new gathering and is in a new hand. The general similarity of format makes it possible that the whole collection from fo. 62 onwards originally formed one book. The statutes of Poore are written in a clear but variable hand of *c.* 1300, with

---

[1] Cf. *Salisbury charters*, p. 128 n. 1 and *Eng. Hist. Rev.*, l. 399 n. 5.
[2] The editor makes many tacit emendations of his text.

very many stupid mistakes, the results of bad reading or mechanical copying, with headings in the original hand and paragraph marks in red. There is no indication of provenance earlier than the xvii c.: the signature of Sir Henry Spelman appears on fos. 1r, 62r, 72v, 74r. This text was the original of Spelman's edition (*Concilia*, ii. 137), which Wilkins used (*Concilia*, i. 599). Bodleian MS. James 26 (S.C. 3863) pp. 171–5, contains extracts from the statutes copied from this manuscript by Richard James in the xvii c.

E. British Museum Harl. MS. 52 fo. 109r.

Title: 'Constituciones bone memorie domini Ricardi quondam Sar' episcopi' in a second xiv c. hand. *Inc.* 'Cum nec rugam . . .'. The statutes, which are followed by those of Bishop Robert of Bingham, come at the end of a long series of provincial and legatine canons with the Clementines, all written in the mid-xiv c. The statutes are written in a coarse charter hand, and contain many errors, some of which have been noted by a contemporary corrector. There is no indication of the original provenance, though it may be said that the collection (which includes articles of inquiry for the visitation of parishes) might well have been made for an ecclesiastical official. Oxford *cauciones* of Master William Darset, 1479 and later, are recorded on fo. 129r. The names of Mr. Hawkyns (1484) and Mr. Wyther (late xv c., fo. 129v) also appear. The volume later belonged to Sir Simonds d'Ewes (title in his handwriting on fo. 1*).

In addition to these manuscripts, which purport to present the statutes as they were published in the diocese of Salisbury, we have other evidence of some textual value in the shape of revised editions of the statutes used elsewhere: in particular, the recensions used in the dioceses of Durham and Canterbury. These will be considered here simply in so far as they elucidate the relations of the texts ABCE, and will call for separate discussion later.

The Worcester manuscript of the statutes (A) is particularly interesting because it preserves at least some features of the original edition, together with numerous corrections and changes. The original text shows the marks of a first recension in its injunctions with time-limits attached: thus the chapter (ch. 70) *Ne sacerdotes extranei admittantur* demands a preliminary examination of unknown priests; the A text alone adds the proviso 'Verumptamen cum talibus infra festum sancti Michaelis proximum misericorditer in officio suo dispensamus quatinus interim de ipsorum ordinatione vita et literatura nobis fidem faciant prout iustum fuerit sufficienter.' This passage (and similar ones in chs. 1 and 76) is deleted in A and omitted from all other texts. Many other changes have been made in A by two hands, A² and A³, involving the alteration of most of the chapter-titles and some additions and deletions in the text. They certainly represent later recensions. Such recensions are implied in the order, common enough in the thirteenth-century statutes, that priests should bring their copies of statutes for correction to each synod. This manuscript may be a copy corrected in the course of years by an archdeacon or parish priest as alterations were announced in successive synods. But certain features of it suggest a still more interesting origin. Some of the corrections are such as would scarcely be made by a parish priest anxious to modernize his copy, unless he were an exceptionally conscientious person. Chapter-titles are submitted to minute alterations, and words are sometimes substituted in the text which do not in any way affect the sense. They can best be explained on the assumption that this is an official copy from the bishop's chancery, with official draft corrections. As such it acquires unique importance among English manuscripts of synodal material.

It is evident that the changes made by A² and A³ on A do not necessarily represent only two revisions of the original statutes. The evidence is the more doubtful because of the difficulty of distinguishing between A² and A³ in A. Some deletions and erasures cannot safely be assigned to one corrector rather than the other. The same warning must be given in regard to the other manuscripts. They likewise contain variants which derive from various recensions, and there is no means of knowing whether any one manuscript preserves one recension exactly; indeed, a study of the variants suggests the contrary. The following conclusions can therefore only be advanced with strong reservations:

1. The A text represents the earliest form in which we know the statutes and gives a version produced 1217 × 1221.

2. The A² text shows comparatively few changes, beyond a general revision of chapter-titles and the deletion of time-limits (cf. above, p. 59). The B text represents something

very close to A². The date of this version appears to be still within the period 1217–21, for there is as yet no mention of the Council of Oxford (1222).

3. CE both belong to a time after the Council of Oxford and introduce references to that council as well as a new chapter on the fraternity of the cathedral fabric (ch. 92). C, the text printed by both Spelman and Wilkins, even contains a final chapter of sentences of excommunication taken bodily from Pecham's Council of Reading (1279); but this late addition does not affect the general character of the version, which textually belongs to the period immediately after 1222; it is probably even earlier than E, which makes several additions to the original text found only besides in the Durham recension.

4. A³ seems to preserve approximately the final version, so far as revision for the diocese of Salisbury goes. It includes most of the variants introduced into the A¹ version by B, C, and E, but in certain cases goes further, altering A¹ and A² where these versions agreed with other manuscripts.[1] It was at this stage, from a version like A³, that the Canterbury derivative was composed; and if the ascription to Stephen Langton in MS. D of this derivative be accepted, it must be dated 1222 × 1228.[2] This accords well enough with the evidence of the Durham derivative, which generally agrees with A³ and the Canterbury derivative against BCE. Both the Canterbury and the Durham versions contain matter additional to any of the texts ascribed to Salisbury, but in no instance do their substantial additions agree: where they both make the same additions to the A text, in each case the like addition is found in A³.[3]

[1] Cf. variants in ch. 109 : et reformatione morum promulgatas AB ; et reformatione morum constituti [sic] omnibus in concilio Oxoniensi a domino Cantuar' editis C ; et reformatione morum promulgata una cum constitucionibus omnibus in concilio Oxon' a domino Cant' editis E ; et reformatione morum promulgatas una cum constitutionibus concilii provincialis apud Oxoniam celebratis [sic] et post presentium lectionem recitandis A³ and Canterbury derivative.

[2] The Canterbury derivative came, however, from a version which still preserved some early features. Thus in ch. 2 : dominorum suorum A and Canterbury derivative ; illorum a quibus requiri debet [debuit C] licentia A³BCE.

[3] A lengthy addition to the AB texts of ch. 66 occurs in texts CE and in the Durham derivative ; in this case, an addition to A by the A³ corrector has probably dropped out : three slanting lines in the A text at this point show that an addition was intended. In ch. 17, following ' precipimus observari ' A³E read

Finally, as an illustration of the sequence of texts, one set of variants shall be quoted from chapter 16:[1]

> aliquid exigant A
> aliquid improbe exigant A[2]
> aliquid improbe exigatur BCE
> aliquid extorqueatur A[3]
> aliquid extorqueatur Canterbury & Durham derivatives.

DERIVATIVES FROM POORE'S STATUTES

Among the earliest, if not the very first, of English synodal statutes, Poore's spread widely within the next generation. The process of their diffusion was a double one: some prelates seem content to copy them practically in their entirety, while for others they provide a store-house to plunder for particularly desirable chapters and well-turned phrases. It need hardly be added that in no case does the copyist name his source; that would have been contrary to usual medieval practice in the matter. In the first category come the copies of Poore used in the dioceses of Canterbury, Durham, and York; in the second, the statutes issued in the dioceses of Salisbury (by Robert of Bingham), Winchester, Exeter, London, Chichester, and Worcester, and those issued at an unknown date in a provincial council of the Scottish Church.

Statutes of Archbishop Stephen Langton (?), *for the diocese of Canterbury*, (*1222 × 1228*).

Two early thirteenth-century texts present us with almost the entire series of Poore's statutes, without the local references to associate them with Salisbury.

D. Brit. Mus., Cotton MS. Julius D. ii fo. 166v.

Title : ' Incipiunt statuta Stephani archiepiscopi in sinodo.' This text, written in a minute mid-xiii c. hand, occurs in a small quarto volume from St. Augustine's Abbey, Canterbury. The various contents of the book, written in the xiii and xiv c., are briefly described by W. A. Pantin, *Benedictine chapters*, i. 4–5 and by W. Holtzmann, *Papsturkunden*, 1. i. 69.

' statuentes ut libere conferantur sacramenta ecclesiastica ' and this phrase is not found in the derivatives. It may, however, be explained as a gloss derived from the IV Lat. Con. 66, from which the whole surrounding passage is taken.

[1] Cf. facsimile.

G. Bodleian, Hatton MS. 67 (S.C. 4075) fo. 76r.

No title. This text, written in an early xiii c. hand, very closely resembles D. It forms the fifth and final part of a volume which contains among other things the Prophecies of Merlin and French sermons of Maurice de Sully, bishop of Paris : but these parts were originally distinct and their provenance is unknown.

J. Bodleian, Rawlinson MS. A. 429 fo. 104r.

No title. This is an imperfect text, written in the early xv c., which breaks off in the middle of ch. 58. It occurs in the midst of a miscellaneous volume of theological and other tracts, more particularly works on confession and penance.

The Cotton manuscript, with its ascription of the statutes to Stephen Langton, was known to Wilkins. He describes it briefly (*Concilia*, i. 572 n.) as a conflation of the Durham statutes (see below), which he regards as the independent work of Richard Marsh, with Poore's Salisbury statutes. But he does not seriously investigate the differences between the D text and the other texts of the Salisbury statutes and consequently cannot express any opinion on the ascription.

When the DGJ texts are compared with the known Salisbury texts, it is found that they agree with A^3 more often than with others.[1] In this they resemble the Durham derivative (whence Wilkins's inference), but a little study shows that they are independent of this. DGJ have substantial additions to the Salisbury text which are not found elsewhere, and omit passages which occur in all other texts. A brief examination of these and other peculiarities is desirable :

Additions. After ch. 7 DGJ add :

> Et quia congnato nomine aliquando culpa tegitur, prohibemus ne rectores ecclesiarum vel vicarii aut sacerdotes in domibus suis mulieres aliquas retineant de quibus suspicio sinistra possit oriri.

At the end of ch. 50 DGJ add precision to the penalties on perjurers in marriage cases :

> quos postquam convicti fuerint vel confessi a legitimis actibus tamquam infames penitus decernimus repellendos et publice tales denunciandos.

After ch. 63 DG add :

> Quod cimiteria claudantur.

---

[1] Cf. above, p. 62. In ch. 107 A^3CE contain an addition not found in the B text of Salisbury or in DG (*Salisbury charters*, p. 162 n. 2).

Ad hec adhicimus precipientes quod admoneantur parochiani quod cimiteria sua in quibus reliquie suorum predecessorum sepeliuntur honeste claudant, et si necesse fuerit, per subtractionem panis et aque benedicte et osculi pacis in ecclesia ad hoc faciendum compellantur; et si protervitas eorum meruerit, arbitrio presidentis ulterius coerceantur.

After ch. 97 DG add:

Statuimus etiam ne moniales onerent se puellulis vel feminas retineant seculares de quibus sinistra suspicio possit oriri, nec aliquas recipiant nutriendas nisi de licentia nostra.

After ch. 107 DG add:

De residentia vicariorum.

Precipimus quod qui vicarius fuerit in ecclesia constitutus in ordine sacerdotali personaliter residens ministret in eadem sub pena amissionis beneficii et una tantum vicaria sit contentus. De personis autem vicarios non habentibus similiter statuimus nisi causa rationabili vel a iudice aprobata vel de licentia diocesani contigerit abesse.

De usuris prohibendis.

Prohibemus sub pena excommunicationis ne quis contractum feneraticium vel speciem usure continentem eccerceat.

De celebratione festorum.

Quoniam turpis est omnis pars que non congruit suo universo, statuimus quod festa consueta uniformiter [per diocesim G] celebrentur nisi alicubi subsit causa specialis a diocesano approbata.

Omissions. The introduction found in all other texts.

Ch. 2 Qui vero . . . postulare.

Chs. 54 and 55.

Ch. 66, excepting the first sentence.

Ch. 81 stops short at *compaternitatem.*

Ch. 86 stops short at *set augeat.*

Ch. 88.

Ch. 92 the passage concerning the fabric of Salisbury (as in F, the Durham version).

Ch. 102.

A few substitutions are significant:

Ch. 44 *penitentiarium episcopi* becomes *penitentiarium nostrum.*
    eius [sc. *episcopi*] *auct.* becomes *auctoritate nostra.*
    ad mandatum episcopi becomes *ad mandatum archiepiscopi.*

Ch. 107 *de episcopatu nostro* becomes *de archiepiscopatu nostro.*

It may be noted that while the additional chapter after

ch. 97 refers to *licentia nostra*, the later additions refer twice
to the licence of the diocesan.

It is clear from the relation of the DGJ version to the
various forms of the A text that it represents a revision
rather than the original of the Salisbury version. The removal
of references to the diocese of Salisbury and the changes of
episcopus and *episcopatus* to *archiepiscopus* and *archiepiscopatus*
alike suggest the possibility that the title in the text from
St. Augustine's, Canterbury, is correct, and that Stephen
Langton in fact borrowed from his brother-bishop of Salisbury and issued this series in a synod of his diocese. If so,
the issue occurred after the Council of Oxford of 1222 which,
although it contributed nothing to the body of the statutes,
is mentioned in ch. 109. Whereas the provincial canons of
Oxford were designed principally for the guidance of the
prelates who attended the council, these statutes, intended
to instruct the parish clergy, had a distinct *raison d'être* and
provided a fitting complement to the provincial canons in the
scheme of ecclesiastical reform. It is perhaps worth insisting
that this DGJ version appears to be framed for the *diocese*
of Canterbury only. This makes it easier to understand why
later borrowings from Poore's statutes do not, apparently,
come from the archbishop's version.

The attribution of these statutes to Stephen Langton is
still open to doubt; but we are on much more insecure
ground when we approach the statutes attributed to his
successor, St. Edmund.[1] For the past five hundred years
St. Edmund has been taken for the author of a series of
forty-one statutes. Lyndwood included many of them in
the *Provinciale*,[2] and they are found in all the printed editions
of *Concilia*. Lyndwood was not prepared to suggest the
occasion of their issue, and later editors have been content
to date them *c.*1236, without assigning them to any particular
ecclesiastical council. No other evidence is known that the

---

[1] The statement of the problem in *Eng. Hist. Rev.*, l. 400–2, is here slightly
modified.

[2] Lyndwood ascribes chs. 16–18 of ' Edmund ' to Archbishop Sudbury (*Provinciale*, v. xvi. 14–16 (pp. 342–3)), and is copied in this by the Oxford editor
of 1679 (appendix ii, p. 59).

archbishop ever held a synod of his diocese or province. While the editors assume that the canons were provincial canons, it has long been observed that their terms imply only diocesan authority.[1] Miss Lang has recently pointed out the original sources of the statutes: 'the first thirty-eight are word for word repetitions of clauses in the Salisbury constitutions [of Richard Poore] without any sort of variation. The thirty-ninth and forty-first clauses are repetitions of clauses in the "Legenda", and the only original contribution is the last part of the fortieth clause concerning tithes.'[2]

St. Edmund had reason both to know and to possess Poore's synodal statutes, for he was canon and treasurer of Salisbury from 1222 to 1234. It seems likely, however, that these statutes which appear under his name were derived from the Canterbury recension described above. The 'Edmund' statutes include nothing omitted by DGJ from the Salisbury series and agree with DGJ in all significant variant readings. But the ascription to St. Edmund needs scrutinizing. Nineteen texts of the statutes have been noted. Several correspond closely to Wilkins's text, but three at least stop short at ch. 38; that is to say, they contain nothing but the selection from Poore.[3] The other texts divide chs. 39–41 from the Poore series by the note: 'In aliquibus libris iste constituciones sunt posite inter constituciones provinciales Oxon' ideo istas ad illas constituciones factas adde, de confirmacione, de decimis, de bonis.'[4] All these texts entitle the statutes 'constituciones provinciales sancti Edmundi Cant. archiepiscopi', but give no further clue to their origin. Lyndwood gives no more information.[5]

[1] Johnson, *Collection*, s.a. 1236, notes to chs. 5, 17, 31; Hefele-Leclercq, v. ii. 1574.

[2] Gibbs and Lang, pp. 118–19. The last part of ch. 40 consists of references to authorities later than St. Edmund's time.

[3] All Souls Coll. MS. 42 fo. 232v; Trin. Coll. Camb. MS. 1245 fo. 119r; Hereford Cath. MS. P. vii. 7 fo. 133r. Lyndwood includes a selection of chs. 1–38 only. Chs. 39–41 occur elsewhere in the Hereford MS. (fo. 159v) headed 'Langetone'. In Harl. MS. 335 fo. 38r, they follow the conclusion of Oxford 1222 without a break.

[4] Exeter Coll. MS. 41 fo. 201r, &c.

[5] While in twelve cases he adopts his usual formula 'Constitutio quæ est Edmundi', he occasionally uses phrases which indicate dubiety: 'Dicitur fuisse Edmundi' (*Provinciale*, p. 71), 'Attribuitur Edmundo archiepiscopo' (pp. 26 160, 204), 'Intitulatur Edmundo in quibusdam libris' (p. 28).

The unanimity of the texts in naming Edmund cannot be regarded as strong evidence in his favour; for these same texts occur only in collections which agree in utterly spurious ascriptions of other texts to Richard at Westminster 1065, and to Langton.[1] On the other hand, it is significant that no manuscript is earlier than the latter end of the fourteenth century; nor in all the thirteenth and fourteenth centuries does any reference to these statutes appear. This evidence is not conclusive condemnation. We must admit the possibility that St. Edmund made excerpts from the derivative of Poore issued by Stephen Langton, added chs. 39–41, and issued the new series as his own diocesan statutes. We might argue that he felt the need for a less lengthy series for his parish priests, and omitted practically all the matter relating to the sacraments because he intended to circulate a distinct treatise on the subject. But the argument is not a strong one. The manuscript tradition is so unsatisfactory that we prefer to regard the title as false and the abridgement as unofficial, made by a private collector, who knew the Canterbury recension of Poore. Admittedly our evidence is negative, but in all respects it corresponds with the evidence against the so-called canons of Westminster 1065 and of Langton at Lambeth: and these can be proved on other grounds to be spurious. In each case a late compiler has made extracts from existing material and provided a new title, and an incorrect one.

Statutes for the diocese of Durham.

F. Durham Cathedral Libr. MS. B. iv. 41 fo. 155r.

Title: 'Constituciones Ricardi quondam episcopi Dunelm*ensis*'. *Inc.* 'Cum nec rugam . . .'. This manuscript, in a xiv c. hand, occurs in the midst of a big series of ecclesiastical law, at the beginning of a section of diocesan statutes for Durham. The whole volume, which was obviously compiled at Durham, and which contains writings from the xiii to the xv c., is described fully by Pantin, *Chapters of the Black Monks*, ii, pp. x–xiii. This text may be the original of Spelman's edition (*Concilia*, ii. 166), although Thomas Rud supposes him to have used M. Wilkins's text (*Concilia*, i. 572) is taken from F and Spelman's edition.

---

[1] With the exception of Bodleian, Rawl. MS. C. 100. Cf. *Eng. Hist. Rev.*, l. 387, 398–400, 402 n. 1.

L. Brit. Mus., Lansdowne MS. 397 fo. 230.

Title: 'Incipiunt constitutiones Ricardi episcopi Dunelmensis'. *Inc.* 'Cum nec rugam . . .'. This forms part of a large volume, mostly written in the xiv c., which belonged to the chancery of Durham Cathedral Priory; its contents may be best briefly described in the words of an inventory of the year 1421 : 'P. Summa dictaminis monachi Ricardi de Pophis et constituciones sinodales ecclesiae Dunelmensis ac constituciones Octoboni legati, cum multis aliis' (*Catalogi Veteres Dunelm.* (Surtees Society, l) p. 124).

M. Durham Cathedral Libr. MS. C. ii. 13 fo. 269va.

Title : 'Constituciones Ricardi quondam episcopi Dunelm*ensis*'. *Inc.* 'Cum nec rugam . . .'. This text, written in the mid-xiv c., is very nearly related to F and is found in a volume which contains much of the same material. Like F, M was in the Durham library in the Middle Ages. It was probably the original of Spelman's edition.

N. Oxford, Jesus Coll. MS. 78 fo. 197r.

Title : 'Incipiunt constitutiones Richardi Dunolm' quondam episcopi Dunolm'.' *Inc.* 'Cum nec rugam . . .'. This is a xvii c. transcript, by Augustine Baker, of F. It belonged at one time to Anthony Wood.

The three fourteenth-century manuscripts of these statutes present very similar texts, without any important discrepancy in contents. They comprise the greater part of chs. 1–97 of Poore's Salisbury series, with minor differences. It is not easy to see why chs. 98–109 should be omitted by any legislator possessed of Poore's whole series, and the easiest explanation of the curtailment may be the right one : that the archetype of our texts had lost its last folio. This is the more likely because the version in Stowe MS. 930 (see below), which apparently belongs to the same tradition, contains chs. 98 and 99. In detail the Durham series shows light re-touching of the original statutes in their A³ recension. Thus in ch. 1 'ut et deus placetur et grex eis commissus edificetur' becomes 'ut et deus in illis honorificetur et grex eis commissus edificetur'. In ch. 53 'id est mundet per confessionem et sanctificet se' becomes 'unusquisque per confessionem mundans et sanctificans'. In ch. 62, to 'vasis decentibus et honestis' is added 'et phialis'. The passage concerning bequests to the cathedral fabric of Salisbury in ch. 92 is naturally omitted, but two other short omissions are probably due to bad copying.[1]

The authorship of this version is not beyond all doubt. It is said to be the work of Bishop Richard, and since Richard Poore was translated to Durham in 1228, he may well have reissued the statutes composed in his southern see. But Poore's immediate predecessor at Durham was Richard Marsh (1217–26), and the possibility cannot be excluded that he, like others, borrowed Poore's work, modifying it only slightly. Both Spelman and Wilkins for inadequate reasons preferred to ascribe the statutes to Richard Marsh and assigned to them a date before the Council of Oxford. But whereas Spelman printed both Salisbury statutes (c. 1217) and Durham statutes (c. 1220) without calling attention to their similarity, Wilkins was led to assign a later date to the Salisbury series (c. 1223) because his text contained references to the Council of Oxford. Noting the similarity of the two sets (Concilia, i. 599b), he treated the Salisbury series of Poore as an expanded version of Richard Marsh's. In the light of the A text of Salisbury this opinion cannot be maintained. Whoever issued the Durham statutes abridged them from the Salisbury series. Moreover, if Marsh issued them, it was between 1222 and 1226; for the character of the text shows that a late version of the Salisbury statutes was being copied; and the fact that the Council of Oxford is not mentioned in the Durham series is explained by the probably accidental omission of those final chapters of Salisbury which refer to the provincial council. But the balance of probability inclines to Poore's own responsibility for this reissue: between 1228 and 1237.

Statutes for the peculiars of the prior and convent of Durham in the diocese of York.

This is a long series of statutes written in a neat hand of the mid-thirteenth century, with rubrications probably by the original writer. They form the first part of the British Museum manuscript Stowe 930, a book from Durham

---

[1] The omission in ch. 49 may be due to haplography: invocantes . . . convertentes; similarly in ch. 50: idem precipimus . . . idem precipimus.

Cathedral Priory, containing chapter statutes and various material suitable to a monastic register.[1] At the end of the statutes, on the blank half of fo. 8r is written, probably contemporaneously: 'Anno gratie m°. cc^{mo}. lxxx^{mo}. kal. Martii hospitatus fuit dominus Petrus de Monteforti miles.'

The statutes are clearly based upon those of Richard Poore; for this reason, probably, a late thirteenth-century hand added a title at the head of fo. 3r, which is now mostly obliterated, but which may be reconstructed as 'Statuta Ricardi quondam episcopi Dunelmensis in sinodo'.[2] But the relationship with Poore's original series is complicated, and the title is probably incorrect. As has been noted, the manuscript comes from Durham Cathedral Priory, and it was probably written there. One might therefore expect the statutes to be those issued in the diocese of Durham. But already we possess a different version of Poore's statutes revised for use in the northern diocese; and certain features of the Stowe manuscript point to another conclusion. Various details connect its version with the diocese of York. The prior and convent of Durham exercised archidiaconal rights in certain parishes in that diocese, and this manuscript almost certainly provides a set of statutes issued by the prior of Durham for the benefit of the priests of the Durham peculiar jurisdiction within the diocese of York. It is based, naturally, upon the current diocesan statutes of Durham, but also makes use of the statutes issued by Robert Grosseteste for the diocese of Lincoln.

The evidence upon which this conclusion rests must be briefly set out. First, as to sources. The greater number of the statutes in the Stowe manuscript (hereafter designated H) are substantially the same as statutes of Bishop Richard Poore, and occur in the same sequence. Although, like the known revision of Poore for the diocese of Durham, they omit the final chapters, they do include two chapters

---

[1] For descriptions of the volume see Pantin, *Benedictine chapters*, i. 32–3 and the catalogue of the Stowe manuscripts. The views expressed upon the origin of these statutes in the following pages owe much to my discussion of the problem with Mr. W. A. Pantin and with Mr. Frank Barlow.

[2] The *incipit* of the text is 'Cum rex celestis glorie . . .' (fo. 3r, formerly fo. 1r).

of the original Salisbury series which do not occur in the known Durham revision (chs. 98, 99). But the close textual similarity of the two versions in other respects encourages one to suppose that the omission of chs. 98–109 in the surviving texts of the known Durham version was accidental, and that H was copied from the version then current in the diocese of Durham.[1] The portions of the Lincoln statutes found in H provide a *terminus a quo* for the compilation: 1240. While the statutes of Walter of Kirkham for the diocese of Durham[2] likewise show knowledge of the Lincoln statutes, the present series has drawn independently from the same source. The portions of H for which no earlier source has been found are few. They include the preamble, small additions to chs. 7, 43, 63 of Poore, and a new chapter at the end; this last reads as follows:

Statuimus etiam quod in singulis ecclesiis in ebor*acensi* diocese ad nostram visitationem spectantibus post susceptionem litterarum nostrarum de visitatione facienda omnes cause tunc temporis mote et non terminate nostre discussioni cum ad partes illas venerimus reserventur.

The circumstances of the H issue are indicated by the following evidence. The preamble would probably reveal its origin without doubt if only it were legible. Unfortunately, stains of damp have obliterated some of the crucial words. Even so, it gives valuable indications. From it we may infer that someone connected with the church of Durham is addressing priests who partake of that church's privileges; and it is stated explicitly that the archbishops of York have confirmed those privileges. The writer refers to the church of Durham as promulgating the statutes ('ea promulgasse seu publicasse cognoveritis', fo. 3v) and speaks of himself as representing that church ('vices agimus ecclesie memorate', *ibid.*). Such language

---

[1] The only divergence hard to explain on this theory is in ch. 50. Here H contains, in common with all the Salisbury texts and the Canterbury derivative, a passage omitted in F: 'Idem fiat de hiis qui malitiose rationabilium testamentorum impediunt executionem'; and it omits the following sentence common to A³DEFG. Although some of the modifications of the original series made in H bring it into line with the version of DGJ, re-shaped for the diocese of Canterbury (the substitution of *archiepiscopus* for *episcopus*, &c.), H includes parts of the original omitted from the Canterbury revision (parts of ch. 2 and chs. 54–5). It cannot, therefore, be derived from the Canterbury revision.

[2] Cf. below, p. 139.

might perhaps come from a bishop of Durham, but it seems more suitable in the mouth of a prior of the cathedral church. The connexion with the northern province is confirmed by the form of the rubric to ch. 54 and by the new final chapter quoted above. The former reads: 'De canone misse habendo secundum usum Eborac' ' (fo. 6v). The latter refers to 'singulis ecclesiis in Eboracensi diocese ad nostram visitationem spectantibus'. This form of reference to the diocese of York suggests an outside authority which, from the preamble, we should suppose to be the prior of Durham.

This supposition is confirmed by a comparison of the borrowings from Poore with their original. One cannot, to be sure, explain all the omissions from the present version on any one principle, but it is significant that these omissions include all the regulations made by Poore for the guidance of his archdeacons.[1] Furthermore, where Poore invoked the archdeacon's action, H provides for other procedure. For example:

<table>
<tr><td>

Poore ch. 9

*Concubine sacerdotum frequenter moneantur a*b archidiaconis.

</td><td>

H fo. 4r

Concubine sacerdotum frequenter moneantur a rectoribus ecclesiarum nostre parochie qui sunt decani nostri.

</td></tr>
<tr><td>

Poore ch. 98

. . . precipimus archidiaconis et decanis *quod, monicione premissa competenti,tales ad claustrum per ecclesiasticam censuram redire compellant. Quod si nec sic . . . induci possint,* iubemus eos *comprehendi.*

</td><td>

H fo. 8r

. . . monemus sacerdotes nostros ut cum aliquis talis inventus fuerit in diocesi nostra *quod, monicione premissa competenti, tales ad claustrum per ecclesiasticam censuram redire compellant. Quod si nec sic . . . induci possint,* denuntietur archiepiscopo ut per eum *comprehenda*tur.

</td></tr>
<tr><td>

Poore ch. 2

Quoniam . . . dispensare possumus, precipimus *quod omnes tales . . .* nostrum *super hoc requirant consilium.*

</td><td>

H fo. 3v

Quoniam . . . dispensare potest archiepiscopus, monemus in domino *quod omnes tales . . .* archiepiscopi *super hoc requirant consilium.*

</td></tr>
</table>

[1] e.g. chs. 3, 4, 8, 38, 83 part 1, 103 of the Salisbury series.

These examples suggest a legislator possessed only of archidiaconal rights, deferring in important matters to the diocesan, who is an archbishop. This deference is seen throughout the statutes, where Poore's 'prohibemus' becomes 'non consulimus' (ch. 58), and his 'precipimus' becomes 'volumus' (e.g. ch. 54). So also, the address 'Filii karissimi' of chapter 12 becomes in H 'Karissimi'. Considered in conjunction with the evidence of the preamble and the provenance of the manuscript, these facts point definitely to the conclusion which has been stated above. The legislator, possessed of archidiaconal rights, addressing priests in the diocese of York, may be either the bishop of Durham or the prior of Durham; for the bishop, like the prior, only possessed archidiaconal rights within his peculiar jurisdiction in the diocese of York. By the time that these statutes were issued, in the middle of the thirteenth century, the spheres of episcopal and conventual authority had been distinguished. Of the two authorities the convent's is most probably behind the statutes. They are preserved in a conventual book and they employ terms natural to a prior of Durham, who speaks of himself as exercising archidiaconal right.[1] Furthermore, whereas the bishop appointed a dean in his peculiar, the prior apparently did not; the latter arrangement agrees best with the phrase in the statutes: 'a rectoribus ecclesiarum nostre parochie qui sunt decani nostri'.

Statutes of Robert of Bingham, bishop of Salisbury (1238 × 1244).
Besides those who were content to reproduce wholly the statutes of Poore, several English prelates made extensive use of them during the next generation. Of these, it is reasonable to mention first Poore's immediate successor at Salisbury, Robert of Bingham. Bingham's statutes appear to have survived only in a single fourteenth-century copy, entitled 'constituciones domini Roberti episcopi Sar'' (Brit. Mus., Harl. MS. 52 fo. 119v). That they belong

---

[1] Cf. 'Robertus de Insula, sacrista Dunelmensis, gerens vicem domini Hugonis, prioris Dunelmensis, fungentis vice ordinaria iure archidiaconali infra libertates S. Cuthberti in Hovedenaschyre et Alvertonaschyre.' (*Durham annals and docts. of the thirteenth century*, no. 134, to be published by the Surtees Society, quoted by kind permission of the editor, Mr. Frank Barlow). Similarly, 'Quia execucioni officii archidiaconalis, quo fungimur in hac parte, personaliter interesse non possumus' (*ibid.*, no. 72).

to Bingham, and not to a successor with the same first name, is shown by the reference to them in the statutes of Bishop Giles of Bridport[1] and by a reference to their ch. 45 in a letter of Robert of Bingham himself dated 11 May 1244.[2] Since they draw freely upon the legatine canons of London (November 1237), they may be dated 1238 × 1244. It was natural that Bingham should borrow from his predecessor. Before his election as bishop he had been for many years a member of the cathedral chapter of Salisbury, and his reputation for theological learning and preaching as well as his activity as diocesan suggest that he shared Poore's interests in a large measure.[3] He may have been content, in his early days as bishop, to reissue the famous statutes of Bishop Poore; even when, probably acting under the stimulus of the legatine council of 1237, he compiled a fresh series, it was issued definitely as a supplement to Poore's statutes. 'Statuta sinodalia sancte recordacionis R. predecessoris nostri innovantes, quedam, adiuti gracia divina et presentis sinodi auxilio et concilio suffulti, duximus adicienda . . .' (fo. 119v). If we analyse Bingham's statutes, we find that they are for the most part an elaboration of certain sections of Poore, together with additions suggested by the legatine canons of 1237. Parts of some twenty-seven chapters of Poore are borrowed verbatim or paraphrased, and at one point three consecutive chapters are referred to explicitly: '*In confessione habeat sacerdos* et cetera usque *in dubiis*—hic legatur constitucio Ricardi episcopi Sar''[4] (fo. 120v). It is worth noting that Bingham appears to have known the decrees of the Fourth Lateran Council, independently of the use made of them

[1] Cf. *Eng. Hist. Rev.*, l. 399.

[2] *Salisbury charters*, p. 283, dated by Macray 15 May 1243. A thirteenth-century note in the Liber Evidenciarum C p. 367 suggests that the *incipit* of Bingham's statutes should read : ' Zelo sanctitatis ut habetur in tribulacionibus'; only the first two words agree with our text. A copy of ' Constituciones Roberti de Byngham Episcopi Sarisburiensis' was contained in a volume of legatine and provincial canons in the library of Titchfield Abbey (shelf-mark : G xix ; *Hants Field Club and Arch. Soc. Papers*, VII. iii (1916), 37).

[3] Cf. Gibbs and Lang, pp. 193, 197 and Russell, *Dictionary*, pp. 131-2.

[4] A reference of this sort may, of course, be the work of a scribe copyist and not belong to the original issue of the statutes. But one may note that these statutes use a similar form of reference to the Fourth Lateran decrees. '*Omnis utriusque sexus* et cetera—hic legatur concilium lateran'' (fo. 120v).

by Poore and Langton. He also seems to have been acquainted with the earliest known statutes for the diocese of Winchester (?1222 × 1228), and at one point uses the same words as are found in ch. 7 of the second statutes of William de Blois, bishop of Worcester (1229).[1]

Statutes of Peter des Roches, bishop of Winchester (1222 × 1228).
These statutes are a tribute to the zeal of Peter des Roches as a diocesan bishop. His ability as administrator of the episcopal estates and his support of the regular canons and mendicant friars have been noticed before now; but the evidence of his interest in the parochial clergy of his diocese is hard to come by.[2] Never much used by modern scholars,[3] and as yet unprinted, the statutes survive in a single early thirteenth-century copy in the Bodleian manuscript, Hatton 92 (*Summary catalogue*, no. 4073) fo. 154r. There is no title: the *incipit* reads 'Licet omnes canonicas sanctiones . . .'. Internal evidence proves the Winchester origin of the statutes and helps to fix the date; for they quote and refer to the council of Oxford 1222; and the reference 'celebrati a domino Cantuarie et eius suffraganeis' (fo. 154r) suggests a date within Langton's lifetime (i.e. before July 1228). The Winchester annals probably give us the actual year of publication: 1224.[4] Under that year the annals read: 'P. episcopus Wyntoniæ in plena synodo excommunicavit molestatores et insurgentes contra iura ecclesiæ.' This agrees with ch. 69 of the statutes (fo. 161v):

Item excommunicationis sentencia innodamus omnes illos qui Wintoniensem ecclesiam vel alias ecclesias nostre diocesis spoliant iure suo vel libertatibus suis vel eis sine iudicio auferunt possessiones quas actenus possederunt.

The statutes are written in a handsome book-hand, but the

---

[1] There are also parallels with the statutes of Worcester III (1240). Cf. below, p. 92.

[2] In the early days of his pontificate he had received a series of mandates from Pope Innocent III, dealing with various types of clerical delinquents and urging the bishop to reform them. These mandates were probably sought by the bishop, to arm him against opposition (*Innoc. III Regest.*, lib. viii nos. 142, 144–8 [Migne, *Patrol. latina*, ccxv. 722–4, Potthast, *Regesta pontificum*, 2594, 2596–600]). There is no clear echo of these mandates in the statutes, composed some twenty years later.

[3] Miss Lang was acquainted with them. Cf. Gibbs and Lang, pp. 112–13.

[4] *Annales monastici*, ii. 84.

text is disfigured by many mistakes. Since the rest of the volume was originally quite distinct and this part bears no mark, the provenance remains unknown.

Of all the synodal statutes[1] which use the statutes of Poore these are at once the earliest and the least dependent. They differ from most others of their age by seldom borrowing the words of earlier legislators. They show acquaintance with the Fourth Lateran Council, the provincial councils of London 1200 and of Oxford 1222, and the statutes of Richard Poore, but the material which these sources provide is re-shaped and usually re-worded. The debt to Poore appears to be but small. Verbal parallels are confined to three chapters. Poore's statutes may have been at the back of others in the Winchester series, but so much in both belongs to the common stock of synodal material of the day that short of verbal identity we cannot presume borrowing. If the bishop of Winchester consciously followed Poore and the other, more eminent, authorities very far, he covered his tracks. He quotes from seven chapters of the Council of Oxford, but rewrites everything else. Very little is left of the pious phrases and preambles of the originals; the language is generally terse and direct. Consequently, a great deal is compressed into a small compass and room is found to add a good many interesting details to earlier injunctions on the same subjects. In their brevity, comprehensiveness, and lack of obvious order these statutes of Peter des Roches resemble the statutes of Robert Grosseteste more than any others; and like them a large part of the series may be the genuine production of the bishop whose name they bear.

Statutes for the diocese of Exeter (?1222 × 1237).

These statutes are only known from a fragmentary copy, as yet unprinted: Bodleian, Ashmole MS. 1280 fo. 103r (formerly fo. 101r). It occurs in the middle of a small volume containing for the most part devotional treatises and sermons; it is written neatly in a very small book-hand of the mid-thirteenth century; the writer, however, often failed to

---

[1] They are described as such in the final chapters: ' hec synodalia statuta ' (fo. 161v).

understand what he was copying and left spaces for hard words or wrote nonsense. The statutes begin (*incipit* 'In Malachia legitur . . .') without any original title, but a fifteenth-century hand adds 'De Constitucionibus vii sacramentorum ecclesie'. So far as it goes, the text agrees fairly exactly with this title. It begins with a section on the secular clergy, their pastoral duties, private life, and ordination. It then proceeds to chapters on baptism, confirmation, and confession, in the midst of which it breaks off abruptly at the end of a folio. The provenance of the volume is entirely unknown.

The statutes may be attributed to a bishop of Exeter by virtue of a passage in ch. 6 (fo. 104r):

[? Precipimus ut si] post instans festum purificacionis beate Marie sacerdos quispiam coram suo superiore convictus fuerit quod capam illicite detulerit manucatam, aut per octo dies suspendatur aut capa illicite delata, vel eius estimacio, fabrice ecclesie Exon' applicetur [. . . (*blank*)] accepcione remota. Hanc autem penam eis tantum infra primi anni specialem [. . . (*blank*)].

A *terminus a quo* is provided by the use of the canons of Oxford 1222, and the absence of any mention of the legate Otto's council suggests (though it does not prove) a date before November 1237. The author of the statutes was therefore probably Simon of Apulia (d. Sept.1223) or William Brewer (1224–44).

We say 'author'; but if the missing portion of the statutes was comparable to what remains, the labours of authorship were slight. The statutes, as they at present stand, show only a preamble and three short chapters which are not directly traceable to other sources.[1] The rest is nothing

---

[1] The most interesting additions are as follows:

Ch. 25 (fo. 106v): . . . In baptismo enim testante iure canonico regeneramur ad vitam, post baptismum vero confirmamur ad pugnam et roboramur contra agones huius seculi. Compellantur eciam parentes ad hoc maturandum, si in hoc precepto fuerint negligentes. Adulti vero qui confirmandi [MS. confirmati] sunt, qui personaliter adire possunt episcopum, si commoniti adire noluerint [MS. noluerunt], compellantur nisi episcopalis remocio dilacionis sue fiat excusacio.

Ch. 36 (fo. 107v): Cum bonorum auctori aliter inherere non possumus nisi cupiditatem que omnium malorum radix est a nobis abiciamus, presentis synodi auctoritate precipimus ne sacerdotes cure parochiali astricti annualia in se recipiant a quoquam, sive aliud missarum honus propter quod servicium ecclesiarum quibus deserviunt in aliquo diminuatur. Et ut liberius a talibus et a quacunque negociacione inhonesta abstineant, districte precipimus ut sacerdotes parochiales

other than a selection of Poore's statutes, to which additions are made at suitable points from the canons of Oxford 1222. The few retouchings seldom go beyond changing the form of words or adding a preamble or explanatory note. As an example of the more extensive retouching we may quote the following chapter:

<table>
<tr><td>

Salisbury ch. 12

Magna nobis, filii karissimi, iniuncta est necessitas pacis observande, cum deus ipse pacis sit auctor et amator, qui non solum celestia et terestria sed etiam terestria adinvicem venit pacificare. Et cum non nisi per pacem temporis et pacem pectoris ad pacem perveniatur eternitatis, monemus vos et *districte precipimus* quatinus *pacem quantum in* vobis *est* cum omnibus habentes, *parochianos* vestros *monea*tis *ut in unitate fidei* et *pacis vinculo unum corpus sint in Christo, inimicitias, si exorte fuerint in* parochia vestra *diligenter sedantes, amicitias copul*antes, *discordantes ad* concordiam *revocantes, quantum in* vobis *est non permittentes quod sol occidat super ira*cundiam*parochianorum* vestrorum.

</td><td>

Exeter ch. 10 (fo. 104v)

Ad hec cum discordancium fratrum oblaciones sive eorum qui pauperes opprimunt a sacerdotibus recipi non debeant neque in sacrario sive in gazophilicio [*sic*] reponi et bonum pacis iuxta officii debitum diligere debeamus, universis nobis subditis *districte precipimus* ut *quantum in* eis *est pacem* habeant erga omnes et singulos; *parochianos* suos*monea*nt propensius et inducant *ut* [*in om.*] *unitate fidei* atque *pacis vinculo unum corpus sint in Christo. Inimicicias si* in parochianis suis sive vicinis *exorte fuerint sedantes, diligenter amicitias copul*ent, *discordantes ad* pacem *revocantes, quantum in* eis *est non permittentes quod sol occidat super ira*m *parochianorum* suorum. Duriciam sive indignationem dominorum sive ballivorum suorum erga sibi subditos temperent, ut innocentes [non] pregraventur.

</td></tr>
</table>

The question, which text of Poore's statutes was used at Exeter, is hard to answer. The closest verbal connexion with existing texts is with F, i.e. the reissue for the diocese of Durham; but a few significant readings agree only with B,[1]

singuli ad minus tres marcas annuas recipiant pro suis stipendiis ab ecclesiarum quibus serviunt rectoribus quos ad hoc precise cum opus fuerit per archi*diaconos* locorum compelli volumus et mandamus.

And cf. the penalty clause in ch. 6, quoted above, p. 77.

[1] Salisbury B, ch. 1 : sevorum ; ch. 49 : *add* et contumaces decimarum detentores.

with E,[1] or with ABE.[2] This may be explained by supposing
that the recension F for Durham was preceded by a closely
similar version for Salisbury, issued after the A[3] recension
and after the Canterbury derivative (DGJ). Otherwise, we
must suppose that the bishop of Exeter was acquainted
with the Durham series in a text which retained certain
characteristics of the BE versions.

Statutes of Fulk Basset, bishop of London (1245 × 1259).

A set of synodal statutes for the diocese of London was
published by the Rev. Canon R. M. Woolley in 1915 from
a Lincoln Cathedral manuscript. At that time he judged
their date to be 'somewhere between 1215–22', but in his
catalogue of the cathedral manuscripts he ascribed the statutes
to Fulk Basset 'on the authority of a fragmentary copy of
these same constitutions belonging to the late Canon Cecil
Deedes of Chichester'.[3] More recently, a third manuscript
(Brit. Mus. Royal 7 A. ix) has been adduced to prove that
the statutes were issued by Roger Niger, bishop of London
from 1229 to 1241.[4] A choice has therefore to be made
between three possible authors. The question of sources
must also be investigated, for there is discrepancy between
Canon Woolley's views and those of Miss Lang, and neither
deals comprehensively with the question. While Canon
Woolley observed that 'in parts [this document] is very
close to and even identical with Poore's constitutions, and
both are evidently based in places on some common source',[5]
Miss Lang says definitely: 'the constitutions are based
almost entirely on those of Master Richard le Poore.'[6]

The first stage in elucidating the matter must be to compare the surviving texts.

A. Lincoln Cathedral Chapter MS. B. 6. 7 fo. 6r [catalogue no.
229].

Title: 'Constitutiones Londonienses'. *Inc.* 'Quia in sacramentorum dispensatione . . .'. The statutes, written in a late xiv c.

---

[1] Salisbury E, ch. 50: De advocatis etiam et quibuscunque.
[2] Salisbury ABE, ch. 22: Aqua vero ubi baptizatur.
[3] *Eng. Hist. Rev.*, xxx. 286 and *Cat. of the MSS. of Lincoln Cath. Chapter
Library* (Oxford, 1927) p. 164.
[4] Gibbs and Lang, p. 118.   [5] *Eng. Hist. Rev.*, xxx. 286.
[6] Gibbs and Lang, pp. 111–12, cf. p. 118.

hand, form the first continuous piece in a theological miscellany, written about 1400. They are very carelessly written, with many nonsensical mistakes. The name of Thomas Carter, as owner, appears twice; the date of acquisition by the dean and chapter of Lincoln is unknown. This text was printed by Canon Woolley (*see above*).

B. Brit. Mus., Royal MS. 7 A. ix fo. 83r.

Title: 'In nomine sancte trinitatis incipiunt prohibiciones et precepta observanda ab omnibus rectoribus ecclesiarum vicariis et sacerdotibus edita a venerabili patre R. London' episcopo.' *Inc.* 'Quia in sacramentorum dispensacione...'. The statutes are written in a hand *c.* 1300 in the midst of a miscellaneous volume by several hands, containing works of Robert Grosseteste, &c. A note on the remainder of a xiv c. index page (fo. 1r) describes this item as 'Prohibiciones et precepta observanda ab omnibus rectoribus ecclesiarum vicariis et sacerdotibus edita a ... Richardo London' episcopo.' The volume belonged to the Austin canons of St. Mary Overy, Southwark.

C. Cambridge, Trinity Coll. MS. O. 9. 28 fo. 29r [catalogue no. 1440].

No title. *Inc.* 'Quia in sacramentorum dispensacione...'. The statutes occur in the midst of a collection of theological and canonical miscellanea, written in several hands of the xiv and xv c. This section is written in a large narrow hand of the early xv c. It is possible that the whole volume belonged to the collegiate church of Warwick in the xv c.

D. Hove, MS. of the Rt. Rev. the Bishop of Lewes, fo. 5v.

Title: 'Synodus London' sub venerabili patre domino Fulcone episcopo consecracionis eiusdem anno [...(*blank*)].' *Inc.* 'Quia in sacramentorum dispensacione...'. The statutes are written in a very small hand in the midst of a miscellany, canonical and theological, probably compiled by a priest of the diocese of London in the middle of the xiii c. The statutes are immediately preceded by a small otherwise unknown series, written in the same hand and entitled: 'Prima statuta venerabilis patris domini F. London' episcopi' (fo. 5r). The little book has had many folios torn or cut out at several points: a gap between chs. 43 and 90 of the statutes is probably accounted for by the loss of two folios after fo. 7. The book belonged formerly to the Reverend Cecil Deedes, prebendary of Chichester (d. 1920).[1]

---

[1] I am much obliged to the Right Reverend the Bishop of Lewes who, in 1932, permitted me to borrow this manuscript to study over an extended period.

From the description of the texts it will be seen that only one manuscript, and that the earliest, gives a clear indication of authorship. D says that the statutes were issued by Fulk Basset. This has the slight support of an item in the catalogue of Dover Priory library (1389): no. 323 'Statuta fukonis londonensis, *inc.* Quia in sacramentorum.'[1] Such of the D text as remains agrees substantially with text A, but by the addition of a passage at the end, demanding that the statutes be generally copied,[2] comes into line with C. Throughout the statutes, C and D are very closely in agreement with each other. B, our only other text with an ascription of authorship, differs from the foregoing texts in omitting both the list of festivals (chs. 94–104) and the addition common to CD. Instead, it adds what appears to be a very brief summary of a few points in the earlier statutes together with some details drawn from the legatine canons of Ottobono; it is followed immediately by the excommunication clause of the Council of Reading 1279. This suffices to show that the bishop 'R.' of the title cannot be Roger Niger: the date of the manuscript and the index reference to Richard suggest that here we have to do with a new edition of Fulk Basset's statutes issued by Bishop Richard Gravesend, bishop of London 1280–1303. Are the textual differences between A and CD such as to suggest different recensions? They seem rather to be the result of independent errors and accidental omissions, together with a few retouchings which cannot be proved to have been official. Judging by the relationship of the texts, we might therefore regard Fulk Basset as the most probable author of the statutes.

An inquiry into the sources reinforces this opinion. The connexion of the London statutes with Poore's attracted the attention of Canon Woolley, who presumed that they had a common source. In fact, while the London statutes reproduce much of Poore's statutes verbatim, there are enough modifications to prove an interesting genealogy. Between Poore and the London series are interposed the Exeter statutes of which we possess only a fragment. The

---

[1] M. R. James, *Ancient Libraries of Canterbury and Dover*, p. 478. Cf. *ibid.*, no. 223 'Statuta curatoribus utilia', no. 392 'Statuta london. in sua', both with the same *incipit*. [2] See above, p. 45.

reliance of the latter upon Poore has already been shown. A comparison of the three series makes the descent indubitable: London's omissions from Poore and the sequence of copying agree with Exeter's; but Exeter contains two chapters of Poore (chs. 26, 34) which are not found in London, and London contains two chapters (chs. 16, 32) of Exeter which were not drawn from Poore. Many elaborations of detail in the course of transmission point the same way; one will suffice for an example.

Salisbury ch. 30	Exeter ch. 18	London ch. 5
ut sic cognoscat et puniat fornicatores, et sic sciat qui legittimi, qui non.	*ut sic cognoscat et puniat fornicatores. Ad alia etiam hec cautela est necessaria.*	*ut sic cognoscat* cum quibus possit matrimonium contrahere, et *ad alia etiam hec cautela est necessaria.*

Borrowings from the Exeter statutes account for some twenty chapters of the London series. What of the sources of the rest? At first sight, it would appear that London drew independently on Poore. In chapter 6, for example, we read that the font is to be kept *sub sera propter sortilegia,* an injunction made by Poore (ch. 22) but not repeated by the Exeter legislator in his borrowing (ch. 20) from this chapter. So also London chapter 12 repeats verbatim Poore's chapter 31 *bis,* which was omitted by Exeter. These likenesses between Poore and London cannot be explained, as may be the likeness of Poore chapters 77, 78, 81, 109 to London chapters 44, 50, 105, by the assumption that the lost portions of Exeter supplied the missing link. But that is still no reason for supposing that the London statutes were directly derived from Poore. Canon Woolley's theory of a common source now deserves attention. The debt of Poore to Odo de Sully, bishop of Paris, has already been noticed (above, p. 55). A close comparison of certain passages in Odo's, Poore's, and the London statutes shows that the London legislator had Odo's work, not Poore's, before him. Thus, the whole of chapters 34–7 of London are derived directly from Odo, whereas Poore made much freer use of the same original. A clear example of the relationship is seen in London, chapter 51:

Paris ch. 7

Prohibeat sacerdos *in ecclesia publice sub excommunicatione ne alter coniugum transeat ad religionem aut recipiatur, nisi per episcopum.*

Salisbury ch. 85

Item doceant sacerdotes frequenter populum et prohibeant sub anathemate *ne alter coniugum transeat ad religionem* nec *recipiatur, nisi per* nos aud per nostram licentiam.

London ch. 51

Prohibeant sacerdotes in ecclesia publice sub excommunicatione ne alter coniugum transeat ad religionem aut recipiatur, nisi per episcopum.

On the same supposition of direct borrowing from Odo we may explain the likenesses to Poore noted above in chapters 6 and 12 of London. The relationship of these statutes may therefore be graphically expressed thus:

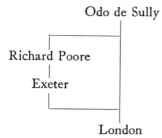

Odo de Sully

Richard Poore

Exeter

London

Consideration of the other sources will help us to fix the date of the London statutes. If London depends on Exeter, itself dependent on the Council of Oxford, Canon Woolley's view that the London statutes should be dated 1215×1222 is at once disposed of. And although the Council of Oxford is not mentioned, it should be noted that it is quoted at length in chapters 79–81, 88–90 of London. Another hitherto unnoticed source determines the date of the London series more exactly. For the sacramental teaching which occupies the first part of his statutes the London legislator seldom went beyond Odo de Sully or Exeter. Chapter 31, however, on the ministry of deacons, is taken directly from Robert Grosseteste's statutes or one of their derivatives. The borrowing from this source becomes more extensive in later chapters on the manners of the clergy (ch. 57), the care of churches (chs. 64–5), &c. (chs. 69–77). These show that the source is one of the Lincoln derivatives rather than the parent text. Hence we arrive at a date for the London statutes in or after 1241.[1] This agrees well with the occurrence in London chapter 85 of words which seem to come from the supplement to the First Council of Lyon, 1245.[2] Our conclusion on the origin and author of these London statutes may be summed up thus. Texts ACD represent statutes compiled by Bishop Fulk Basset between 1245 and 1259.[3] They were reissued with a short appendix, preserved in text B, by Richard Gravesend, 1280 × 1303. The first recension, by Basset, displays very little more originality than do the Exeter statutes from which the bishop of London borrowed. Basset only may be credited with some ingenuity in sewing together a patchwork of many pieces, from several sources. His dependence on earlier legislators can be graphically expressed thus:

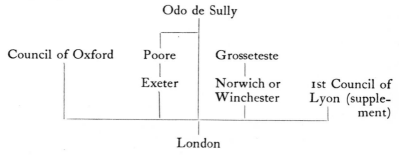

Odo de Sully

Council of Oxford   Poore   Grosseteste

Exeter   Norwich or   1st Council of
            Winchester   Lyon (supplement)

London

Statutes of St. Richard de Wich, bishop of Chichester (1244 × 1253).

The earliest known synodal statutes for the diocese of Chichester are those of Richard de Wich, bishop from 1244 to 1253. One of the three English bishops of the thirteenth century who attained to canonization after death, St. Richard had in his lifetime many connexions with those

---

[1] The earliest date assigned to the earliest (Norwich) derivative of Lincoln is 1240. As Lincoln cannot have been composed before July of this year it is unlikely that the Norwich derivative would be written and copied in London before 1241.

[2] Hefele-Leclercq, v. ii. 1673, *Sext*, v. 11. 1. The passage is also found in Basset's 'Prima statuta', which must therefore also be dated after 1245.

[3] The only dated records of a synod held by Bishop Fulk seem to be two charters dated 13 April 1250 on the morrow of the synod celebrated in the church of St. Paul. Brit. Mus., Harl. MS. 3697 fos. 46, 49.

prelates who were anxious for Church reform in England.[1]
As a scholar and chancellor of the university of Oxford,
he must have known well his older contemporary, Robert
Grosseteste; later he was chancellor to the archbishop of
Canterbury, St. Edmund Rich, the archbishop's companion
in exile, and executor of his will; finally, he was the nominee
of Boniface of Savoy to the see of Chichester in 1244. His
statutes are known in one text only: Oxford, University
Coll. MS. 148, p. 183 (formerly fo. 90r). The title is
'Statuta synodalia domini Ricardi secundi Cycestr' episcopi';
incipit: 'Cum ex iniuncto . . .'. They occur in the middle
of a miscellaneous volume which contains statutes of the
cathedral church of Chichester (to which St. Richard had
made an important contribution) and other matter interesting that church. The various parts of the volume, written
by several hands, were bound together at least as early as
the fifteenth century, and then belonged to the deanery.[2]
The statutes are well written in a late thirteenth-century
hand. There are very few peculiarities of spelling or obvious
errors. Wilkins printed the statutes from this manuscript,
but was unfortunate in his transcriber: his edition has
several gross blunders.[3]

The statutes form a comprehensive, if comparatively
short, series. About one-third is devoted to chapters upon
the sacraments, mainly intended for parish priests, whose
conduct is further regulated in other chapters; the remainder
includes precepts concerning diocesan officials, the regular
clergy, and the Jews. As might be expected from his academic
and official connexions, the bishop shows his acquaintance
with numerous sources from which to compose his statutes.[4]

[1] Cf. Russell, *Dictionary*, pp. 125–7 and Gibbs and Lang, pp. 44–5.

[2] Cf. fos. 40r, 56v, 96r. The connexion of the book with Thomas of Lichfield,
dean of Chichester *c.* 1230–41, assumed in *Archaeologia*, xlv (1877), 160 and
Russell, *Dictionary*, p. 165, cannot be sustained in view of the date of the writing
and of much of the contents.

[3] *Concilia*, i. 688 *seqq.* e.g. ista *for* tria, excipe quando *for* ex qua, generalita-
tem *for* venalitatem, iuncti *for* uicti, omnes *for* quoniam, sibi *for* scribi.

[4] 'The constitutions of Master Richard Wych, Bishop of Chichester, show very
distinctly the influence of Poore, who had been Bishop of Chichester 1215–17, of
the Council of Oxford 1222, and of the Legatine Council of London 1237, and
they embody many decrees of the Lateran Council by name, but there is no
reason to suppose that Richard was using the decrees as an original authority.'
(Gibbs and Lang, p. 111.) It may, perhaps, be properly remarked that there

The contribution of Richard Poore, himself a predecessor in the see of Chichester, is largest in the chapters on the sacraments. Here some sections of Chichester repeat Poore's statutes verbatim; and the borrowing may be observed beyond this, in various passages abridged from Poore. The changes are mostly changes of form and do not affect the general sense of the statutes. In all, Wich drew upon some thirty of Poore's statutes. Did he take them direct from the Salisbury series, or do they come from a derivative? From such evidence as is available we infer that the descent was direct. If we compare the passages most closely alike in the Chichester and Salisbury statutes, we find that Chichester never follows at any significant point the peculiar readings of the Durham versions FH or of the Canterbury version DGJ. Further evidence against dependence on DGJ is the borrowing by Chichester of Poore's statutes, chapter 2 part i and chapters 54, 55: these passages are found in none of the Canterbury texts which we possess. For similar reasons it is clear that Chichester cannot have derived the material from the diocesan statutes of Exeter or London.[1] While the material is too scanty to permit exact identification, we may say that the original of the Chichester text was one of the later Salisbury recensions, embodying some of the peculiarities of E.

The Chichester statutes also draw certain details from a contemporary of Poore. The earliest Winchester statutes have been shown to owe something to the Salisbury series. Bishop Richard Wich seems to have known and used them. Borrowing is evident in two passages:

Winchester ch. 3 (fo. 154r)	Chichester ch. 5
Nullus presbiter presumat celebrare *in vestimentis sordidis vel vetustate attritis,* et *in calice nisi*	*Nullus* sacerdos *in vestimentis sordidis vel* [? *vetustate*] *attritis,* nec *nisi in calice argenteo vel au-*

seems no strong reason for supposing that Wich and other contemporary bishops did not know the Fourth Lateran decrees, as is suggested here and elsewhere by Miss Lang.

[1] Chichester uses Poore chs. 1–2, 10, 26, 28, 36, 45–6, 49, 74, 79, 80, 85, none of which appears in the London series. Exeter contains only a few of these; and others would have occurred, if at all, in the remaining fragment. It has been pointed out that the Exeter statutes resemble the F text of Poore in many readings: this is another reason for discounting their influence on Chichester.

argenteo vel aureo, et illo *integro,* non quassato, cum *duobus palliis benedictis ad minus super altare positis.*

reo, et integro, et in corporalibus mundissimis et *ad minus* in *duabus pallis benedictis super altare positis,* celebret.

The second case indicates the direct influence of Poore in a passage of the Chichester statutes mainly derived from Winchester:

Salisbury ch. 40	Winchester ch. 45 (fo. 158v)	Chichester ch. 7
Rei talium prius mittendi sunt *ad* episcopum vel eius *penitenciarium.* Semper qui mittuntur deferant secum literas continentes genus peccati et circumstantias sufficienter, vel ipse sacerdos cum eis veniat personaliter, alioquin non recipiantur.	*Sacerdotes publice penitentes cum literis suis* rei *veritatem continentibus ad penitenciarium* nostrum *transmittant* [MS. transmittans], et ipsos *revertentes nisi* eis *constiterit de penitencia eis iniuncta tanquam absolutos* non *recipiant.*	*Sacerdotes publice penitentes cum litteris suis veritatem continentibus ad penitentiarium* episcopi *transmittant,* vel in propriis personis cum illis veniant, nec *revertentes* penitentes *tanquam absolutos recipiant, nisi de penitentia eis iniuncta constiterit* per litteras episcopi vel penitentiarii sui patentes.

Not only did Richard de Wich borrow from Richard Poore, both directly and indirectly. It seems that he was also acquainted with Poore's only English source: the provincial canons of Archbishop Hubert (London 1200). Otherwise we can hardly explain the following parallels:

London ch. 12	Salisbury ch. 38	Chichester ch. 11
Si vero incorrecti in negatione perstiterint, indicatur eis purgatio, et non *occasione pecunie captande differatur de die in diem.*	*Si vero* incorrigibiles *in negatione perstiterint, indicatur eis purgatio, que occasione pecunie* oblate vel promisse *de die in diem nullatenus differatur.*	*Si vero incorrecti in negatione perstiterint, indicatur eis purgatio, que occasione captande pecunie de die in diem nullatenus differatur.*

ch. 9	ch. 46	ch. 14
Detentores vero *decimarum* iuxta Rothomagensis concilii constitutum, *si semel,*	*Detentores autem decimarum consuetarum si semel, secundo et tertio commoniti ex-*	*Detentores autem decimarum* debitarum et *consuetarum, si semel, secundo et tertio*

secundo et tertio com- | *cessum suum non emen-* | commoniti sufficienter
moniti, excessum suum | *daverint, usque ad sa-* | *excessum   suum   non*
non emendaverint, us- | *tisfactionem condignam* | *emendaverint,   usque*
que ad satisfactionem | per censuram ecclesi- | *ad satisfactionem con-*
congruam anathematis | asticam compellantur. | *gruam   anathematis*
vinculo feriantur. | | *vinculo feriantur.*

The canons of Oxford 1222 were the only other recent provincial legislation which the bishop of Chichester could use. The regulations of Stephen Langton ('venerabilis patris nostri S. Cantuariensis archiepiscopi') are invoked apropos of archdeacons' fees, and the Fourth Lateran Council and the Council of Oxford seem to be referred to together in the chapters on the conduct of the clergy and on the Jews: 'in generali et speciali concilio'. Finally, the excommunication clause of Oxford is quoted in full.[1] The sparing use made of these important canons can be explained by the fact that while Poore's statutes provided an admirable collection of precepts about the sacraments, &c., for the other administrative subjects to be treated there was more recent legislation of importance and authority surpassing even that of the canons of Oxford. This was the series of canons issued by the Legate Otto at London in 1237.

After Richard Poore, Wich's chief source was Otto. The 'constitutiones domini legati' are frequently cited and provide the bulk of the material relating to the farming of ecclesiastical dignities, the duties of archdeacons, the provision of vicars and chaplains, the conduct of church courts, and the celibacy of the clergy. Generally the relevant canons of Otto's Council of London are quoted in full, but in chapter 14 there is a simple reference: 'Hic recurratur ad concilium generale *De residentia facienda* et *De clericis habentibus plura beneficia* contra concilium' (=London, ch. 13). Besides the canons of London, Wich quotes Otto's constitutions for the Black Monks issued in 1238.[2]

One other possible source remains to be mentioned: the diocesan statutes of Walter de Cantilupe, bishop of Wor-

---

[1] With the original injunction that it be recited four times a year in the churches. Two sections of the Oxford excommunications are not found in our sole text of Chichester: their absence may be due to haplography.

[2] Chichester ch. 18. Otto's constitutions are to be found in Matt. Paris, *Chron. Maj.* (Rolls series), iii. 499.

cester, said to have been issued in 1240. Only one short
passage bears close resemblance to the statutes of Chichester,
but unless a common origin is assumed, it must be regarded
as evidence of borrowing by the latter.[1]

With the synodal statutes of Chichester we have reached
the point where, by about the middle of the thirteenth century,
the statutes of Salisbury lose the pre-eminent importance
which they at first possessed. They no longer provide the
only corpus of sacramental teaching available; their administrative arrangements are antiquated and insufficient, if
judged by post-Ottonian standards. Large traces are found,
to be sure, in some later statutes, notably in the Wells–York
group. But here we cannot be sure of direct descent, for the
derivatives of Poore's statutes were widely diffused. The
descent from Salisbury is made the more doubtful by the
existence of the different versions of *Statuta legenda*, any of
which might have provided identical original material for
the later series.[2] It is significant that while we possess only
four texts of the Salisbury statutes, there are at least thirty-two
texts of the *legenda*. Were Poore's statutes as widely known
as is sometimes maintained, we should expect more manuscripts to have survived. One must therefore dissent definitely from the view quoted at the beginning of this chapter,
that after about 1240 'the rest of the constitutions made by
bishops in the reign of Henry III are all based upon the
Salisbury constitutions'. From this time onwards, the
influence of the statutes of Walter de Cantilupe and Robert
Grosseteste and their derivatives is far more conspicuous.

---

[1] Worcester ch. 27 ('Ne igitur clerici . . .') and Chichester ch. 16 ('Clerici vero comam . . .').

[2] Cf. above, p. 40, and *Eng. Hist. Rev.*, l. 395 *seqq.*

IV

STATUTES OF WALTER DE CANTILUPE, BISHOP OF WORCESTER, AND RELATED TEXTS

IF Bishop Poore provided many of his fellow-bishops with material for their diocesan statutes, Bishop Walter de Cantilupe did a similar service to the next generation. His predecessors in the see of Worcester had attempted nothing so ambitious as the series of statutes which Cantilupe promulgated in a synod of the diocese held in his cathedral church on 26 July 1240. Its preamble proclaims its scope to be similar to that of Poore's statutes: 'Circa mores ministrorum et suorum execucionem officiorum, circa sacramenta prefata et alia que[1] cleri decere credimus honestatem que subscripta sunt duximus statuenda.'[2] Although he covers much of the same ground as Poore (whose statutes he knew), Cantilupe adopts a different arrangement. The first four chapters relate to the dedication and maintenance of churches, and the position of this section is clearly copied from the statutes of Cantilupe's predecessor, Bishop William de Blois. Cantilupe passes next to the subject of baptism, which begins a long series of chapters relating to the administration of the sacraments. Within this framework the legislator finds room to speak of Church services in general under the heading of the Eucharist, and even to append an injunction against sorcery to the chapters on marriage; finally, under the heading *De ordine*, he contrives to press into a formal shape all that he has to say about the life and conduct of the clergy, ingeniously arranging it under the titles of the seven deadly sins. To this is appended a section which might serve as a practical guide to archdeacons in their visitations and form the basis of visitation articles. It opens with the words:

Quia vero multa sunt que clericali honestati conveniunt que longum esset diffuse tractare, que subscripta sunt prohibenda duximus et per archidiaconos diligenter inquiri qualiter se in his habeant subditi sui pro quorum salute statuenda duximus et prohibenda subsequencia cum premissis.[3]

---

[1] que; B qui; ACD quo.
[2] Wilkins, i. 666a.
[3] B text, fo. 216va; Wilkins, i. 673a.

The original edition of the statutes concluded with chapters on miscellaneous topics which found no place in the preceding scheme: the chief sections relate to tithe and to wills.[1] One omission is significant in the light of Walter de Cantilupe's celebrated defence of pluralism at the Council of London 1237;[2] unlike his colleagues of Lincoln, London, Norwich, Salisbury, and Winchester, the bishop of Worcester makes no statute against pluralists. But the whole series, together with the *tractatus penitentialis* which Cantilupe made for the instruction of his clergy,[3] provided an imposing body of law and precept for the diocese of Worcester, and Cantilupe showed the same desire as Poore did that his statutes should be well known and copied by parish priests throughout the diocese.[4]

SOURCES OF CANTILUPE'S STATUTES

Unlike Poore, Cantilupe built on the diocesan statutes of a predecessor. In 1219 Bishop William de Blois of Worcester issued a short series of statutes, of which the chief deal with liturgy and administrative matters.[5] Ten years later, in a synod held on 8 May 1229, he reissued nearly all the first series (omitting only the sections on the commemoration of dead parish priests and others, and on the payment of murage by the clergy), this time incorporated in a larger series. These second statutes of William de Blois, without being conceived on so grand a scale as Poore's, contain a great deal about the parochial ministry, in part taken from the Fourth Lateran Council and the Council of Oxford, and nearly half of them were used again by Cantilupe.[6]

---

[1] The appendix (Wilkins, i. 676), which apparently belongs to a later issue, is mainly concerned with rules for stipendiary priests.

[2] Matt. Paris, *Chron. maj.*, iii. 418–19 (Wilkins, i. 649*a*).

[3] Cf. above, pp. 42–3.

[4] Cf. above, p. 46. The statutes contain no legislation for monks, of whom Cantilupe was a vigorous visitor. Cf. Cheney, *Episcopal visitation*, pp. 34, 89, and above, p. 39.

[5] There is no proof that they were issued in a synod, but we have evidence that a synod was held in this year. Above, p. 17.

[6] William de Blois's statutes were first printed by Wilkins (*Concilia*, i. 570, 623) from transcripts by Henry Wharton : these are contained in his catalogue of the library of Lambeth Palace (now Lambeth MS. 580, fos. 322, 315). Wharton states

As was natural in the year 1240, the canonical authority on which Cantilupe most relied was that of the councils of the Lateran, of Oxford 1222, and of London 1237.[1] All three are often quoted, with or without acknowledgement. In addition, the bishop had a quite recent papal mandate, directed to him on 20 May 1240, to support his statute compelling vicars to reside.[2]

By this time, four other English dioceses—Exeter, Lichfield, Salisbury, and Winchester—all had their episcopal statutes, which Cantilupe might know and use. But he did not borrow much. Poore's statutes for Salisbury are the only ones which leave their mark.[3] If it were proved that Poore's successor, Robert of Bingham, composed his statutes before 1240, we might detect two loans from them in chapters 1 and 6 of Worcester III; but it is equally likely that Bingham, who borrowed from Worcester II, wrote after 1240 and knew Worcester III besides.[4]

THE MANUSCRIPTS OF CANTILUPE'S STATUTES

A. Bodleian, Rawlinson MS. C. 428 fo. 160v.
    Title: 'Constituciones domini W. de Cantilupo Wyg' episcopi super statu ecclesie.' *Inc.*: 'Secundum exhortationem psalmiste . . .'. The statutes are followed by an appendix with the title: 'Subscripte correcciones sunt de constitucionibus pie recordacionis domini W. de Cantilupo' (fo. 168r, printed in Wilkins, i. 676). Written in a hand of the second quarter xiv c., in a collection of ecclesiastical canons procured for the cathedral priory of Worcester by Brother Henry Fouke (professed in 1302). Despite its present shelfmark, the volume was possibly at one time among Tanner's books.

that his transcripts are taken from Lambeth MS. 185, now Lambeth MS. 171 (cf. below, p. 93). The first and second series appear in Lambeth MS. 171 fos. 40r, 37r, and in Bodleian Rawlinson MS. C. 428 fos. 159r, 155r. Among Wilkins's collections in the Bodleian Add. MS. C. 64 fo. 43 are seventeenth-century transcripts of both series, probably from Lambeth MS. 171. The chapters on tithe in Worcester II occur in Oxford, Corpus Christi Coll. MS. 72 fo. 59v, in a fifteenth-century legal collection which possibly comes from St. Augustine's Abbey, Bristol.
    [1] The councils are quoted in the following chapters of Worcester III : IV Lateran, chs. 9, 12, 15, 27, 31 ; Oxford, chs. 25, 32, 45, 49, 55 ; London, chs. 5, 27, 31, 38, 43, 57.
    [2] 'ad residendum compellantur auctoritate domini pape et nostra', ch. 52 (Wilkins, i. 673b). Cf. *Cal. papal letters*, i. 190.
    [3] Probably in chs. 5, 6, 18 ; cf. Poore, chs. 22, 31, 29.
    [4] Cf. above, p. 75.

Either it is the text of the statutes used by Wilkins as 'MS. penes episc. Assaven.' [i.e. Thomas Tanner], or Wilkins used C. A is very closely related to D.

B. Brit. Mus., Cotton MS. Claud. A. viii fo. 212v (formerly 209v). Title: 'Constituciones subscripte sunt venerabilis patris nostri W. de Cantilupo dei gratia Wygorniencis episcopi in sancta synodo˙ sua in cathedrali ecclesia promulgate ad honorem dei et sancte ecclesie in crastino sancti Iacobi apostoli anno domini m⁰ cc⁰ xl⁰, anno pontificatus sui tertio.' A second hand adds approximately the same title. *Inc.*: 'Secundum exhortacionem psalmiste . . .'. Ending: 'Expliciunt constituciones domini episcopi Wygornie' (fo. 218r); followed by an Easter Table, then (without title) by rules for the lectionary throughout the year and a list of double feasts, and then 'Hec sunt festa ferianda ex toto in episcopatu Wygornie . . .', with some miscellaneous notes at the end. Written very carelessly in a xiv c. hand (? early), following verses addressed to Fulk Basset, bishop of London; now bound with various manuscripts originally distinct. This was the original of Spelman's edition (*Concilia*, ii. 240) and is cited by Wilkins as his main authority (*Concilia*, i. 665). The editors of the *Concilia* print the appendixes which follow the Easter Table. There appears to be no way of confirming C. H. Turner's suggestion that fos. 201–19 of this MS. belonged to Worcester Cathedral Priory (*Early Worc. mss.*, p. lxx).

C. Bodleian, Add. MS. C. 64 (S.C. 28419) fo. 24r. Title: 'Constituciones domini Willielmi [*sic*] de Cantilupo Wigornensis episcopi super statu ecclesie.' *Inc.*: 'Secundum hortationem psalmiste . . .'. Followed by the appendix found in A and D. Written in a xvii c. hand in a volume of transcripts used by Wilkins for the *Concilia*. It is a copy of D.

D. Lambeth Palace, MS. 171 (formerly MS. 185) fo. 41r. Title: 'Constituciones domini W. de Cantilupo Wygor' episcopi super statu ecclesie.' *Inc.*: 'Secundum hortationem psalmiste . . .'. Followed by the appendix found in A. Written in a collection of ecclesiastical canons which is very closely related to Rawlinson MS. C. 428 (A), written at about the same date.

It is obvious that the manuscripts are sharply divided, AD on the one hand, B belonging to a different family on the other hand. The variations of the two present several interesting problems. First may be noted the evidence for the date. The B text alone tells us that the statutes were promulgated in a synod on the morrow of St. James the

Greater, i.e. on 26 July 1240, in the third pontifical year of Walter de Cantilupe. But the bishop was elected 30 August 1236, confirmed 20 September 1236, consecrated 3 May 1237, and enthroned 13 October 1237;[1] so that the pontifical year, if correct, is counted from the enthronization, a most unusual method of reckoning. The other elements in the date, however, gain support from the Worcester annalist, who says: 'Episcopus celebravit synodum die sanctæ Annæ', i.e. 26 July, in the year 1240.[2] We are justified in supposing that Bishop Walter promulgated statutes in his synod on this day.

But we cannot go farther and suppose that either B or AD represents the 1240 edition of the statutes. Wilkins conflated two manuscripts. To B, which was the text used by Spelman, Wilkins added the 'correcciones' which form an appendix with a separate title in AD. This title refers, not to corrections of the preceding statutes, but to the correction of the offences of stipendiary priests and others, which is the first subject to be treated in the appendix. While we may assume that the section did not form part of the original series, we can only date it provisionally between July 1240 and February 1266, the time of the bishop's death. The B text, despite its elaborately dated title, itself shows signs of revision; and in its present form cannot be the statutes which Cantilupe issued in his synod of July 1240. This becomes evident if we turn to chapter 65, where there is a clumsy conflation of two forms in B:

Worcester III, ch. 65

A (fo. 167va)	B (fo. 217va)
Precipimus eciam *quod viri religiosi necnon et alii qui contra ius commune decimas possident separatas infra terminum a nobis iam quibusdam statutum*[3] *vel ab officiali nostro statuendum titulum possessionis ostendant.*	*Precipimus quod viri religiosi necnon et alii qui contra ius commune decimas possident separatas* infra festum sancti Michaelis titulum nobis sue possescionis [*sic*] ostendant, *infra terminum a nobis iam quibusdam statutum*[3] *vel ab officiali nostro statuendum titulum* sue *possescionis ostendant.*

---

[1] 'Annales de Wigornia', *Annales monastici*, iv. 428.   [2] *Ibid.*, iv. 432.
[3] MS. *statut'*.

The easiest explanation of this confusion is that the statute originally set the fixed time-limit of Michaelmas, for which the formula contained in A was later substituted.[1] The B text or its archetype introduced the new rule without suppressing the old.

A little farther on, at chapter 72, we encounter another interpolation in the original statutes. The two versions read:

Worcester III, ch. 72

A (fo. 168r*ab*)

Quod autem predecessor noster statuit de festis celebrandis et *observandis ne fiant in eis opera servilia, precipimus ab omnibus uniformiter observari nisi forte aliquid specialiter fiat pro veneracione sanctorum in quorum honore* vel *ecclesie* vel *altaria consecrantur.*

Dictis autem sollempnitatibus festum beati *Nicholai duximus adiungend*um. *Festa autem* Edmundi confessoris *sanctorum Dominici et Francisci in ecclesiis cum novem leccionibus volumus celebrari. Nolumus tamen per hoc opera laicorum fidelium impediri.*

B (fo. 218r*a*)

Quod autem predesessor [sic] *noster statuit de festis celebrandis* [A², in margin: *observandis*] *ne fiant in eiis* [sic] *opera servilia, precipimus ab omnibus uniformiter observari nisi forte* [MS. fortiter] *specialiter aliquid fiat pro veneracione sanctorum in quorum honore ecclesie vel altaria consecrantur.*

Dictis autem solepnitatibus [sic] *beatorum Nicholay* et *Edmundi archiepiscopi duximus adiungenda. Festa autem sanctorum Dominici et Francissi in ecclesiis cum novem leccionibus volumus* super hoc *celebrari. Nolumus tamen per hoc opera layicorum* [sic] *fidelium inpediri.*

The name of St. Edmund cannot have been introduced into this chapter before the year 1247. In the A text Edmund is given a feast of nine lessons: in the B text he has the greater distinction of appearing among 'festa ferianda'. Since we have to judge between the two versions in point of date, it is easier to suppose that the cult of St. Edmund increased than that it soon rapidly diminished. On this supposition A preserves the earlier version of ch. 72.

The variants of this same chapter may throw light on the peculiar addition to the B text which Spelman and Wilkins printed. Cantilupe speaks in ch. 72 of the statute

---

[1] Cf. the deletion of fixed time-limits in the later editions of Richard Poore's statutes. Above, pp. 59–60.

'of our predecessor' on festivals. Unlike similar references in Cantilupe's statutes, this cannot be found in the acknowledged statutes of Bishop William de Blois. The chapter should, however, be compared with the addition to B, for this includes a list of feasts to be observed in the diocese of Worcester.[1] This list, be it noted, does not include the name of Edmund among the *festa ferianda* as the preceding text of ch. 72 does; like A it includes the name of Nicholas and at the end reproduces the A version of ch. 72 relating to Dominic, Francis, and Edmund. Is it not reasonable to associate this section with Cantilupe's reference to what his predecessor ordained about festivals and to regard it (with the other liturgical matter in the B text) as an undated statute of William de Blois, retouched at some time after 1247 with the help of a text like our A text? The scribe of B had this earlier statute by him when he made his copy of Cantilupe's statutes; he was an ignorant and unintelligent scribe, and was quite capable of copying the earlier statute as an appendix without noticing that it was not compatible with the foregoing text.[2]

The examination of these details shows conclusively that the synodal statutes of 1240 were modified on at least two occasions subsequent to 1247. At what time the 'correcciones' found in AD made their appearance we cannot tell; but their absence from B suggests a period relatively late in Cantilupe's life. Thus, while we can point to one or two chapters as indubitably additions, we are left without the means of discovering whether all else belonged to the original core of the statutes. Again one must be content, as so often in this work, to admit uncertainty.

DERIVATIVES FROM CANTILUPE'S STATUTES

That statutes represented by so few texts as these of Walter de Cantilupe should have passed throughout England in the thirteenth century might be a matter for surprise, if the same phenomenon had not already been observed in the case of Richard Poore's statutes. Both these prelates, of

---

[1] Wilkins, i. 677–8.

[2] I am obliged to Mr. Francis Wormald for advice on this part of the Worcester statutes.

whose work the libraries have saved very little, were famous in their own time and their own ecclesiastical circle. Their diocesan statutes were borrowed and reissued. True, the Worcester statutes were never promulgated wholesale in another diocese, as were Poore's; but traces of them in six dioceses argue a wide reputation. The vestiges of Worcester III which have been identified in the statutes of Chichester and Salisbury admit of some doubt;[1] indisputable and more extensive loans appear in the Lincoln statutes of Robert Grosseteste; and besides the indirect influence which Worcester thus exercised over the derivatives from Lincoln, its immediate use is seen in the Norwich and Durham derivatives. These connexions can suitably be dealt with in the following chapter. Here it is proposed to examine another group of statutes which depend even more completely upon Walter de Cantilupe's work. The relationship of the members of the group may be expressed straightway in a simplified form, preliminary to the description of each series in turn:

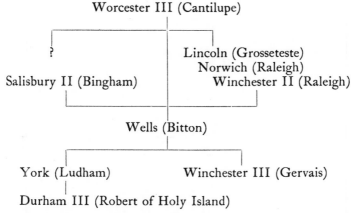

Statutes of William of Bitton I, bishop of Bath and Wells (? 1252 × 1258).

In the year 1342 the bishop of Bath and Wells republished some synodal statutes of his diocese which had been issued by William of Bitton, formerly bishop, declaring them to be still binding upon the bishop's subjects. The

---

[1] See above, pp. 75, 88–9.

document preserved in Bishop Ralph of Shrewsbury's register, which records this, gives the *incipit* of the statutes, 'Quoniam sanctitudo decet domum dei, etc.', but no more, and it leaves in doubt whether the legislator was Bishop William of Bitton I (1248–64) or his nephew, bishop from 1267 to 1274.[1] According to the canon of Wells's history, published by Henry Wharton, William of Bitton I published synodal statutes.[2]

The statutes have hitherto been unknown save for these references, but they are to be found in an unindexed manuscript of the Ottoboni collection in the Vatican Library (Ottobon. cod. lat. 742 fo. 109r). The volume, which is written in two early fourteenth-century hands, contains canon-law works, including in the first part the legatine canons of Otto and Ottobono, the provincial canons of Oxford 1222 and Lambeth 1281, and 'constituciones per episcopum Vellensem in sua diocesi'. The *incipit* of the statutes is 'Quoniam sanctitudo condecet domum dei . . .'. Like many of the Ottoboni collection, this volume belonged formerly to the Duke Giovanni Angelo di Altemps and must have originated in England. The text of the statutes of Wells is neat, but loaded with errors. Fortunately for us, we do not rely upon it alone. The derivatives of York and Winchester, which will be considered below, help to make sense of statutes which, in the Ottoboni manuscript, are frequently distorted beyond recognition. 'Picturis' becomes 'peccaturus', 'in qua' becomes 'nunquam'; whole phrases are carelessly omitted again and again. Maintaining to the last his usual high level of inaccuracy, the scribe writes his colophon, 'Expliciunt constituciones episcopi Wellensis', in the middle of a sentence. These facts add to the suspicions aroused by the final chapters of the York derivative that the Wells version of the statutes is incomplete. The last nine chapters of York, relating to ecclesiastical censures and the payment of tithes, are not found in the Wells statutes. Traces of them are, however, to be seen in

[1] Wilkins, ii. 711, and *Reg. Ralph of Shrewsbury*, ed. T. S. Holmes (Somerset Rec. Soc., vol. x, 1896) ii. 457. Shortly afterwards the decree of republication was withdrawn, since some in and of the church of Wells considered that they were harmed thereby. *Register*, ii. 458. Cf. above, p. 10, n. 4.

[2] *Anglia sacra*, i. 566.

Winchester III, which on other grounds we derive from Wells rather than from York. It seems reasonable to infer that the Wells statutes have been truncated, and provided the original of these chapters in the York series.

The date of the Wells statutes can be fixed within fairly narrow limits. A *terminus a quo* is provided by the reference (fo. 111v*b*) to the 'nova constitucio' concerning the procuration of archdeacons: this must be the constitution 'Ad memoriam' which Innocent IV directed to the English Church on 10 July 1252, at the same time appointing the bishops of Lincoln, London, and Wells as executors of his mandate.[1] The latest possible date for the statutes is shown to be 1258, by their appearance in the diocese of York early in the next year.[2] Certain time-limits named in the body of the statutes suggest publication in an autumn synod.

Together with the related York statutes, the statutes of Wells form a notable addition to the thirteenth-century *synodalia* already known. They are longer than any preceding series published by an English bishop; they cover most of the ground of diocesan administration; and, when seen in connexion with the Winchester second series (likewise unprinted), explain the evolution of Winchester III, the only statutes of that diocese at present in print.

William of Bitton possessed a wide knowledge of the canonical material most useful for his purpose. In the preamble the bishop speaks of the statutes which his predecessors in the see of Wells had published;[3] but it is doubtful whether we ought to attach much importance to such a statement in general terms. It is taken over with the rest of the statutes by the legislator at York, and may be suspected of being common form.[4] Bitton's preamble ends by safeguarding the statutes of the councils of the Lateran, Oxford,

---

[1] *Annales monastici*, i. 300–1 ; Cheney, *Episcopal visitation*, pp. 107–8.

[2] Cf. below, p. 102.

[3] 'Predecessores nostros huic sancte sedi ordinante domino presidentes plurimum laborasse et salubria quedam ad nostrorum reformacionem statuta studiose meminimus aliter novimus edidisse.' Ottobon. MS. lat. 742 fo. 109r*b*.

[4] Cf. the reference in Poore's statutes : 'Ad hec, innovantes predecessorum nostrorum statuta ', which in fact repeats some of the words of Archbishop Hubert's London canons (*Salisbury charters*, p. 149 ch. 62). Hubert had, of course, been bishop of Salisbury, and we cannot preclude entirely the possibility of lost statutes in all these dioceses.

and London. In the body of his statutes he quotes verbatim two chapters of the Fourth Lateran Council (chs. 21, 66) and cites a third (ch. 47) with the chapter 'Cum medicinalis romana' from the appendix to the First Council of Lyon (1245).[1] His reference to the 'nova constitucio' of 1252 on procuration charges has already been noted. Besides borrowing the opening words of the legate Otto's canons to begin his own statutes, Bitton uses several chapters both of Oxford 1222 and of London 1237. But the direct influence of these councils is less obvious in the Wells statutes than is the influence of other diocesan statutes of the southern province. Salisbury, Winchester, and Worcester all make their contributions. The Salisbury statutes of Poore and Bingham obviously inspired some of Bitton's statutes, and occasionally supplied the actual wording for them. The Winchester statutes known to him were not those of Peter des Roches, but a later series which can be best discussed in the next chapter. Anticipating the conclusions reached there, we may say that Winchester II was the work of William de Raleigh between 1247 and 1250, formed on the basis of Norwich statutes derived from Lincoln and of Winchester I.

Bitton's use of these various sources is extensive; and it must be admitted that to represent the Wells series as a derivative of Worcester III distorts the truth and is justified mainly by convenience. The fact remains, however, that Bitton took far more from Cantilupe's statutes than from any other single source. The verbal parallels are too numerous to be worth quoting here and the borrowing extends far beyond verbal parallels. What is more, the arrangement of the Wells series recalls Worcester III. The classification of much of the material under the titles of the seven sacraments is, indeed, not peculiar to them; but the subdivisions of the section *de ordine*, concerning the conduct of the clergy, resemble the Worcester arrangement which has been described. Worcester III, no doubt influenced by the legatine canons of London, devotes more space than most legislators of the time to the conduct of archdeacons; Wells goes farther in the same direction. Looking at the series as a

---

[1] Hefele-Leclercq, v. ii. 1673; *Sext*, v. 11, 1.

whole, we see that despite much retouching and fairly large additions from other sources, Walter de Cantilupe provided the core of Bitton's statutes.[1]

So long as Bitton is concerned with the administration of the sacraments and the conduct of parish priests, he seldom goes beyond recognizable sources in the body of the statute, content to frame the same rule anew and to add here and there some expression of piety. There is more originality about the sections which treat of archdeacons and rural deans and apparitors, testamentary matters, and tithe. It is interesting to observe that several of these chapters anticipate the later chapters of the Council of Lambeth 1261. A chapter directed against clerics who poach fish and game is only found in the Wells and York statutes;[2] so also a chapter dealing with the provision of service-books for parish churches, which deserves to be quoted in full:

De libris abiciendis.

Et quia libri abiecti monasteriorum in plerisque ecclesiis parochialibus appropriatis regularibus assignantur, unde fit quod tam presbiteri quam clerici in ministeriis [Ottobon. MS.: monasteriis] divinis errare coguntur, precipimus quod ammotis libris huiusmodi libri secundum usum predictum[3] infra biennium provideantur ecclesiis memoratis, alioquin ipsarum ecclesiarum proventus in manus nostras transacto biennio capiemus eisdemque faciemus provideri.[4]

Statutes of Archbishop Godfrey of Ludham for the diocese of York (1259) (?).

Lansdowne MS. 397 in the British Museum is a volume used in the cathedral registry or chancery of Durham in the fifteenth century, which contains, along with a work on *dictamen* and miscellaneous letters, synodal statutes of York and Durham, written in the mid-fourteenth century. As far as the Durham statutes are concerned, the texts do not differ greatly from manuscripts still in the cathedral library.[5]

---

[1] The 'correcciones' and other parts of Worcester III which can be shown to form no part of the original statutes of 1240 are not found in the Wells series.

[2] Ottobon. MS. lat. 742 fo. 111va; Lansdowne MS. 397 fo. 249v.

[3] Referring to the preceding chapter, where Wells reads 'usum ecclesie nostre' and York reads 'usum ecclesie (nostre *deleted*) Ebor' vel saltem Sar'.' Wells omits 'usum' at this point.

[4] Ottobon. MS. lat. 742 fo. 110va; Lansdowne MS. 397 fo. 247v.

[5] Cf. above, p. 69.

The volume as a whole has attracted little attention from modern scholars,[1] and the part which concerns us has apparently attracted none at all. On fo. 245r, preceding a text of Archbishop Greenfield's synodal statutes of 1306, is a lengthy series with the simple title 'Constituciones', to which a fifteenth-century hand has added: 'Constituciones ecclesie Ebor''. There is nothing about the statutes to discredit this ascription, and two verbal alterations in this copy serve to confirm it. As originally copied, the statutes demanded liturgical books 'secundum usum ecclesie nostre vel saltem Sar'' (fo. 247v), but the word 'nostre' has been deleted and 'Ebor'' substituted. The colophon reads: 'Expliciunt constituciones Ecclesie', the last word written over an erased word which may have been 'Ebor''. This retouching seems designed to make the statutes applicable, officially or unofficially, to the diocese of Durham. The terms of the statutes throughout do not permit of their being issued for the whole province of York: they are concerned with one diocese only.

The date of the statutes is unusually easy to establish. A chapter on the residence of parsons in their benefices orders those who have dispensations for non-residence to exhibit them 'citra festum beati Petri ad vincula [1 August] anno domini m° cc^{mo} l° nono' (fo. 249v). A similar injunction immediately above and parallels in the statutes of Salisbury II and Wells[2] suggest that about three months' grace was being allowed. This harmonizes with the history of the see of York at this time; for Archbishop Sewal de Bovill had been suspended by the Pope in 1257 and died in May 1258. His successor, Godfrey of Ludham, was elected in July and consecrated at Viterbo on 22 September 1258. These data point to a diocesan synod of York early in 1259.[3]

If Archbishop Ludham can safely be credited with the publishing of these statutes, that is the extent of his performance. For upon examination they prove to be not

---

[1] Cf. Pantin, *Benedictine chapters*, i. 28.

[2] Harleian MS. 52 fo. 122r; Ottobon. MS. lat. 742 fo. 111va.

[3] This date depends on the assumptions that (*a*) the year-date has been preserved uncorrupted in our copy of the statutes, made a century later, (*b*) if correct, the year-date records the *first* publication of the statutes in the diocese of York. The cumulative evidence seems to justify these assumptions.

merely derived from the Wells series, but copied word for word, with a few variations of no importance and a few omissions. The only substantial additions to the Wells series are the last nine chapters, and their absence from the Wells series may be accidental.[1]

The influence of these statutes went farther north. We have already seen that the only text recording the association with York was revised for use in the diocese of Durham, if not for official publication there. A portion of the statutes, at least, did achieve official republication. Robert of Holy Island, bishop of Durham, issued a short series of statutes concerned with tithe and ecclesiastical censures in the year 1276.[2] Chapters 4, 5, and 6 of these statutes are taken verbatim from the York statutes, with the exception of some variants in the excommunication clauses. Robert of Holy Island seems also to have been acquainted directly with Worcester II, if not with Worcester III, for the first chapter of his statutes draws upon ch. 16 of Worcester II.[3]

Statutes of John Gervais, bishop of Winchester (1262 × 1265).

The only statutes for the diocese of Winchester at present in print are those published by Spelman and Wilkins under the name of Bishop Henry Woodlock, dated *circa* 1308. Of recent years this ascription has been discredited, owing to the discovery of a text of the statutes in the register of John de Pontissara, bishop from 1282 to 1304. The editor of the register supposed the statutes to be issued by this bishop about the year 1295.[4] But other manuscripts are available which suggest that this ascription, like the former one, must be abandoned.

A. Brit. Mus., Cotton MS. Otho A. xvi fo. 141r.

Lost. The volume is presumed to have been lost in the fire of 1731.

[1] Cf. above, p. 98.

[2] Wilkins, ii. 28–30. The last part of the text is obviously a distinct document : a mandate from the bishop of Durham's official. It is even doubtful whether it refers to Bishop Robert of Holy Island or not. The dating of the statutes depends on the title in the two known fourteenth-century manuscripts : ' Incipiunt constituciones domini Roberti quondam episcopi Dunelm' anno domini mᵒ ccᵒ lxxᵒ vjᵒ' (Durham Cath. MS. C. ii. 13 fo. 273v*b*; cf. MS. B. iv. 41 fo. 162r [formerly fo. 180r]).

[3] Bishop Walter of Kirkham, a little earlier, showed knowledge of Worcester III. Grosseteste of Lincoln appears to have known both the second and third Worcester series. Cf. below, pp. 121–2.   [4] *Reg. Pontissara*, i. xlii, 207.

Title unknown. Thomas Smith's *Catalogus* (1696) described it as 'Constitutiones cuiusdam sacræ synodi episcopi Wintoniensis, ad clerum suum literis munitæ.' *Inc.*: 'In vinea domini . . .'. The volume cannot have been written earlier than late xiv c. and the Winchester statutes were preceded by the laws of William the Conqueror,&c., acts of an Augustinian general chapter at Southwark, 1309, &c., legatine and provincial canons. A comparison of other texts printed from it by Spelman with those in Arundel MS. 438 (cf. D, below) suggests that Otho A. xvi may have been in part copied from this earlier MS. This text of the statutes was printed by Spelman (*Concilia*, ii. 445) and, probably from Spelman's edition, by Wilkins (*Concilia*, ii. 293). Here, as elsewhere, these editors refer to the MS. as Otho A. xv. No reason appears for Spelman's attribution to Bishop Henry Woodlock. The provenance of the MS. is unknown: an Augustinian house in the diocese of Winchester is indicated by the contents.

B. Winchester, Bishop's Registry, Register of J. de Pontissara, fo. 54v.

Title: 'Hic incipiunt statuta sinodalia Iohannis episcopi Wyntoniensis.' *Inc.*: 'In vinea domini . . .'. Printed from this text with a collation of Wilkins's edition in *Reg. J. de Pontissara*, ed. Cecil Deedes, i. 218.

C. Helmingham Hall, MS. L.J. vi. 16 fo. [48r].

Title: 'Synodus magistri Iohannis Gerveys quondam episcopi Wynton' '(in red, in the original text-hand, repeated approximately in a later hand in black). *Inc.*: 'In vinea domini . . .'. The statutes form the second part of a small octavo volume written in a book-hand *c.* 1300 (not xv c., as stated in *Hist. MSS. Comm. Rep.* i app. p. 61*a*): they are written in one quire consisting now of six folios; and four folios may be missing after the third remaining one (fo. 50). The first part of the volume (fos. 5–47) is the 'Compendium theologie' (cf. Brit. Mus. Royal MS. 9 A. xiv fo. 113). On fo. [47v] is written in a different but nearly contemporary hand: 'Portiuncula ye chirche of angel in Asise consecrata in honore beate Marie quam ecclesiam Franciscus fecit.' Following the statutes is a fragment (fos. 54–5) of a treatise on the Mass, written in another hand of *c.* 1300: it is a bifolio from the middle of a gathering. Fly-leaves at beginning and end (fos. 1–4, 56–8) show that the book was bound after 18 Richard II. The binding is of vellum over wood. The provenance is unknown.[1]

---

[1] I am obliged to the trustees of the late Hon. Lionel Tollemache of Helmingham Hall for the facilities kindly given to me for studying this MS. in 1932, and to Mr. S. C. Ratcliff who, as Secretary to the Historical MSS. Commission, kindly arranged the transfer of the MS. to the Public Record Office for my use.

D. Brit. Mus., Arundel MS. 438 fo. 102v.

Title: 'Incipiunt statuta synodalia Iohannis dicti Gerveys quondam episcopi Wintonie.' *Inc.*: 'In vinea domini . . .'. The statutes occur in a volume written early xiv c., after a copy of the *Sext* and provincial and legatine canons, and preceding the treatise on episcopal election of Laurence of Somercote. The resemblance of the texts of provincial canons with those in Cotton MS. Otho A. xvi (cf. A, above) argues a close connexion between the two manuscripts. The provenance of the MS. is unknown.

E. Oxford, Corpus Christi College, MS. 360 fo. 74r.

Title: 'Constituciones deossidis Wintonnie.' *Inc.*: 'In vinea domini . . .'. Written *c.* 1300 in two hands, the second beginning at the chapter on confirmation. The text is incomplete, ending in the middle of the section on tithe at the foot of fo. 78v. For a description of the whole volume see above, p. 58.

F. Salisbury, Dean and Chapter Muniments, Liber evidenciarum C p. 381*b* (formerly fo. 178r*b*), no. 494.

Title: 'Constitucio domini Iohannis episcopi in synodo Wynton'.' A modern hand (Canon Chr. Wordsworth) has added at the foot of the page: '*Jo.* de Pontissara, cir. 1295.' *Inc.*: 'Inhibemus insuper ne occasione . . .'. A fragment only, consisting of the chapter against archdeacons' exaction of 'gifts' (*Reg. Pontissara*, i. 238). Written in a late xiii c. charter hand immediately after the statutes of Richard Poore. For a brief description of the volume see above, p. 58.

A very brief view of these texts is sufficient to expose the baselessness of the ascriptions to Henry Woodlock and John de Pontissara. The former is probably a worthless conjecture by Dugdale, the editor of Spelman's second volume; the ascription to Pontissara depends on nothing more than the presence of a text in his register. Two other manuscripts, C and D, attribute the statutes definitely to Bishop John Gervais, and these were written at a time when the scribes would hardly have mistaken the work of John de Pontissara for that of a predecessor. Nor do the contents of the statutes belie their title in C and D. It is difficult to suppose that diocesan statutes compiled during Pontissara's time would fail, as these do, to refer to the two great councils of Lambeth, held by the legate Ottobono in 1268 and by Archbishop Pecham in 1281. The councils of Oxford 1222 and London 1237 are both cited. The other discoverable sources agree with the conclusion that these statutes were compiled by John Gervais, bishop from 1262 to 1268. They were probably issued between Michaelmas 1262 and the end of the year 1265.[1]

Since Bishop John Gervais's statutes only claim a place in this chapter as a derivative of Walter de Cantilupe's, a detailed description is unnecessary. It remains simply to be observed that the bulk of Winchester III comes from either Winchester II or Wells.[2] A good deal of this material is reshaped and reworded, to achieve precision, and for the most part the extracts from Winchester II are fitted into the more symmetrical framework of Wells. Apart from these changes, the only additions are in the section on wills, where the influence of the Council of Lambeth of 1261 now seems discernible, and in a few apparently new administrative arrangements. The intermediate position of the Wells series between Worcester III and Winchester III may be illustrated by a simple example:

Worcester III, A (fo. 213rab) (cf. Wilkins, i. 666b)	Wells (fo. 110vb)	Winchester III (*Reg. Pontis.*, i. 225)
Simiteria . . . inhonestum credimus *brutorum animalium sordibus* deturpari, propter quod *precipimus quod honeste claudantur sepe* vel *muro,* canonice com-	Nolentes *quod cymiteria brutorum animalium sordibus* maculentur, *precipimus quod per* ipsos *ad quos de consuetudine onus* claudendi *dinoscitur pertinere,* circum-	*Precipimus* etiam *quod cimiteria fossata sepe vel muro per* eos *ad quos de consuetudine* [D: iure] *onus* huiusmodi pertinet, *honeste claudantur,* ita quod ab eis per hoc

[1] Bishop John, appointed in the Curia and consecrated by the Pope, came into England about Michaelmas 1262 (*Annales mon.*, ii. 353). In 1266, being suspended (probably in Lent) by the legate Ottobono, he set out for Rome and died in the Curia at Viterbo 20 Jan. 1268 (*ibid.*, ii. 104, 106, iii. 240, iv. 180–1, 185, 455). The final chapter of the statutes fixes the Thursday before St. Denis (9 Oct.) as the annual day for the diocesan synod (*Reg. Pontissara*, i. 239).

Among the books given to Westminster in 1623 by John Williams, and lost in the fire of 1694, was a volume of ecclesiastical canons which contained ' Statuta synodalia praesidente Nicholao ep. Wintoniensi ' (J. A. Robinson and M. R. James, *MSS. of Westm. Abbey* (Cambr., 1909) p. 47). These statutes may have been an edition of those of John Gervais revised by his successor, Nicholas of Ely (1268–80).

[2] Canon Deedes's opinion that the statutes were derived from those of Exeter 1287 and Chichester 1289 cannot be sustained in the face of the other sources now brought to light. Cf. *Reg. Pontissara*, i. 207.

pellendis ad hoc faciendum hiis *ad quos* eorum clausio *noscitur pertinere*.	quaque *muro sepe* vel *fossato claudantur honeste*.	immunda animalia arceantur.

Gervais naturally had at his disposal the whole series of Winchester II as well as those parts of it which occur in the Wells statutes. He used both impartially. Where the Wells statutes modify those of Winchester II, Winchester III frequently follows the Wells version. Thus, Winchester II (following Norwich and Lincoln) forbade beneficed clergy and those in Holy Orders to keep taverns (fo. 398v*a*); Wells extended the prohibition to all clerks (fo. 111r*a*), and was followed in this by Winchester III (*Reg. Pontissara*, i. 226). At times, the preference is merely one of form. In many instances, however, Winchester III uses chapters of Winchester II which had found no place in the Wells series, or preserves the Winchester form where Wells had modified it. For example, Wells had repeated the demand of Winchester II for adequate payment of stipendiary priests, without repeating the figures: five marks or sixty shillings, or more according to the church's resources (fo. 399r*a*). Winchester III adopts the five marks figure for a minimum.[1]

We have treated the Wells series as the chief immediate source of Gervais's statutes. But it has already appeared that the Wells and the York series are practically identical. Is there any proof that Gervais plundered Wells rather than York? It is true that a long passage used in Winchester III is found at the end of the York statutes and is not found in the Wells manuscript; but reasons have been given for regarding this as an accidental omission.[2] It is less likely, though possible, that two chapters found only in Wells were

---

[1] *Reg. Pontissara*, i. 227. Text D preserves what appears to be a revised version of this chapter, while failing to cancel the old one found in the other texts. The new chapter is inserted at the end of the section relating to the clergy (cf. *ibid.*, i. 230), and runs as follows :

Et quoniam os bovis alligari nolumus triturantis, et ut eciam ydoneos et bene morigeratos presbiteros in nostra diocesi attrahamus, statuimus quod nullus sacerdos parochialis pro stipendiis annuis minus habeat quam sex marcas exceptis ecclesiis in quibus rectores earum personaliter resident, illisque cum quarum rectoribus propter sui exilitatem nimiam et curam modicam duximus super hoc dispensandum.

[2] Cf. above, p. 98.

originally in the York series as well. They concern litigation before unauthorized judges and the oath extracted
from rural deans and their apparitors;[1] these chapters
appear in a revised form in Winchester III.[2] In detail, too,
several indications point to the dependence of Winchester
upon Wells. Where Winchester III reads 'in kalendario
et aliis libris ecclesie',[3] Wells reads 'in singulis kalendariis
ecclesie et libris' and York reads 'in libris'. Winchester
III[4] agrees with Wells in reading 'ad hoc necessitas
compulerit manifesta', when York reads 'ad hoc sit necessitas manifesta'. These are only slight indications, but
constant in the way they point. Wells seems to precede
York, and seems to be the parent of Winchester III.

These conclusions about the statutes of Wells, York, and
Winchester have not been reached without difficulty and
some misgivings, and even now they are only stated as
hypotheses. Several other attractive theories of their relationship compete for acceptance. These possibilities deserve
statement. William of Bitton I was succeeded in the see of
Wells by Walter Giffard who, within two years, passed on
to the see of York. If we could ignore the date '1259' in
the York statutes, we might suppose that Giffard took the
Wells statutes with him to his northern province. Or there
is another possibility: John Gervais was a friend of Walter
de Cantilupe and was chancellor of York from 1254; might
we not hold him responsible for composing the statutes
for his diocesan at York in 1259? Thence they might be
transmitted to Wells before Bitton died in 1264, and used
at Winchester after Gervais became bishop there in 1262.
Thirdly, supposing that York borrowed from Wells in 1259,
might not John Gervais have used the York series in putting
together his statutes at Winchester? The textual evidence
by which to check these conjectures is lamentably weak.
But even if the hypothesis adopted above is unacceptable,
any interpretation of the evidence leaves us certain about

---

[1] 'Quoniam alique cause . . .'; 'Quoniam nos et officialem . . .' (fo. 111rb).
[2] *Reg. Pontissara*, i. 234, 236 : 'Cum maiores cause . . .'; 'Et quoniam decanorum . . .'.
[3] *Ibid.*, i. 225.   [4] *Ibid.*, i. 226.

two important facts: these statutes of Wells and York and Winchester were all published within the space of about twelve years or less; Walter de Cantilupe's statutes were the chief influence behind this group of three important series. The lesser influence of Winchester II on the same group sets us upon another line which must be separately traced: that leading from the statutes of Robert Grosseteste.

V

THE STATUTES OF ROBERT GROSSETESTE, BISHOP OF LINCOLN, AND RELATED TEXTS

THE reputation of Robert Grosseteste is so firmly established that there seems little reason to accuse historians of neglecting him. His philosophical and scientific works have received a great deal of attention in recent years, and his administrative activity, vividly described by Matthew Paris and other contemporaries, has always been recognized. Many of his letters, which provide a valuable record of his views on the pastoral office, have been in print since 1690. But if we wish to inquire farther into Grosseteste's influence upon later generations, we are put off with vague statements, and are left asking: How did he achieve the popular fame which led to petitions for his canonization? To what extent did his influence persist throughout the fourteenth and fifteenth centuries? The answers to these questions can only result from a thorough survey of all the writings attributable to Grosseteste and the manuscript tradition of them. Then justice will be done to the 'sermons and lengthy theological works' which Luard mentioned only to dismiss.[1] For Grosseteste's pastoral writings were very numerous, and were widely diffused and widely read during the next two hundred years and more. Among them must be reckoned the 'Constitutiones', or statutes designed for the parochial clergy of his diocese, which accompany Grosseteste's collected letters in certain manuscripts. These conform to the usual thirteenth-century type and are comparatively short —they occupy barely ten pages in the Rolls series—but, judging from surviving manuscripts, they circulated far more freely in the Middle Ages than did any other series of English episcopal statutes. Moreover they formed the solid basis of synodal statutes in four other dioceses. Yet these facts have generally passed unnoticed. Of the twenty-three known manuscripts, apart from four copies among the collected letters, only three attribute the statutes to Grosseteste. One other copy attributes them to Archbishop

---

[1] Grosseteste, *Epistolæ*, p. xii. Cf. S. Harrison Thomson's recent work.

Robert Winchelsey, another to Simon Langham, bishop of
Ely; all the rest are content to give the text without naming
the author. The obscurity or inaccuracy of the medieval
copyist has had its natural consequence. The statutes have
been usually neglected or unidentified. They were printed
by Edward Brown in 1690 and reprinted by Samuel Pegge
and by Henry Luard.[1] But, while Spelman omitted them
entirely from his *Concilia*, Wilkins only knew them by the
copy ascribed to Simon Langham and set them in his third
volume under the year 1364. Modern historians have relied
too much on the *Concilia* and fail to observe that Grosseteste
provided the original of much that is found in thirteenth-
century synodal statutes. Some other writers, notably
Gasquet, have drawn upon the 'Langham 1364' version,
unaware that the evidence they cite belongs properly to the
first half of the thirteenth century. This is the less pardonable in view of the prominence given to Grosseteste's statutes
by Luard and Stevenson.

THE MANUSCRIPTS OF THE STATUTES

A. Brit. Mus., Royal MS. 9 A. xiv fo. 193r (formerly fo. 182r).
   No title. *Inc.*: 'Debentes de vobis . . .'. Written in a charter
hand of Edward I's time, in a late xiii c. collection of theological
tracts, lives of saints, &c. They include the tract *Qui bene presunt*,
and the table to the statutes is followed by the tract or sermon on
confession, *Quoniam cogitacio*, attributed to Grosseteste. The provenance of the volume is unknown. On fo. 299 is the name Adam
de Lime (?).

B. Brit. Mus., Add. MS. 6158 fo. 134v.
   No original title; 'Incipit tractatus domini Roberti Grosteth' de
confessione' in a xv c. hand. *Inc.*: 'Debentes de vobis . . .'. Written
in an early xiv c. book-hand in a volume which contains other
material for parish priests, including the tract *Quoniam cogitacio*,
which follows the statutes and precedes the table. The statutes
omit the last chapter and the table is misplaced. The provenance
of the volume is unknown.

C. Brit. Mus., Royal MS. 7 A. ix fo. 115r.
   No title. *Inc.*: 'contemptores et transgressores . . .'. A fragment

[1] E. Brown, *Fasciculus rerum expetendarum . . . una cum appendice* (London,
1690), ii. 410; S. Pegge, *Life of Robert Grosseteste* (London, 1793), p. 315;
Grosseteste, *Epistolæ*, p. 154.

only, consisting of part of the last sentence, followed by the table. Written in a xiii c. book-hand in a volume which contains (in various late xiii c. hands) the tract *Qui bene presunt*, works on penance, several works of Grosseteste, &c. Following the table to the statutes comes the tract *Quoniam cogitacio*. The whole volume belonged to St. Mary Overy, Southwark (O.S.A.).

D. Brit. Mus., Royal MS. 11 B. x fo. 176r.

   Title: 'Constituciones synodales hic incipiunt'. *Inc.*: 'Debentes racionem de vobis . . .'. Written in a late xiv c. book-hand in a volume which contains (in xiv and xv c. hands) the *Pupilla oculi*, instructions for priests, and devotional works. The statutes lack the table, and have the addition found in G, X, and Y. The excommunication clauses of the Council of Oxford are omitted with an 'etc.'. The provenance of the volume is unknown.

E. Cambridge Univ. Libr., MS. Ii. 2, 7 fo. 147v (formerly p. 379).

   Title: 'Statuta synodalia [*sic*] per episcopum loci condita.' *Inc.*: 'Debentes de vobis . . .'. Written in a late xiv c. book-hand in a miscellaneous volume of canons and canon law treatises. The statutes break off before the excommunication clauses of Oxford. The catalogue wrongly identifies them as synodal statutes of Norwich. The volume comes from Norwich Cathedral Priory.

F. Cambridge, Gonville and Caius Coll., MS. 138 fo. 176r.

   No title. *Inc.*: 'Debentes de vobis . . .'. Written in a late xiii c. hand, following the tract *Quoniam cogitacio* in a volume which contains works of William de Montibus and the office of St. Edmund conf. The table of statutes follows. The catalogue fails to identify the statutes. An inscription on the last leaf of the book suggests that the volume belonged to a Cambridge college in the Middle Ages, but M. R. James does not elucidate it.

G. Cambridge, Corpus Christi Coll., MS. 255 fo. 209v.

   Title: 'Incipiunt constituciones sinodales.' *Inc.*: 'Debentes racionem de vobis . . .'. Written in an early xv c. hand at the end of a volume containing the *Pupilla oculi* and instructions for priests. The statutes have the addition found in D, X, and Y. The provenance of the volume is unknown.

H. Brit. Mus., Cotton MS. Nero D. ii fo. 266r (formerly fo. 261).

   Title: 'Constituciones Roberti episcopi Lincoln' rectoribus ecclesiarum vicariis sacerdotibus parochialibus eiusdem diocesis directe.' *Inc.*: 'Debentes de vobis . . .'. Written in a xv c. charter hand. The provenance is unknown. Used by Edward Brown as his main text.

J. Bodleian, Laud misc. MS. 439 fo. 81r.

   No title. *Inc.*: 'Debentes de nobis . . .'. Written in a xiii c. hand in a volume of theological miscellanea which include the tract *Quoniam cogitacio*. The provenance of the volume is unknown.

K. Biblioteca de El Escorial, Latin MS. I. III. 7 fo. 86v.[1]
No title. *Inc.*: 'Debentes de vobis . . .'. Written in a xiii c. hand in a volume which includes the tract *Qui bene presunt*, Innocent III *De contemptu mundi*, and a *liber de penitencia*. The catalogue (Antolín, Madrid, 1911, vol. 2, p. 461) conjecturally identifies the statutes with those of Norwich. On fo. 86r is a letter of presentation to a benefice from the prior and convent of N. to their diocesan, 'J. dei gratia Elnensis episcopo'.

L. Bodleian, Ashmole MS. 1146 fo. 80r.
Title: 'Constituciones domini Roberti de Wynchelsee Cantuar' archiepiscopi.' *Inc.*: 'Debentes de vobis . . .'. Written in a charter hand of mid xiv c. The statutes occur in a legal collection which contains many legatine and provincial canons, mostly written at the same time, apparently for the cathedral church of Chichester, to which the book belonged. The statutes are not identified in the catalogue.

M. Bodleian, Barlow MS. 49 (S.C. 6414) fo. 4r.
Title: 'Constituciones Roberti episcopi Lincoln' rectoribus vicariis sacerdotibus parrochialibus eiusdem diocesis.' *Inc.*: 'Debentes de vobis . . .'. Preceded by the table. Written in a xv c. hand, in fine format. The statutes are followed by the collected letters of Grosseteste (not used by Luard) in the same hand. The rest of the volume was originally distinct. The Grosseteste section formed part of a volume in the library of Syon monastery (N 16), of which another part is found in Oxford, Corpus Christi Coll. MS. 245, ii. fos. 86–179.[2] It belonged to Cotton before passing to Barlow.

N. Bodleian, Rawl. MS. C. 301 fo. 80r.
No title. *Inc.*: 'Debentes de vobis . . .'. Written in a xv c. hand in a paper volume containing sermons and theological miscellanea. The statutes add some excommunication clauses before the table, which breaks off incomplete at the end of a folio. Rawlinson says that he obtained the volume from one of the Kemp family; its earlier history is unknown.

O. Oxford, St. John's Coll., MS. 136 fo. 109r.
Title: 'Hic incipiunt constituciones magistri Roberti Grosseteste Linconiensis episcopi.' *Inc.*: 'Debentes de vobis . . .'. Followed by

---

[1] I am grateful to the Reverend Fr. Angel Custodio Vega, prior of the monastery of El Escorial, for supplying me, in difficult times, with a collation of this text.
[2] I am obliged to Mr. R. W. Hunt for this identification.

the table. Written in a charter hand of Edward I's time, in a volume which contains two collections of sermons and *Physiologus*. One of the collections (*inc.*: Cum appropinquasset . . .) also precedes the T text of the statutes. Documents concerning the vicar of Wycomb (*c.* 1261) occur after the sermons, and other documents of Lincoln diocese (1303 onwards) follow the table to the statutes in another hand. The volume was given to St. John's by Richard Butler, archdeacon of Northampton (1611–12).

P. Oxford, New Coll., MS. 222 fo. 10r.

No title. *Inc.*: ' Debentes de vobis . . .'. Written in a charter hand of Edward I's time, in a volume which contains canonistic and theological excerpts. The provenance of the volume is unknown.

Q. Bodleian, Bodley MS. 312 (S.C. 2123) fo. 144r.

Title : 'Constituciones Roberti episcopi Linc' rectoribus ecclesiarum vicariis sacerdotibus parochialibus eiusdem diocesis directe.' *Inc.*: 'Debentes de vobis . . .'. Written in a xv c. hand. The statutes occur in the midst of collected letters of Grosseteste (beginning without title on fo. 117v), which are now bound with MSS. originally distinct. The Grosseteste section belonged to Thomas Gascoigne (d. 1458) and possibly to the Oxford Franciscans. It was used by Luard.

R. Cambridge, Sidney Sussex Coll., MS. *Δ*. 5. 7 part ii, fo. 20r. [Catalogue, no. 92].

Title : ' Constituciones Roberti episcopi Lincolniensis rectoribus ecclesiarum vicariis sacerdotibus parochialibus eiusdem diocesis directe.' *Inc.*: 'Debentes de vobis . . .'. Written in a xvi c. hand, contained in ' Epistolæ quædam reverendi patris Roberti Grosthead quondam Lincoln. episc. prout repertæ sunt in libro imperfecto manuscripto in bibliotheca Dunelmensi : lviii '. Used by Brown and by Luard.

S. Cambridge, Gonville and Caius Coll., MS. 33 p. 323.

Title : ' Constituciones domini Roberti episcopi Lincolniensis.' *Inc.*: ' Sacerdotes sciant decalogum . . .'. Written in a xv c. hand as a marginal note to a legal MS. of the xiii c. Consists of the table only. Followed on p. 324 (originally blank) by *acta* of a suit before the official of the bishop of Lincoln.

T. Cambridge, Emmanuel Coll., MS. I. 2. 6 fo. 67v [Catalogue, no. 27].

No title. *Inc.*: ' Debentes de vobis . . .'. Written in a very late xiii c. book-hand in a miscellany of theological treatises, &c. (cf. text O). The statutes are followed by the tract *Qui bene presunt*. The table precedes the statutes. The volume contains Salisbury episcopal statutes, but also (in a calendar) the dedication of the church of Sompting, dioc. Chichester.

V. Cambridge, Corpus Christi Coll., MS. 453 fo. 141r.

Title : 'Constituciones Roberti episcopi Lincolniensis rectoribus ecclesiarum vicariis sacerdotibus parochialibus eiusdem diocesis directe.' *Inc.*: 'Debentes de vobis . . .'. Written in a xv c. hand, contained in collected letters of Grosseteste. The provenance of the volume is unknown. Luard's main text : see facsimile as frontispiece to *Epistolæ Roberti Grosseteste*.

W. Cambridge, Peterhouse, MS. 255 part iii fo. 29r.

No original title; in the margin is : 'Sermo in synodo'. The xv c. table of contents says : 'Sermo in synodo Symonis Langham episcopi Eliencis et legati.' *Inc.*: 'Debentes de vobis . . .'. Followed by the table. Written in a good mid xiii c. book-hand in a volume by many xiii c. hands, which contains the *Numerale* and *Similitudinarius* of William de Montibus, Innocent III *De miseria humane conditionis* (i.e. *De contemptu mundi*), sermons, &c. The statutes immediately follow the tract *Quoniam cogitacio*. The volume was bought by Mr. John Warkworth 1462 and given by him to Peterhouse 1481.

X. Oxford, Magdalen Coll., Lat. MS. 104 fo. 153v.

Title : 'Hic incipiunt constituciones sinodales.' *Inc.*: 'Debentes racionem de vobis . . .'. Written in a late xiv c. hand in a volume which contains the *Pupilla oculi* and instructions for priests, as in D, G, and Y. The statutes have the same addition as these texts. The provenance of the volume is unknown.

Y. Bodleian, Bodley MS. 424 (S.C. 2324) fo. 157v.

Title : 'Constituciones sinodales.' *Inc.*: 'Debentes racionem de nobis . . .'. Written in a xv c. hand in a volume which contains the *Pupilla oculi* and instructions for priests, as in D, G, and X. The statutes have the first part of the same addition as these texts. The provenance of the volume is unknown.

This list is a long one, if compared with the usual manuscript survivals of episcopal statutes. It could, however, probably be extended after further search; for most of the early texts signalled here have no titles and have not been identified by modern cataloguers. Many more may remain to be found in volumes of theological miscellanea.

The known texts do not show clear-cut distinctions into families except for the group DGXY. These four copies were written very late in the fourteenth and in the fifteenth century, as an appendix to the *Pupilla oculi*. All have the

title ' constituciones sinodales '. In many details their readings differ from those common to other and earlier texts.
For the purpose of establishing the original they must be
ruled out because of their major differences from the normal
texts; these show that they are the result of a thorough-
going revision, designed to make the statutes suitable for
issue by an archdeacon, in his synods or chapters.[1] The
general fidelity of the other manuscripts to one textual tradition argues unusual care in the first publishing of the statutes
and lack of the revision to be expected had the statutes been
republished in successive diocesan synods.

At first sight, the evidence for the ascription of these
statutes to Grosseteste seems slight. The earliest manuscripts have no title at all and Grosseteste's name appears
first in a carelessly written text (O) of the time of Edward I,
which appears to come from the diocese of Lincoln. The
manuscripts of the collected letters are all so late as to leave
doubts about their evidential value: so also the isolated text
of the statutes with the same title, taken by Brown as his
chief text (H). Is it not possible that we have here the
common phenomenon of a famous name attached arbitrarily
to a familiar document: the sort of error which led to the
false ' Langton ' attributions?[2]

Actually, the evidence is not so weak as it would appear.
Whatever the origin of the manuscript collection of Grosseteste's letters—and this raises a problem as yet unsolved—
its compiler had access to authentic texts and must have
been in a position to distinguish genuine ' Lincolniensia '
from spurious. The title of the statutes which he preserved
at least has nothing suspicious about it. It is also perhaps
significant that six of the early texts which have no title
occur together with another work attributed to Grosseteste:
the tract *Quoniam cogitacio*. The connexion with Lincoln is
slightly reinforced by the four anonymous texts found with
the tract *Qui bene presunt*. Of outside evidence there is
admittedly little. Contemporaries who mention Grosseteste's work of visitation are silent as to his legislating.
Only in one place does Matthew Paris refer to the bishop's

---

[1] For the peculiarities of this version see Appendix I.
[2] Cf. *Eng. Hist. Rev.*, l. 398–400.

'episcopale decretum' ordering beneficed clergy to proceed to the priesthood:[1] this agrees with ch. 30 of the statutes but proves nothing. The internal evidence of the statutes is much more impressive. The following indications of sources will show how nicely the statutes can be connected with papal rescripts to the bishop of Lincoln and the bishop's own mandates to his archdeacons. And when, further, the derivatives of these statutes are considered in relation to Grosseteste's personal circle, the cumulative effect of the evidence is very strong indeed. Short of positive proof, one can hardly ask for more.

Another question raised by the titles of the manuscripts is that of the occasion of issue. Those without title do not assist us, except by showing that in the thirteenth century this document circulated along with homiletic works designed for the instruction of priests rather than with collections of synodal statutes. The texts in the collected letters merely say that the statutes were 'directe' to rectors, vicars, and parish priests of the diocese, a formula which suggests that the original publication took the form of recital at visitations or else issue as a letter through the archdeacons. We know from other sources that Grosseteste was an active visitor and, like his friend Stavensby, bishop of Lichfield, made use of his archdeacons for the publishing of general mandates. But certain manuscripts, without mentioning Grosseteste,[2] describe the statutes as synodal. None of these manuscripts can be less than a century later than the original issue; four of them, it has been seen, contain modifications and additions by an archdeacon. And while they entitle the text 'constituciones sinodales' or 'statuta sinodalia', they do not record the synod in which the statutes were first published. It is easy to presume that the statutes gained the title of 'synodal' at some period after their first issue. A study of their contents favours this presumption. The earliest English episcopal statutes all bear the mark of having been composed for synodal publication. Not so these statutes of Robert Grosseteste. One may go farther and

---

[1] Matt. Paris, *Chronica majora*, v. 279, *s.a.* 1252.
[2] The unusual phrase 'per episcopum *loci*' in the title of the E text may possibly be due to a misreading of 'lincolniensis'.

say that there is no certain proof that this notable reformer ever summoned a synod of his diocese.[1] Maybe this is due to deficiency of records; or it may be that the practical difficulties of assembling the clergy of so large a diocese made Grosseteste neglect the synod in favour of regular visitations and circular letters.[2] One is reminded of the sixteenth-century bishop of Verona, whose excellence Benedict XIV praised; he called only one synod in a pontificate of nineteen years, fulfilling its purpose meanwhile by other ways.[3]

Writing as he did some twenty years after Richard Poore, Grosseteste saw in a different light the need of making diocesan statutes. By this time the decrees of the Fourth Lateran Council had not merely had time to percolate to the extremities of the Church; they had been put verbatim in the 'Extravagantes' of Gregory IX, henceforth to be the official compilation of decretals, and their substance had been repeated in provincial and legatine canons. Apart from legislation, the amount of material available for instructing the priesthood in law and doctrine had grown enormously in the period after the Council. Some of the volumes of miscellanea in which the Lincoln statutes are found give a good impression of this type of literature. Within the same period, the new machinery of provincial chapters and the new activity of bishops in visitation offered alternative ways of dealing with questions of monastic discipline. Grosseteste does not rival Poore or Cantilupe in length and comprehensiveness. He presumably considered that the day was past for reciting canons *in extenso*, and conceived his task to be one of strict compression and strict attention to immediate problems. He limited his statutes still more narrowly by legislating solely for the parochial clergy; he has absolutely nothing to say on this occasion about the conduct of archdeacons and deans or about the monastic

---

[1] Brown prints as Grosseteste's a 'sermo ad sacerdotes in synodo'. *Fasciculus,* ii. 268–70. Cf. S. H. Thomson, *Writings of Robert Grosseteste,* pp. 174, 179.

[2] So also, pentecostal processions to the *matrix ecclesia* in the diocese of Lincoln may have been to other centres besides the cathedral. The words of St. Hugh's mandate on the matter can be thus interpreted (*Eng. Hist. Rev.,* xxx. 288) and the practice was known elsewhere; cf. Berlière, 'Les processions', p. 431.

[3] Benedict XIV, *De synodo diœcesana,* i. 2, § 5.

life. The statutes do not pretend to be a substitute for the canons of the greater councils. Although the bishop speaks with authority to his priests—'precipimus' and 'inhibemus' are his favourite words—he nowhere states the penalties which the laws impose; he confines himself to 'precepta' and 'prohibitiones', to use the term applied to some other diocesan statutes in this century.[1] An excellent example of this is seen in ch. 27[2] of Lincoln, which repeats the prohibition of the selling of sacraments found in ch. 4 of London 1237. The Lincoln statute does not state the penalty for this offence, as declared by the legate Otto: removal from benefice and suspension from office. The only declaration of penalties is at the end of the statutes, where Grosseteste recites in full the excommunication clauses of Oxford 1222. There was special reason for this, in that the council had itself ordered that the excommunications be read quarterly in parish churches and, according to Grosseteste, many churches did not possess a copy of the Oxford canons.[3]

THE SOURCES OF GROSSETESTE'S STATUTES

The Lincoln statutes naturally made use of the Fourth Lateran Council and the Council of London of the legate Otto, as well as the Council of Oxford. But the direct references to, or quotations from, these councils are very few. Chs. 23 and 24 of Lincoln use the wording of the Fourth Lateran decree 16; this passage is, however, found in full in the statutes of Richard Poore (ch. 11), while a note in Lincoln ch. 2 'quemadmodum in generali concilio scribitur' proceeds with a passage similar to the Salisbury statutes ch. 61, which does not appear to belong to the Fourth Lateran or to any other general council. If, for

---

[1] Paris, Mansi, xxii. 675; Rouen, cf. above, p. 56; London, cf. above, p. 80.

[2] The numeration adopted here corresponds to the sections of the table to the statutes (printed by Luard, pp. 164–6), except that the 42nd chapter of the table has been divided into 42 and 43, and the last chapter (not given in the table) is numbered 47.

[3] Both in form and content the Lincoln statutes resemble the earlier circular letter of Grosseteste's friend Alexander of Stavensby, addressed to the archdeacons of the diocese of Lichfield, more than any statutes of the period. But Stavensby wrote a long homiletic introduction and stated explicit penalties for offences.

reasons which will appear, we may date the Lincoln statutes
c. 1241, the legatine canons of London 1237 ought to have
left their mark. Luard, and after him Stevenson, inferred
from the statutes that they were issued after Otto's council;
but it must be admitted that they nowhere copy Otto very
closely. The nearest parallels are in chs. 1, 15, 26, 27, 30
of Lincoln, which recall chs. 3, 7–9, 17, 4, 10 of London
1237. The preoccupation of Otto with the duties of prelates
may explain why his canons leave few traces in statutes
designed exclusively for parish priests. For this latter purpose Grosseteste used one relevant decretal of Honorius III,
which he found either in the *Compilatio quinta* or in Gregory
IX's *Decretals*.[1] Contrary to his usual custom, Grosseteste
took the words of the decretal for his own, to make the
first part of ch. 2 of the Lincoln statutes.

An interesting and less usual connexion may be traced
between the bishop's statutes and the mandates which he
himself received from Rome. When he prohibits the observance of the Feast of Fools, Grosseteste says explicitly
'speciali auctoritate rescripti apostolici penitus inhibemus',
and in four other chapters he legislates by special papal
authority.[2] Three of the papal bulls to which he thus refers
remain in the register of Gregory IX, dated 26 June and
15 July 1236, and 23 January 1239.[3] All three seem to
have been rescripts, in answer to the bishop's requests for
further powers. The history of the mandate of 26 June
1236 is particularly illuminating. On 9 November 1235
Grosseteste persuaded King Henry III, being at Northampton, to issue letters close to his bailiffs there, forbidding
for the future markets and fairs in the cemetery or church
of All Saints, Northampton.[4] Soon afterwards, at some date
unknown, the bishop sent a letter to his archdeacons, in-
forming them of the king's prohibition and suggesting that
the pious monarch would take it kindly if the same were
done elsewhere; the bishop therefore bids his archdeacons
extend the order in respect of holy places throughout their

---

[1] 23 November 1219 : Potthast, *Regesta pontificum*, no. 6166 ; *Compilatio quinta*,
iii. 24, 1 ; *Decretales*, iii. 41, 10.
[2] Ch. 35, cf. chs. 16, 25, 31, 33 (*Epistolæ*, pp. 158–61).
[3] *Cal. papal letters*, pp. 155 (cf. chs. 16 and 33), 178 (cf. ch. 25).
[4] *Close rolls 1234–1237*, pp. 206–7.

archdeaconries.[1] Whether or no there was opposition to this, Grosseteste apparently thought it advisable to have his order reinforced. It was certainly no chance coincidence which caused Gregory IX to write to him on 26 June 1236, to 'put a stop to the practice which obtains in some churches and sacred places of his diocese, of making the house of God a house of merchandise'.[2] Armed with this letter, Grosseteste renewed the prohibition in his statutes 'auctoritate evangelica et etiam de speciali indulgentia apostolica' (ch. 33).

The most important single source upon which Grosseteste drew was the set of statutes issued by his friend Walter de Cantilupe, bishop of Worcester. Although the textual history of these statutes is obscure,[3] their core probably belongs to the month of July 1240, and so provides a later *terminus a quo* for the Lincoln statutes than we have found in its other sources. The proof of the relationship with Lincoln rests on an accumulation of evidence: at one point, Lincoln presents the text of Worcester without the literary ornaments of the latter;[4] at another, it gives more details to elucidate the sense.[5] The first chapter of the Lincoln statutes, describing the irreducible minimum of priestly learning, is ch. 24 of Worcester with only slight retouching. Nine more chapters of Lincoln show traces of the same influence, often with verbal borrowing. One of these parallels suggests that Grosseteste was also acquainted with the statutes of Cantilupe's predecessor, William de Blois: it concerns the presence of laymen in the chancel of the church during service, a topic which is not mentioned elsewhere in thirteenth-century statutes.[6] The significant passages in the Worcester and Lincoln statutes are as follows:

---

[1] *Epistolæ*, pp. 71–2.
[2] *Cal. papal letters*, p. 155; cf. J. L. Cate, 'The Church and market reform in England during the reign of Henry III', in *Medieval and historiographical essays in honor of James Westfall Thompson* (Chicago, 1938), pp. 37–41.
[3] See above, ch. iv.
[4] Cf. Worcester ch. 12 and Lincoln ch. 6.
[5] Cf. Worcester ch. 39 and Lincoln ch. 21.
[6] Except a direct loan from Lincoln, in the Durham statutes of Walter of Kirkham. Wilkins, i. 707b.

Worcester II ch. 11	Worcester III ch. 2	Lincoln ch. 45
Ut *laici* non *sedeant in* choro *inter clericos.*	Nec *laici stent in* cancell*is dum cele-brantur divina,* salva tamen *reverentia pa-tron*orum et subli-mium personarum.	Ne *laici stent* vel *sedeant inter clericos in cancell*o *dum divi-na* ibidem *celebrantur,* nisi forte ob *reveren-tia*m vel aliam ratio-nabilem causam et manifestam hoc solis *patron*is permittatur.

Before leaving the question of Grosseteste's sources, we should notice the connexion of the statutes with the bishop's earlier circular letters and with the articles for visitation in the diocese of Lincoln. The collected letters of Grosseteste include two mandates (dated by Luard with probability 1236) addressed to the archdeacons of the diocese. When, a few years later, Grosseteste framed his more comprehensive series of statutes, it was natural that he should resume some of his former injunctions in similar words.[1] The date of the visitation articles and their relationship to the statutes are somewhat more obscure. Dr. Frere commented upon these articles, describing them as

'set out for Lincoln Diocese, probably under Grossetête's influence, in 1233. This document', he says, 'is the first of a group of closely allied documents. Some similar set of articles must have been used by Grossetête himself for his visitation articles : these are not extant, but the corresponding document, the Injunctions given after visita-tion, or Constitutions, is to hand ; and it agrees not merely in con-tents and general plan but in detail and wording with (*a*) the Articles of 1233 and (*b*) the instructions given by Grossetête to his Arch-deacons in 1236.'[2]

On these articles of '1233' several observations are neces-sary. They are known only from a transcript made by Sir William Dugdale, 14 May 1647, from a manuscript then in the possession of Samuel Roper, Esq., of Lincoln's Inn and Kirby Monachorum (co. Warwick).[3] The document

---

[1] *Epistolæ*, pp. 71–6 nos. 21, 22. Cf. statutes chs. 33, 39–43.

[2] Frere, *Visitation articles*, i. 98.

[3] The transcript is the Bodleian MS. Dugdale 20 fo. 136v, taken from fo. 46v of the original, which Dugdale describes in the following terms : ' ex ms. veteri

itself bears no date: when Dugdale printed it in the second volume of Spelman's *Concilia* (ii. 192–3) he dated it 'a.d. 1230 vel circiter' and when Wilkins reprinted it from Spelman he dated it '1230' without further comment (i. 627–8); Dr. Frere states no reason for dating it *c.* 1233 (p. 87) or 1233 (p. 98). According to the title the articles embody 'Inquisitiones per archidiaconatus episcopatus Linc' in singulis archid*iaconatibus* faciende.'[1] Dr. Frere and others have assumed that Hugh of Wells, bishop of Lincoln, used these articles in his visitations.[2] But the evidence of the manuscript is not sufficient to establish this, and a comparison with the statutes of Grosseteste suggests another conclusion. The table which accompanies the statutes provided a series of short articles which could easily be turned from imperative to interrogative. It would seem as if almost the whole table was treated in this way for the purpose of a visitation, and some new questions were added. The contrary process is inconceivable when we consider the relationship between the Lincoln statutes and the Worcester statutes of 1240. The 45th article, for example—'an aliqui laici sint pertinaces ut stent in cancello cum clericis'—has only one possible place in relation to the chapters of the statutes quoted above (p. 122): it must be derived from the Lincoln statutes. While we need not reject the possibility (put forward by Frere) that Grosseteste's selection of material for his statutes was determined by visitation *comperta*, we must regard the articles rather as a derivative than as a source of the statutes.[3] It is significant that the section of Walter de Cantilupe's

---

(de tempore scilicet regis Henrici tertii) plurima ad abbatiam de Derley in comitatu Derbie necnon historica quædam continente'. The volume has not been traced. It is of some interest that this MS., like the visitation articles of 1252 and 1253, came from a monastery in the diocese of Lichfield.

[1] The printed editions read : 'a singulis archidiaconis faciendae'.

[2] Frere, p. 87 ; Stevenson, *Grosseteste*, p. 126 ; Gibbs and Lang, pp. 107, 160.

[3] The articles preserved by the Burton annalist *s.a.* 1252, 1253 are therefore probably derivatives, once removed, of Grosseteste's statutes. Cf. Frere, i. 98–104 and Gibbs and Lang, p. 160 n. 8. But it is possible that the '1230' series are a shortened form of the articles of 1253.

One detail apparently favouring the early date commonly given to the '1230' articles is the reference (art. 41) to churches dilapidated 'post Oxoniense concilium'; but this cannot refer to anything in the canons of Oxford 1222, and must in fact be a mistake for the 'post Londoniense concilium' (cf. London 1237, ch. 1) which appears in article 18 of 1253 (*Annales monastici*, i. 308).

statutes relating to clerical manners was certainly intended as the basis of visitation articles.[1]

To sum up the evidence obtainable from the manuscripts and the sources : the ascription of these Lincoln statutes to Grosseteste seems justified by internal evidence and by the state of the surviving texts. They were not originally published in a synod. Designed purely for the instruction of parish priests, they deal with details concerning the ministry in as concise a way as possible, without attempting either to repeat or to supplement the canons. Consequently they found a fitting place in the volumes of homiletic tracts which were diffused in large numbers in this period. Their issue, possibly as a circular letter to archdeacons, may be dated after July 1240, and the evidence of derivatives which remain to be discussed will suggest a date very soon afterwards.

DERIVATIVES FROM GROSSETESTE'S STATUTES

The list of manuscripts of the Lincoln statutes itself points to their diffusion outside the limits of the diocese ; and when we take into account the influential position which Grosseteste occupied in the English episcopate of his day, it is easy to see why his statutes should be borrowed for official republication as well as for private reading. Probably the amount of borrowing will never be fully estimated, for bishops and archdeacons alike may have used the series without modification. The version represented by MSS. D, G, X, and Y, which has been mentioned above, may emanate from Lincoln or from any other diocese ; for we cannot attach much importance to the fact that the document which immediately precedes this version in all known texts cites the synodal statutes of Salisbury. But the diffusion can in other cases be fairly clearly traced. Besides the statutes for the Durham peculiars, in which several chapters of Grosseteste are incorporated in a series mostly drawn from Poore,[2] Grosseteste's statutes were soon taken over practically *in extenso* in the dioceses of Norwich, Ely, and Durham. Nor did their influence stop there. From Norwich they

[1] Cf. above p. 90.
[2] Cf. above, p. 70. Chs. 1, 12, 44, 21, 3, 34 of Grosseteste are copied.

passed soon to Winchester, and between 1245 and 1259 Fulk Basset, bishop of London, made use of either the Norwich or the Winchester series.[1]

Statutes of the dioceses of Norwich and Winchester.

Among Wilkins's most important additions to the synodal statutes published by Spelman are those for the diocese of Norwich which he took from the Bodleian manuscript, Digby 99. His text was copied by Mansi, and many later historians have used the statutes. Unfortunately they have generally failed to notice what Thomas Tanner had noticed:[2] that these Norwich statutes are dependent on the Lincoln series of Grosseteste.[3] This provides a valuable clue to the textual history of the Norwich statutes. For the manuscripts of Norwich which Wilkins did not know and the Winchester second series of statutes (also unknown to Wilkins and to later scholars) reveal in a most interesting way the process of accretion and modification whereby synodal statutes were formed.

The relevant manuscripts are as follows:

Norwich.

A. Dublin, Trinity Coll., MS. E. 2. 22 (no. 526) p. 116.

Title (a running title throughout the series): 'Norwyc''. *Inc.*: 'Debentes de vobis . . .'. Written in a late xiv c. hand in a volume of which the first section (pp. 1–130), originally distinct, contains legatine and provincial canons of the xiii and xiv c. The provenance of the volume is unknown.

B. Oxford, Balliol Coll., MS. 301 fo. 197r.

Title: 'Incipiunt constituciones synodales Norwicensis diocesis.' *Inc.*: 'Debentes de vobis . . .'. Breaks off imperfectly at '. . . initium Septembris singulis annis' (cf. Wilkins, i. 735b). Written in a book-hand of *c.* 1400 at the end of a volume which also contains the Sext and legatine and provincial canons of the xiii and xiv c. The provenance of the volume is unknown.

C. Durham, Bishop Cosin's Libr., MS. V. v. 7 fo. [137r].

Title (a running title throughout the series): 'Statuta synodalia.' *Inc.*: 'Debentes de vobis . . .'. Written in a xiv c. hand in a volume which contains tracts on the sacraments, &c., and extracts from legatine and provincial canons, written in several xiv c. hands. The provenance of the volume is unknown.

---

[1] Cf. above p. 84.   [2] *Bibliotheca britannica*, p. 349.
[3] Cf. *Vetus liber archid. eliensis*, pp. 215–16 ; Gibbs and Lang, p. 112.

D. Oxford, Bodleian, Digby MS. 99 fo. lv.

No title. At end: 'Expliciunt. Statut' synodal' alias in synodo promulgat' per Walterum quondam Norwyc' episcopum et additiones postea per Symonem successorem suum firmiter precipimus observari.' [Wilkins treats this as a title to the foregoing statutes, reading: 'Expliciunt statuta synodalia . . . *quæ* firmiter . . .'.] *Inc.*: 'Debentes de vobis . . .'. Written in a late xiv c. hand preceding the 'Stimulus conciencie' of Richard Rolle. This is the text printed by Wilkins, *Concilia*, i. 731–6. The volume belonged formerly to Fr. Johannes Stanys, monk of Thetford.

E. London, Public Record Office, Aug. misc. books 18 (E 315/18) fo. 43r. (The leaves are out of order: the correct order being fo. 47v, fos. 43r–46v, fos. 48r–49r.)

Title (fo. 47v): 'Statuta synodalia.' Near the end, preceding the excommunication clauses of Oxford 1222: 'Hec sunt statuta sinodalia composita a Simone Norwic' episcopo.' *Inc.*: 'Debentes de vobis . . .'. Written in two early xiv c. hands, bound with miscellaneous rentals and memoranda relating to the estates of Battle Abbey (cf. Deputy Keeper's *8th Report on the Public Records*, app. ii. 146). The second hand begins with the chapter 'Precipimus etiam quod' (below, p. 131).

Winchester.

The Winchester statutes are known only from a single copy, hitherto unnoticed:

Liber evidenciarum C of the Dean and Chapter of Salisbury, fo. 397v*b* (formerly fo. 188v).

Title: 'Statuta synodalia.' A xv c. hand has added on fo. 398r, 'Wynton''. *Inc.*: 'Debentes de vobis . . .'. Written in a late xiii c. hand at the end of a small group of provincial and diocesan statutes, immediately following the canons of Lambeth 1261.

The ascriptions in the Norwich manuscripts raise more problems than they solve. The clearest statement is that of Wilkins: that they are synodal statutes of Bishop Walter Suffield (1245–57) with additions by Bishop Simon Walton (1258–66); but this clarity is only achieved by emending the D text. It receives some support from the earlier and better text, E, which describes the statutes as those of Bishop Simon, although they have manifestly undergone a good deal of revision. We have therefore some grounds for regarding the death of Bishop Simon as a final date for the material in D and E: and these texts include between them all that is found in the others. The problem still remains to determine at what date the original core of the statutes was published, and whether Walter Suffield was its author or not. There is the further problem of distinguishing the dates of the several additions.

Unless some new, well-authenticated text comes to light, these problems will never all be solved. There is, however, sufficient evidence to justify conjectures about the original core, though it is obscure and difficult to state in the absence of a printed edition of the texts.

In these synodal statutes of Norwich we certainly possess a set of statutes issued by a thirteenth-century bishop, to which additions were subsequently made. But the state of the texts does not permit us to distinguish one compact original edition with one compact appendix. Additions may have been made, and probably were made, in many successive synods, and those persons who attended the synods and who wrote the copies whence come the existing ones added the new material at varying points in the midst, or at the end, of the first set. The five manuscripts A–E differ widely from each other, both as regards their contents and the order in which they present it. Nor can one hope that any of these texts represents an official edition, an authentic record of the synodal statutes declared by a bishop of Norwich in any one synod. But if we cannot hope to discover the relationship of these texts exactly, at least some indications of what constitute the first form and the last can be had from a comparison of the texts with each other, especially if we invoke the aid of the related statutes of Lincoln and Winchester II. On this basis the five manuscripts of Norwich can be made to yield a version showing (*a*) an early recension of the statutes, (*b*) the whole body of later additions.

The dependence of Norwich upon Lincoln is clear. The original Norwich legislator adopted almost all of the Lincoln statutes, in the same sequence as he found them, making slight modifications.[1] The relationship of Lincoln and

---

[1] The important omissions are Lincoln chs. 7, part of 14, 22, 35, 37–9, 43–7. Besides entirely new chapters introduced in Norwich, a small addition was probably made immediately to ch. 16: Lincoln reads ' vel ballivas teneant ', to which

Norwich to Winchester II can also be established. Unlike the Ely statutes (whose editors supposed them to be based on Norwich, when in fact they are derived independently from Lincoln), Winchester II only knows those parts of Lincoln which appear in Norwich, and knows them in the Norwich form. Therefore, there was a common intermediary or, more probably, Winchester II is derived from Norwich. But Winchester knows Norwich in an early (if not the original) edition, and its form gives a clue to the order of the existing Norwich texts.

Some modifications of Lincoln which figure in certain Norwich texts did not appear in the first edition of Norwich; this is shown by the concurrence of Lincoln and Winchester with Norwich D or AD against the other Norwich texts ABCE or BCE. In one instance (Lincoln ch. 24), Norwich B shows a text bearing many marks of a late recension which yet failed to incorporate the additions found in ACDE; it remains fortunately to confirm the view that Winchester is derived from an early form of Norwich and at the same time to prove that neither A nor B nor D provides that early form intact. On the other hand, it seems that Winchester does not copy the *first* edition of Norwich. For Norwich AD preserve a chapter which agrees with Lincoln ch. 36, whereas Winchester follows the modified form of the chapter found in BCE:

Lincoln ch. 36 and Norwich AD	Norwich BCE	Winchester
Inhibemus quoque ne aliqui sacerdotes celebrent de [D *cum*] *aceto.*	*Inhibemus quoque ne aliqui sacerdotes celebrent* [E quis *sacerdos celebret*] *de* [BE *cum*] *aceto* seu de [E neque cum] *vino corrupto.*	*Inhibemus* etiam *ne aliqui*s *sacerdos celebret de vino aceto* vel *corrupto.*

Yet it is true that, of the remaining manuscripts, A and D probably provide the best material for reconstructing the original edition of Norwich; and for these reasons: as D

Norwich adds 'vel earum firmas'. Mention of apostolic authority is omitted by Norwich from those chapters where Lincoln invoked it by reason of special papal letters.

(Wilkins's text) at present stands, it is avowedly a mixture, 'Statuta synodalia alias in synodo promulgata per Walterum quondam Norwyc' episcopum, et additiones postea per Symonem successorem suum'. Bishop Simon's additions might, to be sure, be inserted in the midst of the earlier statutes, so as to leave the ending unaltered; and some colour is given to this suggestion by the resemblance of parts of the last chapters in D (Wilkins, i. 735*b*) to ch. 46 of Lincoln. Their contents—excommunication clauses—are also suitable to their position. But the arrangement of these chapters in D is apparently muddled (AC offer a more satisfactory form) and another interpretation seems preferable. At an earlier point in D comes a chapter which might well have been the concluding one in a series: that which bids rural deans keep and provide copies of the synodal statutes (Wilkins, i. 734*b*–735*a*). And this is in fact the point at which the A text ends, with a version of the chapter which reads like an earlier form than those of D and CE:

A	D	CE
Et quia non proficit sepius legere et non intelligere, statuimus ut unusquisque decanus statuta synodalia penes se habeat, et copiam fieri procuret in singulis ecclesiis sui decanatus. Et ecclesie in quibus non inventa fuerint tempore visitationis suspendantur. Expliciunt constituciones Norwyc'.	*Et quia non proficit sepius legere et non intelligere, statuimus* [*ut*] *unusquisque decanus statuta synodalia penes se habeat, et copiam fieri procuret in singulis ecclesiis sui decanatus, ita quod si dominus episcopus vel eius officialis per aliquam ecclesiam transitum fecerit et statuta in ea non invenerit,* ipsi per cuius negligenciam steterit quominus statuta synodalia in ea invenianteur, penam infligat.	*Et quia non proficit sepius legere et non intelligere, statuimus ut unusquisque decanus statuta synodalia penes se habeat, et copiam fieri procuret in singulis ecclesiis sui decanatus, ita quod si dominus episcopus vel eius officialis per aliquam ecclesiam transitum fecerit et statuta* synodalia *in ea non invenerit,* decano loci si negligens reperiatur et eciam rectoribus et vicariis necnon et presbiteris ecclesiarum cum per officialem ipsum, si ab eis fuerit requisitus dictorum statutorum copiam habere [C et] non poterunt [C poterint] penam [E pena] infligant. [*sic*][1]

[1] The B text omits this chapter. Neither of the slightly different readings of C and E can be construed without emendation.

Admittedly, A, as it stands, bears marks of revision; but the supposition that this chapter formed the end of an early edition is strengthened by several considerations. It is worth devoting a little space to these, especially as they offer a clue to the subsequent elaboration of the statutes.

In the first place, all the borrowings from Lincoln occur within the section preceding this chapter in D.[1]

Secondly, all the borrowings by Winchester occur within the same section, with the exception of one chapter of Norwich which does not appear in Lincoln or in the D text, although it is found in ABCE:

Reliquias de novo inventas publicare nemo presumat nisi prius auctoritate Romani pontificis fuerint approbate.[2]

This addition occurs at the same point in ABCE and in Winchester, and derives from the same Fourth Lateran decree as the following chapter, ' Nullus predicator questuarius . . .' (Wilkins, i. 734a). These facts suggest that its absence from D may be accidental.

Thirdly, despite the many variations of order in the different texts and despite the fact that chapters additional to the first edition seem to be indifferently inserted in the body of the original text or tacked on to the end, the same chapters in all manuscripts precede the chapter ' Et quia non proficit' (above, p. 129), and these chapters are approximately in the sequence of D. The order of the chapters in Winchester II is the same. These chapters, however, bear some traces of rearrangement. Quite apart from omissions from certain manuscripts which may be ascribed to late cancellation or omission by error,[3] three chapters

---

[1] With the exception of the excommunication clauses already mentioned.

[2] The B text is given here; the only significant variants are: E reads 'nostra' for ' Romani pontificis'; Winchester reads ' publice' for ' publicare'. Fourth Lat. Council ch. 62 reads : ' publice venerari '.

[3] Ch. 19 of Lincoln appears in ABD (cf. Wilkins, i. 733a) and may have been cancelled in the archetype of CE, but this is not likely: it was probably omitted in error, as also Lincoln chs. 9 and 10 from C. The following chapters are found, not only in AD and D respectively, but both also in Winchester ; so that their absence from the other texts can best be accounted for by cancellation :

Quilibet autem rector ecclesie honestum et ydoneum vicarium habeat qui, sicut expedierit, curam gerat animarum. [Wilkins, i. 733a, ad fin.]

Tugurria et domus laicorum erecta in cimiteriis tempore guerre amoveantur, propter inmunditiam fornicationis vitandam, et propter occupationem cimiteriorum. [Wilkins, i. 734b.]

show such variety of order as to suggest that they were not part of the original series:

(i) Ut autem habitus diversitas clericos a laicis faciat discrepare, statuimus etiam. firmiter precipientes ut officiales, decani et sub-decani in suis capitulis et congregacionibus clericorum coram suis prelatis capis clausis utantur. Et ne facilitas venie locum tribuat delinquendi, si [E sed] quos huius statuti inveniemus transgressores sciant se absque gracia et favore graviter esse puniendos . . . noverit se suspensum.

(ii) Precipimus eciam quod nec abbates nec priores obligent se vel domum suam pro seculari [E secularum] persona sine nostra licencia speciali. Pensiones et decimas separatas quas viri religiosi qui non sunt de episcopatu nostro percipiunt in nostra dyocesi in manus nostras sequestramus, inhibentes eos administracionem earundem donec de iure eorum coram nobis docuerint evidenter. [E text, fo. 46r, cf. Wilkins, i. 734*a*.]

(iii) Dolentes referimus quod dum nostri subditi statuta nostra synodalia non observant seipsos illaqueant nosque contempnere non formidant . . . tractantes cum eisdem. [Wilkins, i. 734*b*.]

The first of these chapters appears after the ch. 'Nullus predicator questuarius' in B, after no. ii above in C, and in DE following ch. 25 of the Lincoln series. The various positions of no. ii in the series and its omission by A likewise suggest late insertion. That the omission of no. iii from B and its transposition in CE have the same explanation is confirmed by its substance. It appears to refer to an earlier statute, which may be identified with the ch. 'Cumque non solum' (Wilkins, i. 732*b* = Lincoln ch. 11). Particularly significant is the absence of these three chapters from the borrowed series in Winchester. The absence of the following chapter from Winchester as well as from Lincoln suggests that this too was missing from the earliest edition of Norwich:

Et quia scriptura testante iustus ex fide vivit, ut articuli fidei plenius exponantur, statuimus precipientes ut quilibet sacerdos parochialis· singulis diebus [D *adds* dominicis] ad primam et ad completorium orationem dominicam et simbolum dicat coram suis parochianis in audientia distincte et aperte ad intelligendum. [Conflated text, cf. Wilkins, i. 732*a*.]

The final piece of evidence of the growth of the Norwich statutes is the one demonstrable instance of the substitution of one chapter for another in a later edition. It is interesting to see what happens: AB gives the chapter on clerical garb as quoted above (p. 131); C gives a different version:

Ut autem habitus diversitas clericos a laicis faciat discrepare, et habitus exterior conveniat officio et honore, statuimus firmiter iniungentes ut universi decani et vice-decani in suis capitulis et ubi coram eis iudicium exercetur coramque suis prelatis ac in congregacionibus clericorum cappis clausis decenter utantur. Ne vero facilitas venie incentivum prebeat delinquendi, adicimus [C audivimus] statuendo quod qui huius constitucionis nostre transgressor existat per nos se sciat absque favore vel gracia puniendum. [Cf. Wilkins, i. 735*a*.]

DE contain both of these chapters, when presumably the first ought to have been cancelled. As regards the order, D puts the second chapter after the chapter on rural deans (above, p. 129), so that it stands distinct from what we think to be the first version. In E, on the other hand, it precedes this ending, with much other material not contained in what may be termed the 'core' of D.

The statement of this evidence has necessarily been somewhat involved. The conclusion can at least be stated simply. It seems reasonable to suppose that the earliest edition of Norwich contained the core of the D text printed by Wilkins with the probable addition of the chapter on relics (above, p. 130). The core of the D text included all that precedes the chapter on rural deans (Wilkins, i. 734*b*–735*a*), with the exception of the four chapters quoted above: 'Ut autem habitus', 'Precipimus etiam quod', 'Dolentes referimus quod dum', 'Et quia scriptura'.[1]

No general scheme can be propounded for the sequence of additions and alterations, and it seems impossible to assign even approximate dates to the changes. Furthermore, until an adequate edition of the statutes is published one cannot present the evidence in an intelligible form. Only a few views on the relationship of the manuscripts seem in place here, and they must be taken on trust.

In general, AD stand apart from BCE, and frequently

---

[1] Lincoln ch. 24 remained in its original form, not as it appears in ACDE; Lincoln ch. 30 likewise, as in AD and Winchester; Lincoln ch. 34 likewise, as in D and Winchester; Lincoln ch. 36, as in AD. The chapter 'A sanctis patribus' (Wilkins, i. 734*b*) was in the BCE form, and the final chapter in the form of A, quoted above, p. 129.

preserve the earlier forms of statutes which were later revised.
The latter group shows a division between B and CE. The
general likeness of C and E indeed suggests that they may
descend from the same archetype, a suggestion which would
not hold good for any of the other texts. In five instances C
and E agree in contents against the other texts, their order
is practically identical, and their differences can be explained
by the errors or retouchings of copyists. While CE each
contains more material than any other single manuscript,
their only peculiar additions are two:

(i) After ch. 26 of Lincoln, copied in all the Norwich
texts, C adds: 'et ex nunc decrevimus tales vacare'
(fo. 140r).[1]

(ii) After ch. 16 of Lincoln, copied in all the Norwich
texts, C adds: 'Inhibemus quoque districtius ne quis
sacerdos nec a se missas vel tricenalia celebrari faciat
vel alias lucrativas iniungat hiis qui sibi confitentur
penitencias' (fo. 139r).

It is perhaps worth emphasizing that it does not necessarily
follow from the fullness of CE that their version as a whole
is later in date than those represented by other manuscripts.

A few peculiarities of the manuscripts in respect of particular chapters may be mentioned here, as they illustrate
very clearly the ways of revision and corruption in synodal
texts. The CE addition to Lincoln ch. 26 which has just
been quoted seems to be a temporary administrative order,
which was probably in the original edition only and escaped
cancellation here. The other CE addition repeats in substance ch. 27 of Lincoln, which is common to all the Norwich
texts, and is inserted between two chapters taken from consecutive chapters of Lincoln (16, 17). It can only be explained as a late substitution for Lincoln ch. 27, which ought
to have been cancelled in the archetype of CE. Of other
variants, BCE probably omitted the end of the chapter 'A
sanctis patribus' as an otiose expression of piety by the
first legislator; B may have omitted by haplography the
chapters 'Dolentes referimus quod dum' and 'Adhec omnes
tam prelatos' (Wilkins, i. 734b, 735b), for in CE they occur
together before the chapter 'Dolentes referimus quod

---

[1] E gives corrupt readings of this and the following chapter.

nonnulli'. The omission of the last chapters of the D text by B may be explained by the fact that their contents (the excommunication clauses of Oxford) were unnecessary in a volume which contains the legatine and provincial canons.

So far the only source of the Norwich statutes which has been mentioned is the Lincoln series. But this accounts for rather less than half of Norwich. What was the character of the additional material and whence was it drawn? The strictly pastoral character of Grosseteste's statutes is exceeded by Norwich; the Norwich compilers add a good many new injunctions on similar matters, but swell the statutes with orders to the archdeacons and deans, with other purely administrative orders, and with chapters relating to tithe. Much of this material, while it contains little that is unusual, does not follow slavishly any identifiable canons. Such copying as can be observed comes mainly from the Fourth Lateran Council[1] and the legatine Council of London 1237.[2]

A few passages show that the bishop of Norwich knew the works of others of his English contemporaries besides Grosseteste. Like Grosseteste he probably had the statutes of Walter de Cantilupe before him, for four chapters amongst those outside the original core of Norwich are copied verbatim.[3] Having regard to the great reputation of Richard Poore's statutes, one is surprised to find that, although the bishop of Norwich apparently knew them, he only drew upon them very slightly.[4] A parallel is also found with the Salisbury statutes of Robert of Bingham:

Salisbury (fo. 125v)	Norwich (Wilkins, i. 734*a*).
Ne igitur dum predam sustinemus predones efficiamur, *pensiones et decimas* quascunque, *quas religiosi* seu alii quicunque sine iusto titulo *in nostra diocesi percipiunt*, presentis sinodi auctoritate *sequestramus*.	*Pensiones et decimas* separatas, quas viri *religiosi* qui non sunt de episcopatu nostro *percipiunt in nostra diocesi*, in manus nostras sequestramus.

---

[1] The following chapters are quoted: 14, 18, 19, 62, and there is a reminiscence of ch. 66. Cf. Gibbs and Lang, p. 112.

[2] The following chapters are quoted: 7, 10, 20, 26.

[3] Three parallels to Worcester, chs. 13, 23, 44, will be found in Wilkins's text of Norwich, *Concilia*, i. 735. A parallel to Worcester ch. 65 occurs in text B of Norwich, fo. 198v.

[4] Cf. Poore, ch. 66, and Wilkins's text of Norwich, i. 734*a*.

The likeness here, as in the other parallel passages, suggests that Norwich is the derivative; but since the relevant chapter is probably not part of the original core it does not assist us to date either the Salisbury or the Norwich series.

None of this additional source-material, in fact, carries us any farther towards establishing dates. We have to rely solely upon the connexion of Norwich with Lincoln and Winchester. Resuming that evidence, we may now make a conjecture about the date of at least the core of the Norwich statutes.

The Lincoln statutes were issued after the Worcester series of July 1240 and before Grosseteste's death in 1253. The Winchester second series introduces the festivals of St. Edmund Rich and is thus to be dated in or after 1247. Since it does not mention St. Richard de Wich (whose festival appears in Winchester III), it may probably be dated before 1261. An even earlier limit, 1258, is proved by the borrowings from Winchester II in the Wells series. This gives as extreme time-limits for the original Norwich statutes the years 1241 and 1258, and since we have the authority of the D text for supposing that Simon Walton, bishop-elect from 1 August 1257, only added to earlier statutes, the original core must be the work of either Bishop William de Raleigh, bishop of Norwich 1239–43, or Bishop Walter Suffield, 1244–57. If the dubious authority of the D text is to be accepted completely, Suffield was author of the original Norwich series, and this was used in the diocese of Winchester either by Raleigh, after his translation, or by Aymer de Valence who, after being bishop-elect for ten years, was consecrated at Anagni in May 1260 and died in December the same year. But the alternative is more attractive. There is nothing surprising in the attribution of the Norwich series to Suffield if he enlarged and revised his predecessor's statutes. The most tempting explanation of the parentage of the statutes is the authorship of William de Raleigh for the statutes both of Norwich and of Winchester. He was closely acquainted with Robert Grosseteste; he was a vigorous administrator; what more natural than that he should frame statutes based on Lincoln, and use them again after his translation to Winchester? If this hypothesis is accepted, and it seems probable, we have limited the period within which the Lincoln statutes appeared to 1240 × 1243, and must date Norwich 1240 × 1243 with additions up to 1266; Winchester II falls within the years 1247 × 1249.[1]

Statutes for the diocese of Ely.

In 1917 Dr. Feltoe and Mr. Ellis Minns published *statuta synodalia* of the diocese of Ely, from an early fourteenth-century text in a register of the archdeacons of Ely.[2] The editors presume that the Ely statutes were produced by Bishop Hugh of Balsham (1257–86), and conclude 'that they are closely modelled on or allied to' the Norwich statutes as printed by Wilkins.[3] These statements need emending. The reasons are slender for definitely attributing to Hugh of Balsham either this recension of the statutes or any other; and their relationship to the Norwich series is through common parentage, for they both derive from Lincoln. The manuscripts upon which these conclusions depend are:

A. Cambridge, Gonville and Caius Coll., MS. 204 p. 29.

No title; at end: 'Expliciunt statuta synodalia.' *Inc.*: 'Ad honorem domini . . .'. Written in an early xiv c. hand in a register of the archdeacons of Ely. The text printed by Feltoe and Minns. A xvii c. transcript of it occurs in the Bodleian manuscript, Rawl. B. 278 fo. 61v.

B. Cambridge, Univ. Libr., Add. MS. 3468 fo. 46v.

Title: 'Statuta synodi Eliensis diocesis.' *Inc.*: 'Ad honorem domini . . .'. Written in a xv c. hand in a register containing legal and fiscal material, compiled by officials of the bishops of Ely, xv and xvi c. The volume belonged to Francis Blomefield 1728, William Cole 1752, and Sir Thomas Phillipps (no. 8121).

C. Oxford, New Coll., MS. 98 fo. 142r.

No title. *Inc.*: 'Ad honorem domini . . .'. Written in a xiii c. hand at the end of a volume which contains (in another xiii c. hand) works of William de Montibus. From accounts and lists of manorial tenants at the end we may infer that the volume belonged to Ely Cathedral Priory *c.* 1300. It was given to New College by William of Wykeham.

Whereas A and B give similar texts of the statutes, C is

---

[1] William de Raleigh is said to have died at Tours in Sept. 1250, after staying there about eleven months (Matt. Paris, *Chron. maj.*, v. 178–9; *Ann. Mon.*, ii. 92).
[2] *Vetus liber archidiaconi eliensis*, p. 9. [3] *Ibid.*, p. 215.

a distinct version intermediate between Lincoln and the AB version of Ely. The chief difference between AB and C lies in the latter's omissions. (i) C omits the introductory words which name the bishop of Ely: 'In primis nos N., permissione divina episcopus Elyensis'.[1] (ii) C also omits a group of chapters, found in AB but not in Lincoln, which deal with the examination of the parochial clergy, with their duty as confessors, with baptism in necessity, and with the commemoration of St. Etheldreda.[2] (iii) C stops short of a long section at the end of AB.[3]

These omissions do not involve any of the borrowings from Lincoln; on the other hand, C copies Lincoln (and, in a corrupt passage, extends it) where AB work over the ground more fully and introduce the first group of chapters mentioned above.[4] In other details, besides, C agrees with Lincoln against AB and is thus proved to be no mere abridgement of the latter. The question then arises: Can we regard C as an earlier version of Ely synodal statutes?

The references to the bishop of Ely and to St. Etheldreda are both missing, and there is no suggestion of synodal authority or publication. Probability still favours the Ely ascription. C's variations from the Lincoln original do not agree with the Norwich variants; they do agree with those of Ely; the text is an early one and the book belonged to Ely. The very re-editing of the C text in AB offers a presumption in favour of successive synodal publications. Moreover, the C text may not give the original series untouched. That is suggested by the uncomfortable sequence of the Lincoln peroration and the chapters on clandestine marriage and clerical garb. For these chapters resume subjects touched on in the preceding statutes,[5] and it is improbable that they were issued at the same time.

---

[1] *Vetus liber*, p. 9.

[2] *Ibid.*, pp. 9–10: 'Item statuimus propter animarum pericula . . . specialis memoria habeatur.'

[3] At '. . . vestibus non utantur' (*ibid.*, p. 14), omitting 'Item quoniam dignum est . . .' to the end.

[4] The passage in C reads: '. . . septem ecclesiastica sacramenta, et hii qui sunt sacerdotes maxime parochiales sciant que exiguntur ad vere confessionis et penitencie sacramentum, formaque [*sic*] baptizandi exercere illud [*sic*] nisi subfuerit necessitas, scilicet timor mortis pueri baptizandi. Sciat etiam quilibet . . .'. Cf. Lincoln ch. 1 and *Vetus liber*, p. 9.   [5] *Vetus liber*, p. 14, cf. p. 12.

We therefore conclude that the original Ely series was taken from the Lincoln series with only slight modifications.[1] At a later date, the chapters just mentioned were added. This constituted the C text in its present state. Still later, new chapters were added near the beginning and at the end and the AB version came into being.

The sources of these statutes, other than the Lincoln series, do not enable us to fix narrow time-limits to the several versions. Neither the original text nor the addition in C contains anything later than Lincoln; for the alteration of 'Council of London' to 'Council of Lyon' in text A[2] is incorrect: London appears correctly in BC and the reference is to ch. 14 of Otto's council of 1237. Some of the additions peculiar to AB can be dated after the legatine Council of London 1268. The corrupt reading of A, 'constitucionem beati Gregorii'[3] is replaced in B by 'constitucionem legati', and refers to chapter 2 of Ottobono's council. The passage relating to the religious orders is mostly derived from the decretal *Cum ad monasterium*,[4] but Ottobono is also mentioned, and described as 'quondam legatus'. From all this it may be conjectured that the original series and its first revision (C) were issued between 1241 and 1268, and that the revision represented by AB took shape between 1268 and the early fourteenth century.

Statutes of Walter of Kirkham, bishop of Durham (1258 × 1260).
F. Durham, Cathedral Libr., MS. B. iv. 41 fo. 152r (formerly fo. 170r).
    Title: 'Prologus constitucionum synodalium Dunolm'.' (And, following the prologue: 'Hic incipiunt constituciones Walteri episcopi Dunolm'.'). *Inc.*: 'Cum sit ars artium . . .'. Written in a xiv c. bookhand in a volume described above, p. 67. This may be the text printed by Spelman (*Concilia*, ii. 294), although he more probably used M. Wilkins (*Concilia*, i. 702) used F and Spelman's edition.
L. Brit. Mus., Lansdowne MS. 397 fo. 258r (formerly fo. 229r).
    Title: 'Hic incipiunt constituciones domini Walteri episcopi Dunelm'.' (A xvi c. hand adds 'Kirkham' after 'Walteri'). *Inc.*:

[1] Omissions are Lincoln ch. 2 part i, chs. 7, 9–12, 15–20, 22–3, 25–6, 35–7, 39 part i, 40, 44–5.
[2] *Vetus liber*, p. 14.   [3] *Ibid.*, p. 10.
[4] Which had been published in England by the legate Otto among his statutes for the Black Monks in 1238. Cf. Matt. Paris, *Chron. maj.*, iii. 505–6.

'Cum sit ars artium . . .'. Written in a xiv c. hand in a volume described above, p. 68.

M. Durham, Cathedral Libr., MS. C. ii. 13 fo. 268r.

Title : 'Prologus constitucionum synodalium Dunelm'.' (And, following the prologue : 'Hic incipiunt constituciones Walteri episcopi Dunelm'.'). *Inc.*: 'Cum sit ars artium . . .'. A text closely related to F. Written in a mid xiv c. charter hand in a volume described above, p. 68. This was probably the original of Spelman's edition.

N. Oxford, Jesus Coll., MS. 78 fo. 191r (formerly fo. 185r).

A xvii c. transcript of F, by Dom Augustine Baker.

These statutes of Walter of Kirkham were confessedly intended as a supplement to the comprehensive series published by his predecessor, Richard Poore. But just as at Salisbury Robert of Bingham found it useful to cover some of the same ground as Poore's statutes, here abridging and there extending, so Kirkham produced a more compact and manageable series than Poore provided. He also went beyond Poore to deal with questions which were probably of special importance in the northern diocese: questions of chapels in large parishes, and of the duties of archdeacons and rural deans. Poore's statutes form the background of Kirkham's. They are safeguarded in the prologue: 'statutis bone memorie Ricardi quondam episcopi Dunelmensis quatenus observata fuerint et admissa in suo robore duraturis';[1] priests are recommended to read chapters 2 and 53;[2] a penalty contained in ch. 9 is invoked explicitly;[3] and other sections of Kirkham recall, without quoting, Poore chapters 10, 14, 43, 109. But for a short, practical corpus of injunctions for the parochial clergy Kirkham went to his contemporary Grosseteste, and incorporated more of Grosseteste's statutes than are to be found in the statutes of either Norwich or Ely. The omissions are few and mostly unimportant.[4] While the order of the original Lincoln series has been revised and some chapters of it are entirely rewritten or expanded, it forms, as at Norwich and at Ely, the core of the new statutes.

---

[1] Wilkins, i. 704a. Cf. above, p. 10 n. 4.
[2] *Ibid.*, i. 704b, 705a.   [3] *Ibid.*, i. 706a.
[4] Lincoln chs. 19–21, 25–6, 35, 37–8, 43.

The borrowings from other sources are not extensive. The Fourth Lateran Council is quoted or referred to at several points; the orders for dedicating churches and chapels and about the residence of rectors[1] are reminiscent of the Council of London 1237. That Kirkham was acquainted with Cantilupe's statutes for Worcester is suggested by identity of matter at two points accompanied by some agreements in wording:

Worcester III ch. 17	Durham, L (fo. 260v, cf. Wilkins, i. 707*b*)
Nec extranea persona de qua per denunciacionem constare non pótest an legitima sit *ad contrahendum matrimonium* aliquatenus *admittatur, nisi* super hoc per literas prelati sub cuius iurisdictione prius steterat fidem faciat episcopo vel archidiacono loci vel officiali eorundem.	Prudenter vero caveant rectores vicarii et sacerdotes parochiales ne aliquis extraneus *ad contrahendum matrimonium* in eorum parochiis *admittatur, nisi* prius ipsis de eius habilitate legitimis constiterit documentis.

Worcester III ch. 56	Durham, L (fo. 259v and Wilkins, i. 705*b*)
Precipimus eciam quod *viri religiosi vicarios presentent* ad ecclesias suas quas habent in proprios usus *in quibus nondum sunt vicarii constituti.*	*Precipimus* et iniungimus ut [*viri religiosi*] *vicarios* ad suas ecclesias *in quibus nondum sunt vicarii constituti,* nobis personas ydoneas re*presentent.*

Finally, the introduction to the excommunication clauses of Durham can hardly be independent of the title and preamble to the articles drawn up in 1258 at Archbishop Boniface's Council of Merton or Westminster:[2]

Merton or Westminster	Durham (Wilkins, i. 708*a*)
Articuli qui *dissimulari* non *poss*unt absque *interitu salutis eterne* animarumque periculo et subversione ecclesiastice libertatis ac ecclesiasticarum personarum preiudicio manifesto. Cum *ecclesia anglicana* non solum contra iura divina et	Quia *ecclesia anglicana oppressionibus* suarum libertatum in pluribus articulis *multipliciter* deformatur, quos *dissimulare non poss*umus sine *interitu salutis eterne.* . . .

[1] It may be noted that Kirkham does not refer to the papal mandate on the subject addressed to him 18 Jan. 1255; cf. *Cal. papal letters*, i. 310.

[2] Wilkins, i. 736*b*; cf. *Eng. Hist. Rev.*, l. 402–3.

statuta canonica sed eciam contra
libertates a regibus, principibus,
et aliis regni magnatibus sibi
concessas . . . *oppressionibus* nefa-
riis *multipliciter* attrita sit. . . .

The context of the passage in the articles of Merton
makes it extremely unlikely that it was borrowed from
Kirkham's statutes, even could we suppose that a council
at which the bishop was probably not present would use
the wording of his synodal statutes. So we are provided
with a means of fixing the date of the statutes (at least in
their present form) within quite narrow limits. There is
little information about Kirkham's activity as diocesan.
Prominent in earlier days as a royal servant, he seems to
have withdrawn from public affairs before the critical period
of 'baronial reform', and by then he was an old man. It
was then, it seems, that he held the synod in which the statutes
were published: between the council of June 1258 and his
death in August 1260.

VI

CONCLUSION

IT is to be hoped that readers of this volume will attach more importance to the details in the foregoing chapters than to these final generalities. The statement in the Preface should warn the historian against expecting much from a Conclusion. For the material which has been examined in these studies was not selected because it seemed to form a compact body or to provide by itself a key to the history of the thirteenth-century Church. It was selected for treatment because any profitable historical discussion must be contingent upon a solution of the textual problems. Those aspects of the historical subject which have been well treated before were purposely omitted; and only some of the diocesan statutes which present problems of text or affiliation have been mentioned.

To obtain a general view of the episcopal legislation of thirteenth-century England one would have to take into account the statutes for the archdeaconry of London attributed to Bishop Roger Niger,[1] the statutes sent out to his archdeacons by Alexander of Stavensby, bishop of Coventry and Lichfield, the third series of Salisbury statutes, printed by Wilkins as the work of Bishop Giles of Bridport,[2] the second series of Chichester, and finally the great series issued by Bishop Peter Quivil at Exeter in 1287. In addition, there are the so-called *legenda* of Oxford and the dubious *statuta quædam* found in a Burton Abbey manuscript.[3] From one point of view, the episcopal statutes are

---

[1] Printed from Liber L (MS. W.D. 4), fo. 63, in the muniments of the Dean and Chapter of St. Paul's, by W. Sparrow Simpson, *Registrum statutorum et consuetudinum ecclesiæ cathedralis sancti Pauli Londinensis* (London, 1873) p. 190. Other texts, some containing many interpolations, still await comprehensive study: Cambridge Univ. Libr., MS. Gg. 4, 32 fo. 108r; Brit. Mus., Harl. MS. 335 fo. 11r; Harl. MS. 335 fo. 8r; Harl. MS. 535 fo. 1r (in English translation); Durham, Bishop Cosin's Libr., MS. V. v. 7 fo. [168r]; Henry Huntington Libr., MS. HM 932 fo. 2r; Dublin, Trinity Coll., MS. E. 2. 22 (cat. no. 526) p. 131; Worcester Cathedral Libr., F. 172 fo. 155 (in English translation).

[2] Cf. above, p. 49.

[3] Cf. above, pp. 40, 53 and *Eng. Hist. Rev.*, l. 385–98. Statutes of a bishop of Llandaff which occur in Brit. Mus. Royal MS. 8 B. xv fo. iii may belong to the thirteenth or fourteenth century. The statute of Walter de Gray, archbishop

seen to form only one part of a literature which requires treatment as a whole. The homiletic element in them was always strong and links them with the large body of popular pastoral theology which was growing rapidly in this age. What was said in Chapter II about the production of official manuals for priests only touches the fringe of a much bigger subject; and the pastoral writings of English bishops are represented by much more than these few treatises. Roger de Weseham addressed instructions to his clergy which have survived in a miscellaneous volume.[1] Robert Grosseteste, who in his statutes demanded that the parish priests should learn the ten commandments and other essential doctrine, did much to cater for their needs in his other writings.

The last three chapters have emphasized a common feature of the statutes: a large part of each series usually repeats material common to all, and each usually makes some peculiar addition or change. From the constant repetition one gets an idea of the common policy and centralized government of the thirteenth-century Church. Only a great organization, rich in personalities as in traditions and material wealth, could produce such a determined general attack as this represents upon ignorance and indiscipline. But there is another aspect of the matter. The repetition—not merely extensively, throughout the dioceses of England, but also in time, throughout the century—suggests the inveteracy of the evils which the statutes combated. In his canons demanding the elementary education of parish priests and their observance of the law of celibacy John Pecham went no further than Robert Grosseteste, and Robert Grosseteste no further than Richard Poore. Although all parish priests were expected to possess copies of synodal statutes, these were lacking in seven out of sixteen churches in the jurisdiction of St. Paul's Cathedral in 1297;[2] and the

of York, known only by his reference to it in 1228, may have been diocesan or provincial (cf. *Reg. W. de Gray*, Surtees soc., 1870, p. 20). Likewise the constitution of Archbishop William Wickwane, preserved in the York collection of 1518 (Wilkins, iii. 673).

[1] See below, appendix II.

[2] *Visitations of churches belonging to St. Paul's* (Camden Soc., N.S. 55) pp. 2–62 *passim*.

confusion among existing texts reflects the carelessness with which they were often copied.

Of one thing we can be certain. The appearance of similar statutes in one series after another does not mean that their repetition became mere common form. The occasional modifications show how much attention was paid to local conditions and how much local custom was incorporated. The general dependence of statutes upon visitation *comperta* and the experience of the courts christian can only be inferred, not proved; but it is possible in a few cases to connect a statute with a specific papal mandate. Thus diocesan statutes, if used judiciously, can be made to yield a good deal of evidence about liturgical peculiarities, or the practice of different regions in the matter of mortuary payments, or the jurisdiction allowed to inferior prelates. The sacramental teaching is especially valuable, for it is both detailed and closely related to the practice of the time. We may find here useful evidence upon such subjects as baptism by immersion, the age of confirmands, communion by the laity in both kinds, and penitential discipline.

These textual studies show, too, how the character of the diocesan statutes depended, not merely on a universal law of the Church and a centralized administration, but also on a constant interchange of ideas among the English hierarchy. Miss Gibbs's study of the personnel of the English episcopate in the reign of Henry III prepares us for this. The English bishops were men brought up in the same traditions, often connected with each other by common service of the king or by earlier acquaintance in universities and cathedral closes. The truism needs no stressing. But it is worthy of note that the English bishops both knew each other and had frequent occasion to meet each other in the thirteenth century. The number of ecclesiastical assemblies at which they met is far more than those which are recorded by legatine or provincial legislation,[1] and the service of the

---

[1] Cf. the list of ecclesiastical councils in *Handbook of British chronology*, ed. F. M. Powicke (Royal Hist. Soc., 1939) pp. 356–60. There were also many occasions for discussion at the consecration of bishops, and some unofficial assemblies, such as those at Dunstable and Hailes in 1251 (*Annales mon.*, iii. 181; *Hist. MSS. Comm. Rep.*, iii app., 358*b*).

king came increasingly to demand the attendance of bishops in secular councils and parliaments. Along with these facts one should remember the influence of the papal government of the Church. A glance at the *Calendar of papal letters* shows how often mandates came from the Curia to two or three English bishops, involving work which brought them together. The measures to be taken for the rule of their dioceses must have often been discussed in these meetings, and although every cathedral and diocese had its own customs, there was evidently no reluctance to borrow from elsewhere. The northern province borrows and even cites the canons of southern councils.[1] Nor was the connexion confined to the relationship of individual bishops. Since one cannot tell to what extent bishops were personally responsible for writing the statutes which they promulgated, it is of interest to see links also formed between cathedral chapters. Cathedral statutes were transmitted from see to see, through Normandy and England;[2] chapters combined in litigation against their diocesans or metropolitan.[3] Great monasteries, too, had reason to be concerned with other bishops besides their own diocesans, through the possession of distant priories and appropriated churches. Thus St. Albans had interests in the diocese of Durham, and Durham had its region of peculiar jurisdiction in the diocese of York.

From the provenance of surviving texts of diocesan statutes one may learn almost as much about their circulation as one can from their contents; and it suggests a wide diffusion. The Winchester second series is known only from a muniment book of the dean and chapter of Salisbury, while a York series is found only in a Durham manuscript. Doubtless because of its churches across the Thames, the Augustinian house of St. Mary Overy, Southwark (itself in the diocese of Winchester) possessed a copy of the London statutes. For a like reason Norwich statutes occur in a text from Battle Abbey.

[1] Cf. *Eng. Hist. Rev.*, l. 216 n. 3.
[2] Cf. H. Böhmer, *Kirche und Staat*, p. 97, and H. Bradshaw and C. Words-worth, *Lincoln Cathedral statutes* (Cambridge, 1892–7) i. 101 *seqq.* and vol. ii.
[3] Cf. *Hist. MSS. Comm. Report, Wells* (1907) i. 99. For continental examples, see A. Luchaire, *Manuel des institutions françaises*, p. 58, and H. Nelis in *Revue d'histoire ecclés.*, xxv (1929) 447–70.

The exigencies of arranging intractable material have led to the treatment of certain statutes purely as 'derivatives' of others. To a careful reader, however, it must have been obvious that this is little more than an unavoidable formality. The Norwich statutes provide more material additional to the statutes of Grosseteste than the latter added to his sources. The textual problems have brought into special prominence three great prelates of the thirteenth century: Richard Poore, Walter de Cantilupe, and Robert Grosseteste. But some allowance must be made for the uncertain authorship of their statutes and for the other influences which helped to determine the shape of their 'derivatives'. Above all, their statute-making has significance only when it is seen as part of a more extensive activity, operating in the Latin Church in the thirteenth century as never before or since.

THE MODIFIED VERSION OF THE LINCOLN STATUTES

IT has been pointed out above (p. 115) that certain texts of Grosse-teste's statutes, listed as D, G, X, and Y, show the marks of revision for use by an archdeacon. All the texts of this version are very late, and it is not possible to say when or where it was composed. In each of the four manuscripts the statutes are preceded by the *Pupilla oculi* and by a short series of instructions to parish priests. The latter work begins: 'Sacerdos parochialis multa debet suis parochianis diebus dominicis prout expedire viderit proponere . . .' and ends with a lengthy passage about excommunication. The instructions, besides drawing upon the canons of Lambeth 1268 and Reading 1279, twice cite the synodal statutes of Salisbury; in one case the reference is to Poore, ch. 28, in the other it seems to be to Bingham, ch. 10. But we shall hardly be justified in the inference that the instructions were written in the diocese of Salisbury or that the version of the statutes originated there.[1]

The principal differences between the normal text of Lincoln and this version are as follows:

Ch. 1. DGXY read 'Quicunque vult, et dicitur symbolum Athanasii' for 'Quicunque vult, qui cotidie ad primam in ecclesia psallitur'.

Ch. 2. DGXY omit 'quemadmodum in generali concilio scribitur'.

Ch. 5 is omitted.

Ch. 10. DGXY omit 'neque in sacris ordinibus si eos postea acceperit, ministrare presumat'.

Chs. 29–30, 33 are omitted.

Ch. 43. DGXY read 'in annua anniversaria solempnitate matricis ecclesie eorum' for 'eorum in annua visitatione matricis ecclesie'.

Ch. 44. DGXY read 'Precipimus etiam districtius inhibentes ne quisquam scienter concubinas clericorum, nisi forte transitum facientes, in hospitio suscipiat; et hoc solempniter in singulis ecclesiis denuntietur. Item nullus simul clericum fornicatorem et suam concubinam in eodem hospitio suscipiat.'

Chs. 46–7. DGXY read 'Item excommunicationes in consilio Oxon' promulgate ad terrorem malefactorum et eorum malicie refrenationem singulis annis in singulis ecclesiis innoventur,

---

[1] The instructions also appear as an appendix to the *Pupilla oculi* without the addition of the statutes: Bodleian, Bodley MS. 182 (S.C. 2082).

quarum principii tenor talis est : Ex autoritate dei patris omni-potentis et cetera.

Volumus igitur sicut statuta sunt canonice a vobis reverenter et firmiter observari. Sciant contemptores seu transgressores si inde convicti fuerint seu confessi se per vos canonice fore puniendos.'

There immediately follows (without the table found in the normal texts):[1]

Accepimus etiam quod dissimulando pertransire non possumus nec debemus quod quidam sacerdotes parochiales ignorantie tenebris involuti aut falsa pietate detenti clavibus eis collatis abutentes excommunicatis a suis superioribus a domino papa vel a diocesano vel a consiliis tam generalibus quam provincialibus penitentiam iniungunt [D iniungant] antequam ab eo qui habet potestatem absol-vendi fuerint absoluti; cum igitur tales sacerdotes animas talium non curant sed circumveniunt et semetipsos, prohibemus ne quis tales ad penitentiam admittat nisi in articulo mortis, et tunc sub conditione tali quod si convaluerint adibunt illum qui habet pote-statem eis absolutionis beneficium impendere. Percussores clericorum vel detentores eorum in carcere vel in vinculis violenter incendiarios denuntiatos sortilegos cum re sacra vel demonibus immolantes vel abutentes sacramentis vel aliud quam deum honorantes, communi-cantes cum excommunicatis a domino papa scienter vel in crimine falsarios literarum domini pape vel procuratores falsis literis utentes et quos consilium provinciale Oxon' excommunicacionis vinculo innodavit precipimus sub pena predicta[2] superioribus reservari.

Cum secundum canonicas sanctiones abbates priores ecclesiarum prelati curam animarum habentes celebrationi sancte sinodi debeant interesse vel se canonice excusare, decanis nostris firmiter iniungi-mus quatinus beneficia eorum qui presenti synodo non comparu-erint vel se non excusaverint ut tenentur, teneant sequestrata propter suam inobedienciam donec super hoc a nobis aliud receperint man-datum et beneficia eorum, similiter qui defectus ecclesiarum suarum in visitationibus inventos hactenus suplere neclexerint. Iniungimus insuper virtute obedientie omnibus decanis nostris ne aliquis admittat de novo aliquem novum capellanum ad celebrandum divina in archi-diaconatu nostro donec fuerit presentatus.

Expliciunt constitutiones synodales.

---

[1] The D text (fo. 177v) is given, without noting unimportant variants.
[2] Y reads *dicta* and ends at this point.

APPENDIX II

THE *INSTITUTA* OF ROGER DE WESEHAM

THE following text is found in a mid-thirteenth-century manuscript in the Bodleian Library, Bodley MS. 57 (Summary catalogue 2004) fos. 96r–97v. The volume, which is described fairly fully in the *Summary Catalogue of Western MSS.*, seems to come from Leicester Abbey. The *Instituta* are followed immediately, on fo. 97v, by a short moral piece entitled *Quomodo facienda est triaca*; inc.: 'Dicitur quod illi qui triacam faciunt . . .'. This text of the *Instituta* is noted in Tanner's *Bibliotheca*, and a few lines of it are quoted by Samuel Pegge in his *Memoirs of the life of Roger de Weseham* (London, 1761) p. 58.

Instituta magistri Rogeri de Weshaam episcopi Coventrensis.

Quoniam secundum apostolum nemo potest aliud fundamentum ponere preter quod positum est, Jesus Christus,[1] et secundum apostolum Petrum non est aliud nomen datum hominibus super terram in quo oporteat homines salvos fieri;[2] in quo nomine fundata est ecclesia et solidata, que est congregacio hominum catholica, id est universalis. In quo eciam cotidie signa magna et sanitates fiunt[3] in ecclesia per oraciones fidelium. In quo eciam sacramenta ecclesiastica consecrantur, que sunt: Baptismus, confirmacio, penitencia, eukaristia, unctio extrema, ordo, et matrimonium; ac sine quo effectum in nobis habere non possunt. Et sunt septem dona spiritus sancti, que sunt: Timor, pietas, sciencia, consilium, fortitudo, intellectus, sapiencia; [ac sine quo][4] in nobis proficere non possunt. Sine quo eciam septem virtutes, scilicet: Fides, spes, karitas, prudencia, temperancia, fortitudo, iusticia in nobis sufficere non possunt. In quo eciam septem peticiones oracionis dominice—videlicet: Sanctificetur nomen tuum, et cetera que secuntur[5]—exaudiuntur et inpetrantur. Sine quo eciam octo beatitudines que enumerantur in ewangelio Matthei, ubi dicitur: Beati pauperes spiritu; beati mites; beati qui lugent; beati qui esuriunt et sciciunt iusticiam; beati misericordes; beati mundo corde; beati pacifici; beati qui persecucionem paciuntur[6]—neque in presenti neque in futuro optineri possunt neque haberi. Sine quo eciam decem mandata domini—que sunt: Non habebis deos alienos; non assumas nomen dei tui invanum; memento diem sabbati observare; honora patrem et matrem; non occides;

---

[1] 1 Cor. 3, 11.   [2] Act. 4, 12.   [3] Cf. Act. 4, 30.
[4] *ac sine quo*, omitted in the MS., seems required to make sense.
[5] Matth. 6, 9.   [6] Matth. 5, 3–10.

non mechaberis; non furtum facies; non falsum testimonium dices; non concupisces uxorem proximi tui; non concupisces rem proximi tui [1]—salubriter fieri vel observari non possunt. Sine quo eciam septem mortalia peccata—que sunt: Superbia, invidia, ira, accidia, avaricia, gula, luxuria—vitari non possunt nec purgari, nec hereses nec horrores nec scismata eliminari vel evacuari. In quo eciam omnia bene fiunt omnino et contra quod nichil bene fieri potest, quoniam sine fide Iesu Christi inpossibile est placere deo [2] nec absque eo est salus animarum.[3]

Nos igitur qui racionem reddituri [4] sumus de animabus subditorum nostrorum vocati sicut credimus et speramus per conspiracionem divinam et ad curam et regimen animarum ipsarum, volumus, in visceribus Iesu Christi obsecramus, et [fo. 96v] desideramus quod fides Iesu Christi operans per dilectionem, sine qua quasi mortua est fides, per nos ac per vos pure, integre, et expresse subditis nostris innotescat, non solum in ydiomate latino, immo in proprio ydiomate sub verbis magis notis ac congruis prout deus vobis ac nobis inspiraverit. Volumus eciam quod de fide et de suis articulis fiant frequenter menciones [5] in ecclesiis ad populum et predicaciones aliquando simpliciter et sine discucione, magis initentes exemplis quibus congrue possunt quam racionibus subtilibus vel inquisicionibus vel discucionibus; fides cum sit principium christianorum et supponenda est, non inquirenda nec discucienda, sed pro re notissima et certissima firmiter habenda et tenenda, iuxta illud Salomonis: Perscrutator maiestatis opprimetur [6] a gloria; [7] et in Ecclesiastico: Noli scrutari multipliciter, [8] quod intelligendum est precipue de hiis que ad fidem pertinent. Possunt autem sicut credimus articuli subsequentes [9] absque dubietate doceri de fide ac predicari, dummodo verbis congruis et simplicibus.

¶ Primus articulus est quod credere debemus unum et summum bonum esse, a quo est omne bonum et nichil mali, culpe carens principio et fine, omnium rex, conditor, et gubernator, attingens a fine usque ad finem fortiter et disponens omnia suaviter, [10] deus scilicet ac dominus, unus in essencia ac trinus in personis.

¶ Secundus articulus est quod in persona filii, non in persona patris, nec in persona spiritus sancti conceptus est in utero virginis de spiritu sancto.

¶ Tercius articulus est quod natus est de virgine in utraque substancia, divina scilicet et humana, suscipiens ex ea beatam humanitatem et in nullo minuens divinitatem, suscipiens quod prius non erat, non diminuens quod erat.

[1] Exod. 20, 3–17.   [2] Hebr. 11, 6.   [3] Cf. Act. 4, 12.
[4] Cf. Hebr. 13, 17.   [5] MS. m̄cones.   [6] MS. opprimentur.
[7] Cf. Prov. 25, 27.   [8] Ecclus. 3, 24.   [9] MS. obsequentes.
[10] Cf. Sap. 8, 1 and the antiphon O sapiencia.

¶Quartus articulus est quod in carne humana voluntarie passus est, pro omni salute pendens in cruce. Ad quem articulum pertinent sputa, flagella, obprobria, contumelie, alieque carnis passiones et penalitates.

¶Quintus articulus est quod post mortem est sepultus. Ad quem articulum pertinent ea que circa sepulturam acta fuerint, utpote unctio corporis conditi cum aromatibus, lapidis suppositio, militum custodia, et alia huiusmodi.

¶Sextus articulus est quod in anima descendit ad inferos et eduxit ac eruit animas sanctorum virorum de potestate diaboli. Ad hunc articulum pertinet credere quod omnes anime qualescunque [1] sint ante passionem dominicam ad inferos descenderunt, in tenebris sedentes, lucem et liberacionem exspectantes, et siqua similia.

¶Septimus articulus est quod tercio die resurrexit a mortuis gloriose. Ad quem articulum reducere possumus glorificacionem corporis et anime Iesu Christi, et mortis victoriam, et consimilia.

[fo. 97r] ¶Octavus articulus est quod [2] in carne et anima glorificata eadem in qua natus est et passus celos ascendit. Ad quem articulum pertinet sessio ad dexteram dei patris, ac pociorum bonorum fruicio, et pro nobis intercessio, et siqua similia.

¶Nonus articulus est quod venturus est ad iudicium in humana specie, et vivos ac mortuos iudicaturus. Ad quem articulum possunt reduci et [quod] [3] terribilis apparebit in iudicio, et quod veniet cum discipulis, et cetera.

¶Decimus articulus est quod nos omnes resurgemus in resurreccione generali, recepturi prout gessimus in corpore sive bonum fuerit sive malum. Ad quem articulum pertinet [4] corporum nostrorum et animarum nostrarum glorificacio, ac immutacio, et innovacio salvandorum, non autem dampnandorum, et consimilia.

¶Undecimus articulus est quod sacramenta ecclesie animas sanctificant. Ad hunc articulum reducere possumus quod sacramenta nove legis efficiunt quod figurant; item quod extra ecclesiam et absque sacramentis non est salus.

¶Duodecimus articulus est quod idem ipse, qui fuit creator et conditor, gubernator, redemptor et salvator, erit omnium bonorum misericors retributor ac malorum iustus ultor quorum non fuit auctor. Ad quem articulum pertinet quod supra meritum remunerabit iustos, et citra meritum puniet dampnandos, in omnibus iusticiam servans et misericordiam.

Ex hiis ergo manifestum est quod summopere vitanda sunt ac reprobanda ea que fidem Iesu Christi destruunt, obnubilant, vel obtenebrant. [5] Et quoniam [6] vitari non possunt nisi innotescant, volumus

---

[1] MS. quantumcunque.   [2] MS. quod est.   [3] MS. *omits* quod.
[4] MS. possunt.   [5] MS. obtenuant.   [6] MS. quam.

sub compendio per graciam dei quedam ex eis que nostre occurrunt memorie declarare. In primis enim hereses que manifeste opponuntur articulis fidei, et sunt ab ecclesia et a viris ecclesiasticis reprobate et dampnate; utpote heresis ariana, et pelagiana, et cetera. Sunt et alia que originem sumpserunt ab artibus magicis quas adinveniunt demones et hominibus tradiderunt, ut per quosdam deceptos alios decipere cotidie satagunt. Ex quibus sunt incantaciones, coniuraciones, divinaciones, sortilegia, maleficia, observaciones dierum et horarum in agendis negociis, et sompniorum observaciones. Ad hec omnia pertinent ligature remediorum et excecrabilium caracteres, in quibus omnibus ars demonica[1] est, [fo. 97v] ex quadam pestifera societate hominum et angelorum malorum exorta. Que quidem[2] omnia sunt a christianis vitanda, repudianda, atque dampnanda. Nec sunt illi soli dampnandi qui hec faciunt, sed qui huiusmodi scienter et prudenter consenciunt vel ab hiis consilium deposcunt. Prohibita sunt enim in veteri testamento et novo; unde in Exodo scribitur: Maleficos non pacieris vivere;[3] et in Levitico: Non augurabimini, nec observabis sompnia, neque figuras aereas et[4] stigmata facietis,[5] et cetera. Contra hoc habebis remedium in Deutronomio, unde dicitur: Prophetam suscitabo eis de medio fratrum suorum;[6] ipsum sicut me audite. Dicit dominus Moysi, qui propheta Iesus Christus est, qui est via, veritas, et vita,[7] ad quem in necessitatibus, in tribulacionibus, in periculis recurrendum est; qui dicit de seipso in ewangelio: Venite ad me omnes qui laboratis et onerati estis et ego reficiam vos;[8] qui et dicit: Ego sum lux mundi, subiungens: Qui sequitur me non ambulat in tenebris,[9] et cetera. Et quia[10] predicta mala sectatores et fautores suos elongant a deo, et ipsius fidem contaminant ac demonibus[11] ac eorum tradicionibus nephariis approximare faciunt, iubemus firmiter sub pena anathematis ne quis de cetero aliquid de predictis facere presumat, vel ab eorum auctoribus consilium vel auxilium requirat, vel ipsis aliquatinus consenciat. Sed unusquisque vestrum omnia ista et consimilia in vobismetipsis et vestris subditis destruere faciat et adnichilare; recurrendo ad ipsum qui est fons omnis sapiencie et sciencie et contra omnia mala sufficiens remedium, de quo scriptum est: Omnis sapiencia a domino deo est,[12] et alibi: A deo est omnis medela.[13]

---

[1] MS. demon.   [2] MS. Quedam *for* Que quidem.   [3] Exod. 22, 18.
[4] Levit.: aliquas aut.   [5] Cf. Levit. 19, 26 and 28.
[6] Deut. 18, 18.   [7] Ioan. 14, 6.   [8] Matth. 11, 28.
[9] Ioan. 8, 12.   [10] MS. qui.   [11] MS. demonia.
[12] Ecclus. 1, 1.   [13] Ecclus. 38, 2.

BIBLIOGRAPHY

ABRAHAM, LADISLAUS. 'Ius canonicum particulare in Polonia tempore decretalium Gregorii IX', *Actus congressus iuridici internationalis Romae*, iii (Rome, 1936) 409–14

ADDLESHAW, G. 'Diocesan synods', *Theology*, xxix (1934) 262–71.

ANDRIEU-GUÎTRANCOURT, PIERRE. *L'archevêque Eudes Rigaud et la vie de l'Église au xiiie siècle d'après le ' Regestrum visitationum'*. Paris, 1938.

Annales Monastici, ed. H. R. Luard, 5 vols. (Rolls series, 1864–9).

BARION, HANS. *Das fränkisch-deutsche Synodalrecht des Frühmittelalters* [511–1046] (Kanonistische Studien und Texte, ed. A. M. Koeniger, v and vi). Bonn, 1931.

BENEDICT XIV, Pope (Prosp. Lambertini). *De synodo diœcesana libri tresdecim* [second ed.]. Rome, 1755.

—— *The diocesan synod*, being some chapters from the treatise 'De synodo diœcesana', selected and done into English by W. R. V. Brade. London, 1926.

BERLIÈRE, URSMER. 'Les processions des croix banales', *Bulletin de la classe des lettres, . . . de l'académie royale de Belgique*, 5e série, viii (1922) 419–46.

BIERBAUM, MAX. 'Diözesansynoden des Bistums Münster', *Römische Quartalschrift für christl. Altertumskunde*, etc., xxxv (1927) 381–411.

BIGELOW, MELVILLE M. *History of procedure in England from the Norman Conquest: The Norman period (1066–1204)*. Boston, 1880.

BOTTEO, ENRICO DE. *Tractatus de synodo episcopi et de statutis episcopi synodalibus*. In *Tractatus illustrium in utraque . . . facultate iurisconsultorum*, XIII. ii (Venice, 1584) fos. 378d–407c.

BOUCHEL, LAURENT (BOCHELLUS, L.). *Decretorum ecclesiæ gallicanæ . . . libri octo*. Paris, 1609.

BOYE, MARTIN. 'Die Synoden Deutschlands und Reichsitaliens von 922–1059. Eine kirchenverfassungsgeschichtliche Untersuchung.' *Zeitschr. der Savigny-Stiftung für Rechtsgeschichte*, xlix, kanonistische Abt. xviii (1929) 131–284.

—— 'Quellenkatalog der Synoden Deutschlands und Reichsitaliens von 922–1059', *Neues Archiv der Gesellschaft für ältere deutsche Geschichtskunde*, xlviii (1929) 45–96.

Calendar of papal letters. Calendar of entries in the papal registers relating to Great Britain and Ireland: Papal letters, vol. i, A.D. 1198–1304, ed. W. H. Bliss. London, 1893.

CHENEY, C. R. *Episcopal visitation of monasteries in the thirteenth century*. Manchester, 1931.

—— 'Legislation of the medieval English Church', *Eng. Hist. Rev.*, l (1935) 193–224, 385–417.

—— 'La date de composition du "Liber Poenitentialis" attribué à Pierre de Poitiers', *Recherches de théologie ancienne et médiévale*, ix (1937) 401–4.

CHURCHILL, IRENE J. *Canterbury administration*, 2 vols. London, 1933.

Corpus iuris canonici. Decretum Gratiani [etc.] *una cum glossis*. ad exemplar romanum diligenter recognitae. Editio ultima. 3 vols. Paris, 1612.

Corpus iuris canonici, ed. E. Friedberg (Leipzig, 1881).

DANSEY, WILLIAM. *Horae decanicae rurales*, 2nd ed., 2 vols. London, 1844.

DE CLERCQ, CARLO. *La législation religieuse franque de Clovis à Charlemagne: Étude sur les actes des conciles et les capitulaires, les statuts diocésains et les règles monastiques, 507–814.* (Université de Louvain. Recueil de travaux . . . d'histoire et de philologie, 2ᵉ série, fasc. 38.) Louvain and Paris, 1936.

Decretales Gregorii Papae IX, see *Corpus iuris canonici*.

Decretum Gratiani, see *Corpus iuris canonici*.

DIETTERLE, J. 'Die "Summae Confessorum" von ihren Anfängen an bis zu Silverius Prierius', *Zeitschrift für Kirchengeschichte*, xxiv–xxviii, 1903–7.

DOBIACHE-ROJDESTVENSKY, OLGA. *La vie paroissiale en France au xiii siècle*. Paris, 1911.

DURANDUS, GUILLELMUS. *Instructions et constitutions de Guillaume Durand le Spéculateur*, ed. Jos. Berthelé and M. Valmary. (Archives du départm. de l'Hérault, Documents et inventaires complémentaires, tome v, fasc. i.) Montpellier, 1905. Extrait des *Mémoires de l'académie des sciences et lettres de Montpellier*, Section des lettres, 2ᵉ série, tome iii.

ELY. *Vetus liber archidiaconi eliensis*, ed. C. L. Feltoe and E. H. Minns (Cambridge Antiq. Soc., 8vo publ. xlviii, 1917).

ESPEN, Z. B. VAN. *Ius ecclesiasticum universum*. 4 vols. Louvain, 1753.

FINKE, HEINRICH. *Konzilienstudien zur Geschichte des 13. Jahrhunderts.* Münster, 1891.

FOURNIER, PAUL. *Les officialités au moyen âge.* Paris, 1880.

FRERE, W. H. *Visitation articles and injunctions of the period of the Reformation.* i. *Historical introduction.* Alcuin Club collections 14, 1910.

GAVANTI, BARTOLOMEO. *Praxis exactissima diœcesanæ synodi cum theoria celebrandæ.* Altera editio. Venice, Giunta, 1634.

GIBBS, MARION, and LANG, JANE. *Bishops and reform 1215–1272.* Oxford, 1934.

GOUSSET, TH. (ed.). *Les actes de la province ecclésiastique de Reims,* vols. 1 and 2. Reims, 1842–3.

GROSSETESTE, ROBERT. *Epistolæ Roberti Grosseteste,* ed. H. R. Luard. (Rolls series, 1861.)

HASKINS, CHARLES HOMER. *Norman institutions.* Harvard, 1918.

HAUCK, ALBERT. *Kirchengeschichte Deutschlands.* Vol. iv (5th ed.) 1925, vol. v, pt. i (1st ed) 1911.

—— 'Synoden', *Realencyklopädie für prot. Theologie und Kirche,* ed. J. J. Herzog and A. Hauck, xix (Leipzig, 1907) 262–77.

—— 'Die angeblichen Mainzer Statuten von 1261 und die Mainzer Synoden des 12. und 13. Jahrhunderts', *Theologische Studien Th. Zahn dargebracht* (Leipzig, 1908), and separately.

HEFELE, C. J., etc. *Histoire des conciles,* ed. H. Leclercq, 9 vols. Paris, 1907-38.

HEYDENREICH, JOHANNA. 'Zu den Trierer Synodalstatuten des xiii. Jahrhunderts', *Zeitschr. der Savigny-Stiftung für Rechtsgeschichte,* lvi, kanonistische Abt. xxv (1936) 478–85.

HINSCHIUS, PAUL. *System des katholischen Kirchenrechts, mit besonderer Rücksicht auf Deutschland.* 5 vols. and vol. vi, part i. Berlin, 1869–97.

HOLTZMANN, WALTHER. *Papsturkunden in England,* i and ii (Abhandlungen der Gesellschaft der Wissenschaften zu Göttingen, phil.-hist. Klasse, neue Folge xxv, dritte Folge 14–15), 1930–1, 1935–6.

HOSTIENSIS (Henricus de Segusia). *Henrici cardinalis Hostiensis . . . lectura in quinque decretalium gregorianarum libros.* Paris, Jean Petit and Thomas Kerver, n. d.

INNOCENT IV, POPE. *Apparatus Innocentii.* [Colophon :] *Apparatus domini Innocentii quarti super toto volumine decretalium.* Venice, 1495.

JOHNSON, JOHN. *A collection of all the ecclesiastical laws . . . of the Church of England.* . . . 2 vols. London, 1720.

JUSSELIN, M. 'Statuts synodaux et constitutions synodales du diocèse de Chartres au xive siècle (1355)', *Revue hist. de droit franç. et étrang.*, 4e série, viii (1929) 69–109.

LAVOYE, MADELEINE. *Le texte original des statuts synodaux de Jean de Flandre.* Liège, 1934 (reprinted from *Bulletin de la Société d'art et d'histoire du diocèse de Liège*, vol. xxv, 1934).

LUCHAIRE, ACHILLE. *Manuel des institutions françaises: période des Capétiens directs.* Paris, 1892.

LYLE, E. K. *The office of an English bishop in the first half of the fourteenth century.* [Philadelphia], 1903.

LYNDWOOD, WILLIAM. *Provinciale . . . cui adjiciuntur constitutiones legatinae d. Othonis et d. Othoboni.* . . . Oxford, 1679.

MANSI, J. D. (ed.). *Sacrorum conciliorum nova et amplissima collectio.* 31 vols. Venice and Florence, 1759–98.

MARTÈNE, E., and DURAND, U. *Thesaurus novus anecdotorum,* iv: *Varia concilia, episcoporum statuta synodalia,* etc. Paris, 1717.

MASKELL, WILLIAM. *Monumenta ritualia ecclesiae anglicanae.* 3 vols. London, 1846–7.

PANORMITANUS (Nicolaus de Tudeschis). *Prima* [etc.] *pars abbatis Panormitani super primo* [etc.] *decretalium.* . . . Lyon, 1516–17.

PANTIN, W. A. (ed.). *Documents illustrating the activities of the general and provincial chapters of the English Black Monks 1215–1540.* Royal Hist. Soc., Camden 3rd series, vols. 45, 47, 54, 1931–7.

POLLOCK, FREDERICK, and MAITLAND, FREDERICK WILLIAM. *The history of English law before the time of Edward I.* 2 vols. 2nd ed. Cambridge, 1898.

POMMERAYE, F. *Sanctæ Rotomagensis ecclesiæ concilia ac synodalia decreta.* Rouen, 1667.

PONTISSARA, JOHN DE. *Registrum Iohannis de Pontissara episcopi Wyntoniensis (1282–1304),* ed. C. Deedes (Canterbury and York Soc. and Surrey Record Soc., 1915–24).

POTTHAST, AUGUST (ed.). *Regesta pontificum romanorum (1198–1304).* 2 vols. Berlin, 1874–5.

RICHARDSON, H. G. 'The parish clergy in the thirteenth and fourteenth centuries.' *Royal Historical Soc. Transactions,* 3rd series, vi (1912).

RIGAUD. *Regestrum visitationum archiepiscopi Rothomagensis: Journal des visites pastorales d'Eude Rigaud, archevêque de Rouen (1248–69)*, ed. Th. Bonnin. Rouen, 1852.

RUSSELL, J. C. *Dictionary of writers of thirteenth-century England.* (Bulletin of Inst. of Hist. Research, special supplement no. 3.) London, 1936.

Salisbury Charters. Charters and documents . . . of Salisbury, ed. W. Rich Jones and W. D. Macray. (Rolls series, 1891.)

SCHREIBER, GEORG. *Kurie und Kloster im 12. Jahrhundert.* (Kirchenrechtliche Abhandlungen, ed. U. Stutz, 65–8.) 2 vols. Stuttgart, 1910.

SCHULTE, F. VON. *Die Geschichte der Quellen und Literatur des canonischen Rechts.* 3 vols. Leipzig, 1875–80.

Sextus liber decretalium, see *Corpus iuris canonici.*

SPELMAN, HENRY. *Concilia, decreta, leges in re ecclesiarum orbis britannici. . . .* vol. 2 (1066–1531). London, 1664.

STEVENSON, FRANCIS SEYMOUR. *Robert Grosseteste, bishop of Lincoln.* London, 1899.

SWEET, ALFRED H. 'The English Benedictines and their bishops in the thirteenth century', *American Hist. Rev.*, xxiv (1919) 565–77.

TEETAERT, AMÉDÉE. *La confession aux laïques dans l'église latine depuis le viiie jusqu'au xive siècle.* Paris, 1926.

THOMASSIN, L. *L'ancienne et la nouvelle discipline de l'Église*, ed. M. André. 7 vols. Bar-le-Duc, 1864–70.

THOMSON, S. HARRISON. *The writings of Robert Grosseteste, bishop of Lincoln 1235–1253.* Cambridge, 1940. [This important work appeared too late to be used in Chapter V, above.]

VETULANI, A. 'La pénétration du droit des décrétales dans l'église polonaise au xiiie siècle', *Acta congressus iuridici internationalis Romae*, iii (Rome, 1936) 387–405.

Vetus liber, see ELY.

WAKE, WILLIAM. *The state of the Church and clergy of England, in their councils, synods, convocations, conventions, and other publick assemblies. . . .* London, 1703.

WERMINGHOFF, ALBERT. *Verfassungsgeschichte der deutschen Kirche im Mittelalter.* 2nd ed. Leipzig, 1913.

—— 'Verzeichnis der Akten fränkischer Synoden von 742–843', *Neues Archiv der Gesellschaft für ältere deutsche Geschichtskunde*, xxiv (1899) 457–502.

158 BIBLIOGRAPHY

WERMINGHOFF, ALBERT. 'Verzeichnis der Akten fränkischer Synoden von 843–918', *ibid.*, xxvi (1901) 607–78.

WHARTON, HENRY. *Anglia sacra.* 2 vols. London, 1691.

WILKINS, DAVID (ed.). *Concilia Magnæ Britanniæ et Hiberniæ.* 4 vols. London, 1737.

WOOLLEY, R. M. 'Constitutions of the diocese of London, *c.* 1215–22', *Eng. Hist. Rev.*, xxx (1915) 285–302.

INDEX OF MANUSCRIPTS

GENERAL INDEX

Bishops are indexed under the names of their dioceses, and popes under *Rome*.
Diocesan synods are indexed under the names of their dioceses, and other councils
under *Councils*.

Addleshaw, G., 2 n. 3.
Alcester, abbot of, 23 n. 4.
Amiens, diocese of, 44 n. 1.
Angers, diocesan statutes of, 22, 46.
Archdeacons, 5 n. 4, 21–2, 30, 39, 43–4,
  46, 72, 88, 100–1, 116–17, 120, 122,
  134, 139, 142.
Autun, diocesan statutes of, 56.
Aylesbury, co. Buck., 24.

Barnwell, priory of, 20, 21 n. 2.
Bath, diocese of, *see* Bath and Wells.
— prior of, 25.
Bath and Wells, bishops of:
  Reginald, 23 n. 4.
  Savaric, 27.
  Walter Giffard, 108.
  William of Bitton I, 97–101, 108.
— diocesan statutes of, 44, 97–103.
— — synods of, 17, 19 n. 2, 23 n. 4, 25.
Battle, abbey of, 23, 126, 145.
Berlière, U., 18 n. 4.
Binham, priory of, 24.
Bodmin, co. Cornw., 28 n. 4.
Bonn, provost of church of, 25.
Botteo, Enrico de, 1, 9–12 notes, 14.
Bradenstoke, prior of, 24 n. 3.
Bury, abbey of St. Edmund of, 20, n. 11.

Cahors, diocese of, 18 n. 1.
Cambrai, bishop of, 19.
Canterbury, archbishops of:
  Baldwin, 26.
  Boniface, 21 n. 2, 85.
  Edmund Rich, 65–7, 85, 95, 135.
  John Pecham, 32, 45, 143.
  Richard, 29.
  Robert Winchelsey, 110–11, 113.
  Simon Sudbury, 65 n. 2.
  Stephen Langton, 52, 62–5, 67.
  Theodore, 14 n. 3.
  Thomas Arundel, 49–50.
— cathedral priory of, 27.
— diocesan statutes of, 35, 61–5, 71 n. 1,
  79, 86.
— — synods of, 18 n. 6, 21, 25 n. 6, 26–
  7, 29.
Carcassonne, diocese of, 18 n. 2.
Cardiff, co. Glam., 20.
Cauciones, 59.

Cemeteries, 43, 63–4, 106–7, 120–1, 130
  n. 3.
Chabham, Thomas of, 49, 54.
Châlons, diocesan statutes of, 48.
Chapter, archidiaconal, 5 n. 4, 46.
— cathedral, 14–15, 26, 44, 145.
— provincial, of Black Monks, 23 n. 4.
Chartres, diocesan statutes of, 56.
Chester, bishop and diocese of, *see* Coventry
  and Lichfield.
Chichester, bishops of:
  Richard Poore, *see* Salisbury.
  Richard de Wich, 84–9, 135.
— diocesan statutes of (1244 × 53), 24,
  44, 84–9.
— — — (1289, 1292), 36, 106 n. 2, 142.
— — synods of, 17, 19 n. 2, 23.
Cistercian Order, 23–4.
Clermont, diocesan statutes of, 24.
Cluny, abbey of, 24 n. 5.
Coggeshall, abbey of, 23.
Combe Martin, chapelry of, 28.
Conches, abbot of, 27.
Council, provincial, 3, 6–8, 37, 145.
Councils:
  Basel, 15, 41.
  Cognac, 32.
  Lambeth (1261), 101, 147.
  — (1281), 40.
  Lateran III ('I'), 55.
  — IV, 7, 15, 30–1, 34–7, 51–2, 55,
    57, 61 n. 3, 74, 76, 85 n. 4, 91–2,
    99–100, 118–19, 130, 134, 140.
  London (1200), 55, 76, 87, 99 n. 4.
  — (1237), 74, 88, 91–2, 100, 105, 119–
    20, 134, 138, 140.
  — (1268), 32, 81, 138.
  Lyon (1245), 84, 100.
  Merton (1258), 140.
  Narbonne (1227), 30.
  Oxford (1222), 32, 40, 51, 61, 65, 75–
    8, 83, 88, 92, 99–100, 105, 119.
  Paris (1213), 15 n. 6, 57.
  Reading (1279), 32, 61, 81, 147.
  Regensburg (1209), 30.
  Reims (1213), 57.
  Rouen (1213), 57.
  Scottish church, 62.
  Toledo IV (633), 6.
  — XVI (693), 7, 13.
  Tours, 14, 32 n. 3.